Ahlam F. Sawsaa

Ontological Engineering approach of developing Ontology of Information Science

Anchor Academic Publishing

Sawsaa, Ahlam F.: Ontological Engineering approach of developing Ontology of
Information Science, Hamburg, Anchor Academic Publishing 2015

Buch-ISBN: 978-3-95489-448-2
PDF-eBook-ISBN: 978-3-95489-948-7
Druck/Herstellung: Anchor Academic Publishing, Hamburg, 2015

Bibliografische Information der Deutschen Nationalbibliothek:
Die Deutsche Nationalbibliothek verzeichnet diese Publikation in der Deutschen
Nationalbibliografie; detaillierte bibliografische Daten sind im Internet über
http://dnb.d-nb.de abrufbar.

Bibliographical Information of the German National Library:
The German National Library lists this publication in the German National Bibliography.
Detailed bibliographic data can be found at: http://dnb.d-nb.de

All rights reserved. This publication may not be reproduced, stored in a retrieval system
or transmitted, in any form or by any means, electronic, mechanical, photocopying,
recording or otherwise, without the prior permission of the publishers.

Das Werk einschließlich aller seiner Teile ist urheberrechtlich geschützt. Jede Verwertung
außerhalb der Grenzen des Urheberrechtsgesetzes ist ohne Zustimmung des Verlages
unzulässig und strafbar. Dies gilt insbesondere für Vervielfältigungen, Übersetzungen,
Mikroverfilmungen und die Einspeicherung und Bearbeitung in elektronischen Systemen.

Die Wiedergabe von Gebrauchsnamen, Handelsnamen, Warenbezeichnungen usw. in
diesem Werk berechtigt auch ohne besondere Kennzeichnung nicht zu der Annahme,
dass solche Namen im Sinne der Warenzeichen- und Markenschutz-Gesetzgebung als frei
zu betrachten wären und daher von jedermann benutzt werden dürften.

Die Informationen in diesem Werk wurden mit Sorgfalt erarbeitet. Dennoch können
Fehler nicht vollständig ausgeschlossen werden und die Diplomica Verlag GmbH, die
Autoren oder Übersetzer übernehmen keine juristische Verantwortung oder irgendeine
Haftung für evtl. verbliebene fehlerhafte Angaben und deren Folgen.

Alle Rechte vorbehalten

© Anchor Academic Publishing, Imprint der Diplomica Verlag GmbH
Hermannstal 119k, 22119 Hamburg
http://www.diplomica-verlag.de, Hamburg 2015
Printed in Germany

In the name of Allah, the Beneficent, The Merciful

(رَبَّنَا آتِنَا فِي الدُّنْيَا حَسَنَةً وَفِي الْآخِرَةِ حَسَنَةً وَقِنَا عَذَابَ النَّارِ)

"Our Lord gives unto us in the world that which is good, and guard us from the doom of Fire."

(The Holy Quran, 2:201)

To my family

The near and far

Acknowledgments

First of all a special thank to my Lord Almighty Allah. We always keep the deficit in the description of words of thanks, especially to people who provide with tenderness without borders, the lines of thanks are always extremely difficult to formulate.

I would like to thank Professor Zhongyu (Joan) Lu, for her support, encouragement, and guidance from the initial to the final level, enabling me to develop an understanding of the subject, and her excellent feedback on the related paper and articles produced during the research project. Her encouragement has a big impact on my learning in finding pieces of knowledge and solving challenges.

I am heartily thankful to Julie Wilkinson and Violeta Holmes for their guidance and advice during these years.

Also, great thanks to all the staff of the Computing and Engineering School at the University of Huddersfield who inspired me to do my research. A big thank to everyone who participated in Ontocop's project.

Also, all the people were at my side; my sincere and faithful husband for his great and magnificent support, and the three essences of my life: Khalifa, Tasnim and Noor.

A great thanks also to all who gave me a helping hand to reach the end of my journey.

Abstract

Ontology has been a subject of many studies carried out in artificial intelligence (AI) and information system communities. Ontology has become an important component of the semantic web, covering a variety of knowledge domains. Although building domain ontologies still remains a big challenge with regard to its designing and implementation, there are still many areas that need to create ontologies. Information Science (IS) is one of these areas that need a unified ontology model to facilitate information access among the heterogeneous data resources and share a common understanding of the domain knowledge. The objective of this study is to develop a generic model of ontology that serves as a foundation of knowledge modelling for applications and aggregation with other ontologies to facilitate information exchanging between different systems. This model will be a metadata for a knowledge base system to be used in different purposes of interest, such as education applications to support educational needs for teachers and students and information system developers, and enhancing the index tool in libraries to facilitate access to information collections. This thesis describes the process of modelling the domain knowledge of Information Science IS.

The building process of the ontology of Information Science (OIS) is preceded by developing taxonomies and thesauruses of IS. This research adopts the Methontology to develop ontology of Information Science OIS. This choice of method relies on the research motivations and aims, with analysis of some development ontology methodologies and IEEE 1074-2006 standards for developing software project life cycle processes as criteria. The methodology mainly consisted of; specification, conceptualization, formalization, implementation, maintenance and evaluation. The knowledge model was formalized using Protégé to generate the ontology code. During the development process the model has been designed and evaluated.

This research presents the following contributions to the present state of the art on ontology construction;

- The main achievement of the study is in constructing a new model of Information Science ontology OIS. The OIS ontology is a generic model that contains only the key objects and associated attributes with relationships. The model has defined 706 concepts which will be widely used in Information Science applications. It provides the standard definitions for domain terms used in annotation databases for the domain terms, and avoids the consistency problems caused by various ontologies which will have the potential of development by different groups and institutions in the IS domain area.

- It provides a framework for analyzing the IS knowledge to obtain a classification based on facet classification. The ontology modelling approach is based on top-down and bottom–up. The top-down begins with an abstract of the domain view. While the bottom-up method starts with description of the domain to gain a hierarchal taxonomy.
- Designing Ontocop system a novel method presented to support the developing process as specific virtual community of IS. The Ontocop consists of a number of experts in the subject area around the world. Their feedback and assessment improve the ontology development during the creating process.

The findings of the research revealed that overall feedback from the IS community has been positive and that the model met the ontology quality criteria. It was appropriate to provide consistency and clear understanding of the subject area. OIS ontology unifies information science, which is composed of library science, computer science and archival science, by creating the theoretical base useful for further practical systems. Developing ontology of information science (OIS) is not an easy task, due to the complex nature of the field. It needs to be integrated with other ontologies such as social science, cognitive science, philosophy, law management and mathematics, to provide a basic knowledge for the semantic web and also to leverage information retrieval.

Publications

1. Sawsaa, A. & Lu, J (2009). A Generic Model of Knowledge Mapping Through Virtual Communities of Practice in Information Science (IS). Conference proceeding. World Congress in Computer Science, Computer Engineering, and Applied Computing, Las Vegas, Nevada.12-15 July 2009.
2. Sawsaa, A. & Lu, J (2010). Ontocop: A virtual community of practice to create ontology of Information science (IS). Conference proceeding. World Congress in Computer Science, Computer Engineering, and Applied Computing, Las Vegas, Nevada 12-15 July 2010.
3. Sawsaa, A. & Lu, J (2010). Ontology of Information Science (IS) based on OWL conference proceeding. The International Arab Conference on Information Technology (ACIT2010).
4. Sawsaa, A. (2010). A virtual community. The 3th Scientific Research Symposium for Libyan Students in UK Universities. Sheffield Hallam University, 12th June 2010.
5. Sawsaa, A. & Lu, J. (2011) 'Extracting Information Science concepts based on Jape Regular Expression'. In: WORLDCOMP'11 - The 2011 World Congress in Computer Science, Computer Engineering, and Applied Computing, 18-21 July 2011, Las Vegas, Nevada, USA
6. Sawsaa, A. & Lu, J. (2011) 'Virtual Community of Practice Ontocop: Towards a New Model of Information Science Ontology (OIS)' International Journal of Information Retrieval Research, 1 (2), pp. 55-78. ISSN 2155-6377
7. Sawsaa, A., ZHAOZONG, M. & LU, J. (2012) Using an Application of Mobile and Wireless Technology in Arabic Learning System. IN LU, Z. J. (Ed. Learning with Mobile Technologies, Handheld Devices and Smart Phones: Innovative Methods. USA, IGI Global. pp. 171-186. ISBN978-1-4666-0936-5
8. Sawsaa, A. & Lu, J. (2012) Developing a Domain Ontology of Information Science (OIS). IN SHONIREGUN, C. A. & AKMAYEVA, G. A. (Eds.) International Conference on Information Society (i-Society 2012) June 25-28, 2012,. London, UK, i-Society 2012 Technical Co-Sponsored by IEEE UK/RI Computer Chapter. pp 462-467.
9. Sawsaa, A. & Lu, J. (2012) Extracting Information Science Concepts based on JAPE Regular Expression. International Journal of advanced Computer Science (IJEC) , in press

10. Sawsaa, A. & Lu, J. (2012) Building an advance domain ontology model of Information Science (OIS). Journal of the American Society for Information Science and Technology (JASIST), in press

11. Sawsaa, A. & Lu, J. (2012) Building Information Science (OIS) Ontology with Methondology and Protégé. Journal of Internet Technology and Secured Transactions (JITST) 2 (1/2), ISSN 2046-3723. In press.

12. Sawsaa, A. & Lu, J. (2013) Extracting Occupational Therapist concepts to develop domain ontology. The Seventh International Conference on Digital Society (ICDS 2013) February 24 - March 1, 2013 - Nice, France.

Posters:

1. Sawsaa, A. and Lu, J. (2011) 'ONTOCOP: Virtual Community Of Practice to build Ontology of Information Science'. *University of Huddersfield 2009*

2. Sawsaa, A. and Lu, J. (2009) A Generic Model of Knowledge Mapping Through Virtual Communities of Practice in Information Science (IS)

Table of contents

ACKNOWLEDGMENTS IV

ABSTRACT V

PUBLICATIONS VII

TABLE OF CONTENTS IX

LIST OF FIGURES XVII

LIST OF TABLES XXI

ACRONYMS XXIII

PART 1: FUNDAMENTAL ISSUES 1

1   CHAPTER 1: INTRODUCTION 2

     1.1. PROBLEM IDENTIFICATION 3

     1.2. AIMS AND OBJECTIVES 4

     1.3. METHODOLOGY AND IMPLEMENTATION 5

     1.4. CONTRIBUTIONS 6

     1.5. MOTIVATION OF STUDY 8

     1.6. THESIS ORGANIZATION 9

2   CHAPTER 2: RESEARCH BACKGROUND 12

     2.1 ONTOLOGY OVERVIEW 12

         2.1.1 Historical and philosophical perspective of the ontology 13

             2.1.1.1 Definition of ontology 14

         2.1.2 Ontology Theoretic 16

             2.1.2.1 Category Theory 16

             2.1.2.2 Mereotopolgy Theory 17

         2.1.3 Referencing and meaning in the ontology 19

         2.1.4 Ontology spectrum 20

             2.1.4.1 Thesaurus 20

- 2.1.4.2 Taxonomy 21
- 2.1.5 Approaches for modelling ontology: 24
  - 2.1.5.1 Top-down approach 24
  - 2.1.5.2 Bottom–up approach... 24
  - 2.1.5.3 Middle out approach 25
- 2.1.6 Structure of ontology... 26
- 2.1.7 Ontology Categorization 27
  - 2.1.7.1 Informal ontology 29
  - 2.1.7.2 Formal ontology... 29
  - 2.1.7.3 Domain ontology 29
- 2.1.8 Related Research 30
- 2.1.9 Designing Criteria for ontology 35
- 2.1.10 Ontology evaluation approaches 36
- 2.1.11 Ontology Engineering Methodologies 39
  - 2.1.11.1 CYC Method 40
  - 2.1.11.2 Uschold & King Method... 40
  - 2.1.11.3 Gruninger & Fox Method... 41
  - 2.1.11.4 SENSUS Methodology 42
  - 2.1.11.5 Methontology 42
  - 2.1.11.6 Comparison of Methodology 46
  - 2.1.11.7 Evaluation of ontology methodologies 49
- 2.1.12 Techniques Involved 50
  - 2.1.12.1 Ontology languages 50
  - 2.1.12.2 Resource Description Framework RDF, and RDFs... 51
  - 2.1.12.3 Web Ontology Language (OWL) 54

- 2.1.12.4 Comparison of ontology languages 57
- 2.1.12.5 Ontology Tools 58
- 2.1.12.6 Ontologua server 59
- 2.1.12.7 OntoSaurus 59
- 2.1.12.8 WebOnto 59
- 2.1.12.9 OilEd: 59
- 2.1.12.10 Cmap tools 60
- 2.1.12.11 Protégé 60
- 2.1.12.12 Web Protégé 60
- 2.1.12.13 General Architecture for text engineering(GATE) 60
- 2.1.12.14 Comparison of ontology tools 61

2.2 INFORMATION SCIENCE (IS) 63

- 2.2.1 Overview 63
- 2.2.2 Definitions 63
- 2.2.3 Relationship of information science with other sciences 65
- 2.2.4 Information Science Taxonomy 67
  - 2.2.4.1 Universal decimal classification (UDC) 69
  - 2.2.4.2 Library of Congress Classification (LCC) 69
  - 2.2.4.3 Colon Classification Scheme (CCS) 69
  - 2.2.4.4 The advantages of Facet analysis system (FAS) 70
  - 2.2.4.5 Classification Research group (CRG) 72
- 2.2.5 Why Information Science Taxonomy: 72

2.3 KNOWLEDGE MANAGEMENT (KM) AND VIRTUAL COMMUNITIES OF PRACTICE (VCOPS) 74

- 2.3.1 The Main components of knowledge management. 74
  - 2.3.1.1 Data 74

        2.3.1.2 Information 75

        2.3.1.3 Knowledge 75

   2.3.2 Knowledge Management 76

   2.3.3 Knowledge Engineering (KE) 78

   2.3.4 Knowledge Representation (KR) 79

   2.3.5 Virtual Communities of practice (VCops) 81

   2.3.6 Communities of Practice (Cops) 81

   2.3.7 Virtual communities of practice (VCops) 83

   2.3.8 Summary 88

PART 2: METHODOLOGY OF CREATING ONTOLOGY OF INFORMATION SCIENCE (OIS) 89

3   CHAPTER 3: METHODOLOGY EMPLOYED 90

   3.1   THEORETICAL APPROACHES 90

       3.1.1 Taxonomy of OIS ontology approach 91

   3.2   THE METHODOLOGY TO BE ADOPTED 94

   3.3   TECHNIQUES AND TOOLS TO BE EMPLOYED 94

   3.4   ESTABLISHING THE ONTOLOGY MODEL 95

       3.4.1 Conceptual aspect 95

       3.4.2 Computational aspect 96

   3.5   INTRODUCING OIS DESIGN METHODOLOGY 96

       3.5.1 Designing ontology model 96

       3.5.2 Designing ontocop website tool 100

       3.5.3 Summary 100

PART 3: IMPLEMENTATION 101

4   CHAPTER 4: MODELLING DESIGN OF OIS ONTOLOGY 102

   4.1   BUILDING CONCEPTUAL MODEL 102

XII

- 4.1.1 Specifications 102
  - 4.1.1.1 Identifying the purpose and the scope 102
  - 4.1.1.2 Knowledge acquisition 104
- 4.1.2 Conceptualisation of IS entities ontology 109
  - Identification of concepts and relations 109
  - 4.1.2.1 Building Glossary of terms of IS 110
  - 4.1.2.2 Building Concepts taxonomy 110
  - 4.1.2.3 Building ad hoc binary relation: 116
  - 4.1.2.4 Build the concept dictionary 116
  - 4.1.2.5 Define ad hoc binary relation 117
  - 4.1.2.6 Define instance attributes 117
  - 4.1.2.7 Create class attributes table 118
  - 4.1.2.8 Define constants 118
  - 4.1.2.9 Define formal axiom 119
  - 4.1.2.10 Define instances 119
- 4.1.3 Conceptual Model of OIS Ontology 119
- 4.2 BUILDING COMPUTATIONAL MODEL – FORMALIZATION: 121
  - 4.2.1 Actors 123
    - 4.2.1.1 Person 124
    - 4.2.1.2 Institution 125
  - 4.2.2 Domains 126
  - 4.2.3 Kinds 126
  - 4.2.4 Practice 127
    - 4.2.4.1 Information Service 128
  - 4.2.5 Studies 129

	4.2.5.1	Information economics studies	129
4.2.6		Mediator	130
4.2.7		Methods	131
4.2.8		Resources	132
4.2.9		Tools	133
4.2.10		Philosophy and theories	133
4.2.11		Legislation	133
4.2.12		Societal	134
4.2.13		Time	134
4.2.14		Space	134
4.2.15		OIS Components	136
	4.2.15.1	Classes	136
	4.2.15.2	Axioms	142
	4.2.15.3	Properties	143
	4.2.15.4	Individuals	148
4.2.16		Usage Class Tab	149
4.3		Ontocop - a system of visualisation of IS knowledge	151
4.3.1		System Requirements	151
4.3.2		System Architecture	151
4.3.3		System implementing	152
	4.3.3.1	Technical features	152
	4.3.3.2	Aesthetic Features	153
4.3.4		System developments	153
4.3.5		Description and potentials of Ontocop components	157
4.3.6		Summary	160

PART 4: RESULTS & DISCUSSION 161

5 CHAPTER 5: RESULTS AND DISCUSSION 162

5.1 RESULTS 162

5.1.1 Evaluation OIS ontology 162

5.1.1.1 Ontology validation 162
5.1.1.2 Ontology verification 166
5.1.1.3 Use case scenario of evaluation 166
5.1.1.4 Results of Evaluation 169

5.1.2 Results of Ontocop System 175

5.2 DISCUSSION AND ANALYSIS 177

5.3 REVISED OIS MODEL 184

PART 4: CONCLUSION & FUTURE WORK 187

6 CHAPTER 6: CONCLUSION & FUTURE WORK 188

6.1 CONTRIBUTIONS 188
6.2 ACHIEVEMENTS 190
6.3 FUTURE WORK 191

BIBLIOGRAPHY 194

APPENDICES 205

A. EVALUATION REPORT 205
B. TAXONOMY OF IS 205
C. GLOSSARY 205
D. INVITATION LETTER ONTOCOP 205
E. INFORMATION ABOUT PARTICIPENTS PROCESS 205
F. LIST OF ONTOCOP'S PARTICIPANTS 205
G. GETTING INITIATION OF PARTICIPENTS PROCESS 205

H.	EXAMPLES OF A COLLECTED DATA	205
I.	LETTER SENT TO PARTICIPANTS	205
J.	RESPONSE EMAILS FROM PARTICIPENTS	205
K.	EVALUATION TAXONOMY	205
L.	PART OF OIS ONTOLOGY IN OWL FORMAT	205
M.	LESSONS LEARNED	205

List of Figures

FIGURE 1-1 THESIS ORGANIZATION 11

FIGURE 2-1 THE MEANING TRIANGLE 19

FIGURE 2-2 RELATIONS BETWEEN TERMS IN THESAURUS 21

FIGURE 2-3 SIMPLE TAXONOMY 22

FIGURE 2-4 SPECTRUM OF ONTOLOGY. 23

FIGURE 2-5 ILLUSTRATION OF MIDDLE-OUT APPROACH 25

FIGURE 2-6 GUARINO'S PROPOSAL FOR ONTOLOGY MODULARIZATION 28

FIGURE 2-7 AN EXAMPLE OF ONTOLOGY ROLE 34

FIGURE 2-8 CONCEPTUAL MODELLING 44

FIGURE 2-9 SEMANTIC WEB LANGUAGES 51

FIGURE 2-10 SEMANTIC NET IN RDF, RDFS 53

FIGURE 2-11 INFORMATION SCIENCE RELATIONS WITH OTHER SCIENCES 66

FIGURE 2-12 KNOWLEDGE MAP OF INFORMATION SCIENCE 67

FIGURE 2-13 DIFFERENCES BETWEEN DEWEY & RANGANTHAN CLASSIFICATION 70

FIGURE 2-14 CLASSIFICATION OF KNOWLEDGE IN ONTOLOGICAL DIAGRAM 77

FIGURE 3-1 THE MAIN COMPONENTS OF OIS ONTOLOGY 91

FIGURE 3-2 TAXONOMY OF LIBRARY SCIENCE MODULE 93

FIGURE 3-3 DOMAIN ONTOLOGY OF OIS DEVELOPING PROCESS 99

FIGURE 4-1 THE MAIN COMPONENT OF IS DOMAIN 103

FIGURE 4-2 SCREENSHOT OF IS GAZETTEER 105

FIGURE 4-3 ANNOTATIONS OF IS TERMS 107

Figure 4-4 annotation of IS concepts 108

Figure 4-5 result accuracy 109

Figure 4-6 Conceptualisation activities 109

Figure 4-7 shows Top-Down method 111

Figure 4-8 concept Taxonomy of OIS ontology 112

Figure 4-9 Bottom–up methods 113

Figure 4-10 fragment of OIS Taxonomy 115

Figure 4-11 ad hoc binary relations 116

Figure 4-12 part of conceptual model of OIS ontology 120

Figure 4-13 Upper-level of OIS ontology 122

Figure 4-14 Main Actors class 124

Figure 4-15 Person class 124

Figure 4-16 Institution Class 125

Figure 4-17 Domains Class 126

Figure 4-18 Kinds class 127

Figure 4-19 Practice concepts 128

Figure 4-20 Information service class 129

Figure 4-21 Information Economics studies class 130

Figure 4-22 Mediator class 131

Figure 4-23 Methods class 132

Figure 4-24 Resources class 132

Figure 4-25 philosophy and theories class 133

Figure 4-26 visualizing OIS by OWLViz 135

Figure 4-27 methods of defining class in OWL 137

Figure 4-28 defined class in owl 141

Figure 4-29 an example of disjoint class 142

Figure 4-30 object properties 143

Figure 4-31 InversOf relation 145

Figure 4-32 Individuals of OIS ontology 148

Figure 4-33 properties assertions of OIS ontology 149

Figure 4-34 usage class tap in protégé 150

Figure 4-35 website layout 152

Figure 4-36 Ontocop Forum 154

Figure 4-37 Ontocop chatting page 154

Figure 4-38 : Ontocop chatting page 155

Figure 4-39 Ontocop Members list 155

Figure 4-40 Ontology Page 156

Figure 4-41 Feedback Page 156

Figure 4-42 FQA Page 157

Figure 4-43 Contact Page 157

Figure 5-1 circular classes 164

Figure 5-2 inferred class hierarchy 165

Figure 5-3 part of OIS ontology verification results 166

Figure 5-4 Evaluation of IS taxonomy 167

Figure 5-5 snapshot of OIS ontology on WebProtégé 168

Figure 5-6 OIS documentation 168

Figure 5-7 ontology consistency 170

Figure 5-8 Consistency of is-a and part-of –relationships 171

Figure 5-9 completeness of ontology 171

Figure 5-10 Clarity of OIS ontology 172

Figure 5-11 ontology generality 172

Figure 5-12 semantic data richness of the ontology 173

Figure 5-13 The General assessment on OIS ontology 175

Figure 5-14 participants of Ontocop 175

Figure 5-15 visitors of Ontocop 176

Figure 5-16 satisfaction levels with the OIS ontology 181

Figure 5-17 evaluation criteria at level 3 182

Figure 5-18 Searching on WebProtégé 184

Figure 5-19 ontology matrices 185

Figure 6-1 Architecture of system design approach 189

Figure 6-2 Interface of OIS ontology searching 192

Figure 6-3 Relationships between ontologies 193

List of Tables

TABLE 2-1 SIMILARITY BETWEEN ONTOLOGY AND CATEGORY THEORY 17

TABLE 2-2 DIFFERENCES BETWEEN TAXONOMY AND ONTOLOGY 23

TABLE 2-3 ONTOLOGY CATEGORIES 30

TABLE 2-4 DOMAIN ONTOLOGIES 33

TABLE 2-5 APPROACHES OF ONTOLOGY EVALUATION 36

TABLE 2-6 AN OVERVIEW OF LEVELS OF ONTOLOGY EVALUATION 39

TABLE 2-7 IMPLEMENTATION OF METHONTOLOGY 45

TABLE 2-8 COMPARISON BETWEEN METHODOLOGIES 48

TABLE 2-9 METHODOLOGY STANDARDS 49

TABLE 2-10 COMPARISON BETWEEN SEMANTIC LANGUAGES 54

TABLE 2-11 OWL CONSTRUCTORS 56

TABLE 2-12 OWL AXIOMS INTERPRETATION AND FACT 57

TABLE 2-13 COMPARISON BETWEEN ONTOLOGY LANGUAGES 58

TABLE 2-14 GROUPS OF ONTOLOGIES TOOLS 58

TABLE 2-15 COMPARISON BETWEEN ONTOLOGY TOOLS 62

TABLE 2-16 COMPARISON BETWEEN COMMUNITIES OF PRACTICE 87

TABLE 4-1 THE SCOPE OF IS DOMAIN 103

TABLE 4-2 PART OF THE GLOSSARY OF TERMS OF OIS ONTOLOGY 110

TABLE 4-3 CONCEPTS CLUSTERING 114

TABLE 4-4 CONCEPTS DICTIONARY 117

TABLE 4-5 PART OF THE AD HOC BINARY RELATION OF OIS ONTOLOGY 117

TABLE 4-6 SHOWS PART OF INSTANCE ATTRIBUTES OF OIS ONTOLOGY 118

TABLE 4-7 A SECTION OF THE INSTANCE ATTRIBUTES TABLE OF OIS ONTOLOGY 118

TABLE 4-8 A SECTION OF CONSTANTS TABLE OF OIS ONTOLOGY 118

TABLE 4-9 THE INSTANCE TABLE OF THE OIS ONTOLOGY 119

TABLE 4-10   TYPES OF RELATIONS BETWEEN TERMS 144

TABLE 5-1 INCONSISTENCE CLASSES 163

TABLE 5-2 THE QUESTIONS IN OIS ONTOLOGY SURVEY 169

TABLE 5-3 LEVEL 3 OF SATISFACTION ON ONTOLOGY BASED ON SPECIFIC CRITERIA 182

Acronyms

AI	Artificial Intelligence
ANNE	A Nearly New Information extraction System
CLIPS	C Language Integrated Production System
COC	Community of Commitment
CoI	Community of Interest
Cops	Communities of practice
DARPA	Defence Advanced Research Projects Agency
GATE	General Architecture for Text Engineering
IE	Information Extracting
IS	Information Science
JAPE	Java Annotation Patterns Engine
KE	Knowledge Engineering
KR	Knowledge Representation
LOOM	Language for Object Oriented Methods
Nop	Network of practice
OCML	Operation Conceptual modelling Language
OIS	Ontology of Information Science
Ontocop	Community of Information Science website
OWL	Web Ontology Language
RDF	Resource Description Framework
SGML	Standard Generalized Mark-up Language
VCops	Virtual Community of practice

VCs	....	Virtual community
W3C	....	World Wide Web Consortium
XML	....	Extensible Mark-up Language

Part 1: Fundamental Issues

1 Chapter 1: Introduction

Recently, the development of domain ontologies has become increasingly important for knowledge level interoperation and information integration. They provide functional features for AI and knowledge representation. Domain Ontology is a central foundation of growth for the semantic web that provides a general knowledge for correspondence and communication among heterogeneous systems. Particularly with a rise of ontology in the artificial intelligence (AI) domain, it can be seen as an almost inevitable development in computer science and AI in general.

Ontologies are useful for different applications to be able to share information between heterogeneous data resources. They are also essential for enabling knowledge-level interoperation of agents, when these agents are interacting to share a common interpretation of the vocabulary. Moreover, it is useful for human understanding and interaction to reach a consensus amongst a professional community.

Although there are a range of domain ontologies on the semantic web such as Gene Ontology (GeneOntology, 2009), Biological science ontology (Sabou 2005), CIDOC-CRM ontology of culture heritage documentation, FRBR in Bibliographic and NCI cancer ontology (Golbeck et al., 2008), there still exists a lack of domain ontologies, which has led to the loss of knowledge in specific domains. This is a significant problem for scholars and researchers who need to be able to access information within their interest area.

Ontology provides a vocabulary for metadata description with machine understandable terminology. Ontology provides a format for explaining and understanding terminology and the knowledge contained in a software system. By using shared concepts and terms in accordance with a specific approach, a lot of information remains in people's heads. It is discussed in 2.3.

However, information science (IS) is a fast paced discipline and communication technology is rapidly increasing, so it is imperative to take advantage of this development. IS is a multidisciplinary field and it has gained the fundamental root of its theory from different related fields. The analysis includes the three branches of the field, which are; Library Science, Archival Science and Computer Science. Meanwhile it overlaps with other sciences, as stated in Section 2.2, e.g., communication, cognitive science, philosophical science, management, social science and marketing. More precisely, the relationships between information and marketing can be subdivided into marketing information, marketing information services, marketing of library services.

These kinds of relationships need logical ontology to clarify their relations and the science boundaries, amongst others. Therefore, Information Science still needs identity.

However, there is a lack of IS ontology representing the unified model that combines all concepts and their relationships. Moreover, IS as any domains which use the natural language. It contains a lot of jargon which needs to be in a formal language for programming or logic. Alternatively, integration of the computer with the internet has led to the emergence of new concepts in the field of IS such as , Electronic Library, Virtual Library, Library Without Walls, Digital Library and Information Management, as well as Nerve Centres. Even the information concept itself has strong and complex relations with other concepts, for example some people have defined it as fact, energy, data, and symbols. Also, it can be composed with other words such as; information age, information revaluation, information crisis, information explosion. However, there are 400 definitions for information in the literature (Yuexiao, 1988). It is hard to differentiate between these concepts. Even within the same field, there is still confusion over defining information - everyone defines it based on his background, for example librarians know it in term of facts, and data can be in containers such as journals, books and documents. The computer scientists conceive it as small units such as bits and bytes.

Consequently, modelling the IS domain necessarily assumes the need to represent the correct picture of the whole domain, and any changes in the domain will have to be added to keep the model up to date (Mommers, 2010, Yuexiao, 1988).

Our consideration is that in developing an ontology of Information science OIS to define its boundaries, and avoid ambiguous concepts.

Therefore, there is a lack of unified model of domain knowledge, because of the inconsistency in structure of domain which led to difficulty of using and sharing data in syntax and semantic level.

1.1. Problem Identification

Information Science is seeking its identity and it is one of the many domains which use natural language including much jargon. Also, integration of the computer with the internet has led to emerging concepts in the field of IS such as , Electronic Library, Virtual Library, Library without walls , digital Library It is hard to differentiate between them.

Furthermore, its structure led to lack of a unified model of domain knowledge. This led to lack of a unified model of domain knowledge, and difficulty of using and sharing data at syntax and semantic levels. The OIS ontology provides a standard terminology and shared representation of domain concepts.

Therefore, the ontology of information science is missing in ontological engineering area. Our consideration is that developing ontology of Information science to define its boundaries, and to avoid the concepts ambiguous.

The research problem of the study was defined as the following:

Q. How an ontology of Information Science (OIS) model can be developed to visualise the IS domain, and how the model could capture and represent this knowledge?

To achieve the primary objective, the researcher asks questions to be answered through this study such as:

- What domain knowledge does the ontology represent?
- What is the level of knowledge that the ontology will represent?
- Which knowledge representation techniques and languages should be used?
- What are the relations that will be used to structure the knowledge, and which structure for the ontology will it have e.g. tree, graph, and its main components of ontology (e.g., classes, instances, relations, rules)?
- What is the value of tools such virtual community of practice ontocop? Could they be valuable in supporting the developing process?
- Does the developing process of the ontology follow designing criteria?
- Is the ontology evaluated based on specific criteria?

1.2. Aims and Objectives

The aim of this research is to develop a generic model of ontology that visualize domain knowledge of IS that serves as a foundation of knowledge modelling for applications and aggregation with other ontologies.

The visualisation stage provides an extensible and commonly understood semantic framework by describing the terminology of the domain. Achieving this aim in the current study will fulfil the following Objectives:

- Building a conceptual model for establishing a better analysis framework to understand, classify and compare various classes of Information Science.

- providing a framework to make it possible to share a common understanding of Information Science by:
    o Identifying the key objects of IS domain and relationships.
    o Providing a specification of information requirement for both developers and end users, to be used in different applications.

1.3. Methodology and Implementation

The aim of this part is to investigate whether the results found in the literature study could be applied in practice by focusing on ontologies in a specific area. For this purpose, the virtual community of practice (Ontocop) was designed to visualise the area of Information Science (IS). Also, to involve other people as member of VCops by using some process of negotiation, to give us feedback on the ontology it is been developed. Additionally, they will help the researcher to assist and evaluate the ontology. There are many different methods for asking for feedback and analysis what the results are.

The literature review will be used in this research to address the research problem as identified by Saunders, et al (2000). It will be include the key of academic theories through the chosen area, and revealing that knowledge of your chosen area is new. Beside explain how the research relates to previous published research, to justify arguments by referencing prior works. Furthermore, enabling readers to find the original work you cite through apparent reference.

Regarding building the ontology, a methodology for building ontologies decides the main development stage and proposes guidelines for each stage dependent on use of the ontology. Many methodologies have been proposed since the 1990s to build ontologies. Each one has a different approach, such as Methontology, and SENSUS. Gòmez-Pérez et al. (2004) have made comparisons between these methods, and have pointed out that these methods have common development stages most of them have conceptualisation, requirements analysis, formalisation, implementation, maintaining and evaluating. Hence, there seems to be no general agreement on methodology to building and design ontology, due to the fact that it depends on its application and purpose of using it Noy and McGuinness (2009). To build a new ontology from scratch, or reuse another ontology, it should be built according to present needs and the purpose from it (Pinto and Martins 2001).

In this study, a new approach is proposed for designing a system to build ontology through sharing and reusing knowledge between members of communities of practice of Information Science (IS). The first step is building the ontology through the (VCops).

The second step is building ontology of Information Science (OIS). In this sense our approach to visualise the knowledge of IS domain, will be as depicted in Chapter 3.

1.4. Contributions

In this research the main contribution presented through this thesis is:

- Creating ontology of Information Science OIS model to unify IS knowledge. The OIS ontology is a general model for the domain, enabling the integration of a large amount of information resources. It designed to be flexible, reusable for other implementations, and compatible in knowledge base systems rather than imposing a specific solution.
- The model has fundamental roots in a framework based on analysis of the knowledge of IS domain; our framework is to identify the domain boundaries and relationships among them by providing IS taxonomy. Although there are many classification systems in the world none of them represent this in a formal way. In this study OIS taxonomy will be represented in OWL formal presentation; the taxonomy approach is described in Section 3.1.1.

  The model has defined 706 concepts which will be widely used in Information Science applications. It provides the standard definitions for domain terms used in annotation databases for the domain terms, and avoids the consistency problems caused by various ontologies which will have the potential of development by different groups and institutions in the IS domain area.
- Design VCops (Ontocop) to support and assess the development process as specific virtual community of IS. The Ontocop consists of a number of experts in the subject area around the world. Their feedback and assessment improve the ontology development during the creating process.

The structured ontology was developed as a specific model of IS domain by following Methontology based on the IEEE standard (1996, 2006) for development software life cycle process. It mainly consists of the four main stages described in Section 3.3. The methodology and tools of design ontology was determined based on the experiments of Uschold and Grüninger M.(1996), Noy and McGuinness, (2001).

The designing evaluation tool is presented in Section 4.1. The research tools adopted were;

1. Design a virtual community of practice (ontocop) evaluation ontology model.

2. The study used information extraction (IE) techniques to annotate the key entities of IS using JAPE grammar and General Architecture for Text Engineering (GATE) for data annotation; more details can be found in Section 4.1.1.2.

The principle resources that have been used are domain experts through Ontocop, who were consulted to assess the ontology based on their experience and knowledge.

This research attempts to improve understanding of the distinctions among information science as a whole. Therefore, it is seeking to describe the constituents of the IS field, and ideally to put these into set theoretical foundations in Section 3.1.

The research does not provide any a priori assumptions of using precise details about the IS domain, insofar as it is a generic model intended to provide a control vocabulary that can be applied for IS applications. It is important to note that the ontology model does not cover the range of individuals and extending relations. Nevertheless, it defines the concepts that serve as the foundation of IS, such as Actors, Methods, Domains, etc, which need to be extended in future use with corresponding ontologies.

OIS ontology is structured as a combination of domain and an upper ontology. The upper ontology contains a foundation of the ontology. It offers very general entities with subclasses, attributes, objects that give potential sources of integration with other ontologies. The IS domain has a strong relation with others.

The reason behind that, however, is that the domain ontology presents specific concepts of the domain in eclectic ways, which are often incompatible and incomplete. These kind of ontologies need to be merged and shared with other ontologies into more general representation. Also, it should be well-matched to the equivalent semantic area with corresponding ontology. Particularly in the IS domain, this consists of a complex combination. By using a common foundation, ontology provides basic elements for emerging domains ontologies automatically. The ontology model is a comprehensive scope covering three branches that are closely related to the domain; library science, archival science, and computer science.

The purpose of the OIS model is not to serve a broad spectrum of librarians, academic staff, publishers, information service providers only insofar it takes into account a variety of applications. Entities, relationships and attributes are the basic components of the model; these elements were derived from logical analysis of IS data.

Furthermore, the research describes the strategy and method developed to build the domain ontology of IS. It believes that this research offers significant advantages to modelling domain knowledge, in term of the contents of developing the IS ontology. This study created domain ontology and it is not considered task and application ontology. The main purpose of the OIS ontology is to provide a unified model of domain knowledge that supports knowledge sharing and the exchange of data among databases.

1.5. Motivation of study

Ontology is not just identifying classes as entities and their relations and concept hierarchy but also specifying them by using specific ontology representation languages. OIS ontology seeks to provide a formal model of Information Science domain that is formulated in description logic. OIS ontology aims to represent domain knowledge to use independently of any application.

The motivation will be therefore at these possible levels:

- Ontologies represent knowledge about the real world. Nowadays, with growing attention to ontology, IS needs ontology. The problematic situation is identification of IS itself, especially the overlap between it and library science, computer science and archives science. On the other hand, there are many attempts to change the identity of the science to Knowledge science rather IS(Zins, 2007a). From this perspective we need a serious attempt to challenge the identity of IS through identification of its boundaries and relations with other fields, through this research, in Section 2.2.
- Information Science just as any other scientific field requires a framework for organising its knowledge, especially with the fast speed of development disciplines. The terms data information and knowledge still have definition issues, although there have been many attempts to define and distinguish between them, precise definition is still problematic (Zins, 2007a, Wiederhold, 1986, Bubenko and Orci, 1989).
- Providing a consensual knowledge model of the IS field to be used by application ontologies. Hence, developing ontology enables the application to manage complex and disparate information. Also, changing the semantic web structure from surface composition to be captured in the application logic.
- Using a virtual community of practice as a way of sharing knowledge. Although there has been extensive discussion about the use of communities of practice in this way, no formal academic research has been identified relating specifically to the context of evaluating ontology via VCops in the Information Science domain.

1.6. Thesis organization

This research is structured into 5 parts and 6 Chapters. Each part is preceded with a brief introductory section to explain how the work presented in the Chapter fits in the overall structure of the research.

Part 1: presents the fundamental issue of the research. Chapter 1 provides the identification of the problem, and the aims, objectives and motivation of the study, research methods, and research organisation. Furthermore, to solve the problem identified we create ontology in Chapter 4.

The second Chapter 2 presents a survey of the previous studies to provide contextual information on the main components of the research; Section 1, which is about ontology for semantic web overview, presents the origin of the ontology, and introduces the formal definition of an ontology that supports the communication between human and machine. Additionally, it introduces types of ontologies and provides techniques to represent ontologies based on web standards languages e.g., XML, RDF. Furthermore, it presents a comprehensive framework of ontology layered for the semantic web. Section 2 is about Information Science as domain of the ontology, as well as Section 3 which is about knowledge management and virtual communities of practice. This part explores related work to provide the background to the research.

Part 2: presents methodology of creating ontology of Information Science OIS in Chapters 3 in two sections. The Section 1 provides the theoretical model of the current study. The Section 2 presents the methodology that has followed in the research to design OIS ontology.

Part 3: implementation of OIS ontology model Chapter 4 in two sections, which provides the functionality of the implemented tool environment for ontology engineering called Protégé. It provides a numbers of screenshots and examples of the running system. Section 1 presents the model design and Section 2 presents the ontocop system design.

Part 4: Results and Discussion, in Chapter 5, has two sections. Section 1 provides our approaches to evaluating OIS ontology. These approaches are based on a number of ontology quality criteria, to consider the question of how this Information Science ontology will be used and whether it will be useful, and if the answer is yes, which context or application ontology will use it, as identified in Chapter 4.

Part 5: consists of one Chapter 6 of conclusion and future work, to draw together the contributions this research offers, and a direction to future work. Figure 1 gives a graphical overview of how to construct the research.

Appendices are at the end of the thesis. The evaluation report is found in Appendix A. Appendix B includes Taxonomy of IS. Appendix C includes the Glossary of IS terms. The ontocop collection is included in Appendix D, which also contains the invitation letter to invite participants to ontocop, and E contains information about participation process. The members list is found in Appendix F; Appendix G is about getting initiation of participant's process – it explains how members can start using the ontocop. Appendix H contains examples of the database of participants; Appendix I contains the letter of setting at ease starting of participants, and Appendix J contains the response emails of agreement to the participation. Appendix K consists of the feedback on evaluation taxonomy. Appendix L is a part of OIS ontology OWL file. Finally, some lessons learnt during the study can be found in Appendix M.

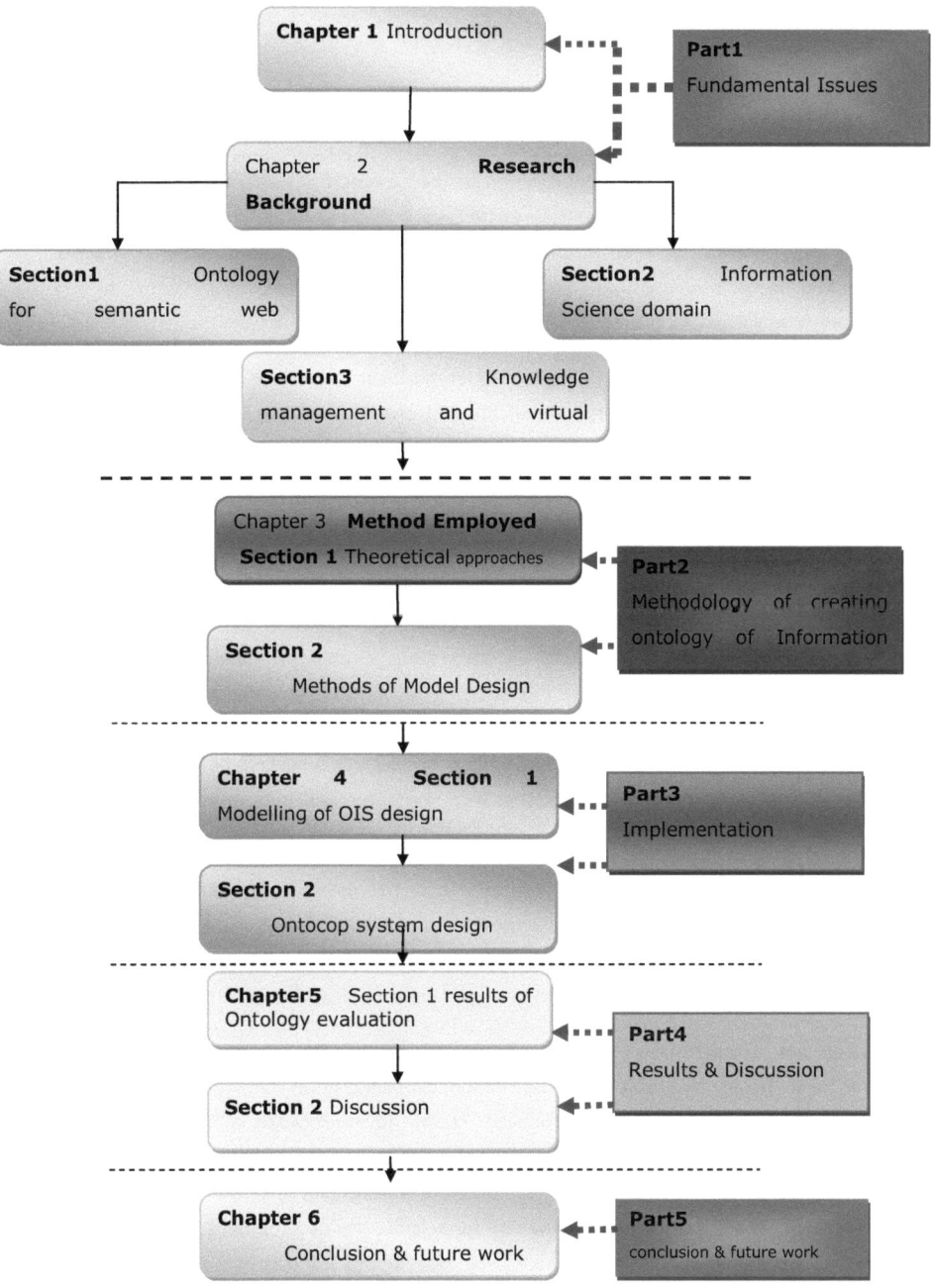

Figure 1-1 Thesis organization

2 Chapter 2: Research Background

The literature review gives the background to the research process, which consisted of three main aspects to find out the theoretical background essential to this project. These aspects were: ontological engineering, Information Science, and Communities of Practice within knowledge management. The following sections provide an overview of key literature relevant to this project.

Firstly, however, the background starts with some basic definitions to establish what is meant by ontology and what the significance of creating ontology is. The survey will come back to the three key aspects of this study and review literature on these; firstly, ontology.

2.1 Ontology Overview

Ontology plays an important role to use as a source of shared defined terms – for instance metadata – which can be used in a specific domain (Gaoyun et al., 2010). The concept of ontology became popular in the 1990s. Ontology's meaning can change according to the context of where it is used – for instance in philosophy, computers, linguistics, mathematics or social science. It is defined differently in work relating to computer science. Barry Smith (2003) said that ontology is a science of the existence of beings, and as such it has a relationship with computer and information science as a field.

Interest in the area of ontology in computer science has grown in recent years (Amira et al., 2007, Bhatt et al., 2009). In the early 1990s, ontology definitions as a term within computer science emerged. Computer science defined ontology based on knowledge systems (KMS) as a classification of knowledge (Guarino, 1997).

Ontology has a long history of development which predates computer science. This section will begin by reviewing the historical background of ontology, and the philosophical perspective will be introduced. Then, moving forward to defining ontology based on comparing the original use with its current use in computer science will be combined, which will lead to a formal definition of an ontology that will be the basis for this research. Then, the thesis will move on to describe the development of ontology and share an explanation of the benefits of developing ontologies. It summarising approaches to modelling ontology with some examples of ontologies. Finally, we summarise some methodology, and explain the tools such as Protégé and the languages used for representing ontologies.

2.1.1 Historical and philosophical perspective of the ontology

To understand the ontological foundation for the ontology of Information Science it required reviewing diverse approaches to the notion of this concept. This section reviews some of the literature that is relevant to philosophical ontology. We explore some views from logicians that have influenced this project.

The ontology concept came from a branch of philosophy. Philosophers used ontology as a synonym of metaphysics - that means anything comes after the physical (Smith, 2003). Consequently, they defined it as a theory related to the study of relationships between beings (Webster's, 2010).More accurately, ontology is the study of things categories that may exist or already do exist in some domains (Sowa, 2000).

Back to the history from a philosophical perspective, Aristotle (384-322BC) invented ontology as a study of the ways that the universe is organised into categories. The category is the highest level of universal obtained from those domains; all other universals reorganised their hierarchies that need the top levels of categories, such as City, Man, and Organism. In (1200-1600) medieval scholars developed a common control vocabulary for talking about these universals in terms of sorts of reality. Descartes only initiated a movement of epistemology as a centre of philosophy rather than ontology or metaphysics until around (1960-61) by differentiating between mental and physical subspecies which had not been a problem for Aristotle. Brentano (1838-1917) denied the differences between philosophy and science; he said they are one and the same. Husserl (1859-1938) influenced by Brentano, invented formal ontology as a discipline distinct from formal logic. He showed how philosophy and science had become detached from the real life world or ordinary experience (Calero et al., 2006).

Philosophical ontology is a way of describing reality by providing a comprehensive classification of entities. That means organising all kinds of relations by classes or entities collectively (Merrill, 2011).

In general, methods of philosophical ontology are derived from philosophical methods. These methods include theory development, and testing and modifying them. Furthermore, these methods were similar to Aristotle's view.

Many philosophers had made distinctions between logic, computation models and ontology. Robert Poli (2003) has discriminated further between Husserlian formal ontology, descriptive and formalized ontologies. This distinction appeared from discussion of the main role of logic in these formalisms of ontology. Husserl's logical view had asserted that logic is an essential part of formal ontology (Poli, 2003). The group of

AI has followed this theory where the formal ontology contained concepts, logical axioms, theorems and mereology. However, according to Tim Berners-Lee's semantic web tower, logic is the top layer above ontology vocabulary (BERNER-LEE, 2001). More interestingly the technical and knowledge representation aspects have been using a robust concept of Web Ontology Language (OWL) as W3C recommendations are based on the description logic.

Recently, ontology has become associated with AI and information systems. AI logicists have focused attention on the knowledge-based craft. In 1980 McCarthy recognized the overlap between philosophical ontology and building logical theories of AI systems. McCarthy (1980) confirmed that developers of logic based on intelligent systems need to accumulate everything that exists to build the ontology.

Nirenburg and Raskin (2001) emphasize that ontological semantics is a theory of meaning in a Natural Language Process (NLP) that supports many applications such as information extracting and machine translation. Crucially, however, a good ontology requires choosing concepts that have to be covered and reasonably consistent. The ontology designers decide how to arrange and organise the concepts to be included (Nirenburg and Raskin, 2001, Nirenburg and Raskin, 2004).

In the interim, a similar view of overlap with philosophical ontology was proposed by Joan Sowa; ontology is to be considered as catalogue for possible global use that puts everything together and defines how it works (Sowa, 1984).

The AI community prefers to use the concept of ontology in knowledge engineering without much overlapping with the field of philosophical ontology. They work under the title of "ontology" that is related to logical semantics and logical theory.

Alexander et al., (1986) initially used the concept in the AI sense. This concept has been grown considerably in different fields of Database Management Systems (DBMS), knowledge engineering, domain modelling and conceptual modelling.

2.1.1.1 Definition of ontology

Since the AI community discovered the power and knowledge within their systems, ontologies can refer to an engineering artefact to present a formal specification developed with AI, or an informal specification for human users. The AI community defined ontology as:

"Ontology is a theory of what entities can exist in the mind of a knowledgeable agent". (Wielinga and Schreiber, 1993)

In 1993 Tom Gruber coined the concept Ontology in a sub-field of computer science. Gruber gave us the most widely-shared definition of ontology as a conceptual model:

"An ontology is an explicit specification of conceptualisation."(Gruber, 1993a)

But his definition has many interpretations, which are that ontology can provide a specification of conceptualisation of generic notions such as space and time or domain application. A number of researchers in the computer science community have attempted to clarify and formalise the ontology definition further such as (Guarino, 1998).

Guarino and Giaretta (1995) highlighted the importance of terminological classification, to avoid misunderstandings over an ontology as a conceptual framework at knowledge level and an ontology as an artefact at symbol level, used for a specific purpose. The concept was further developed in 1999 when Welty and his colleagues described a range of information artefacts that had been classified as ontology. (Welty et al., 1999)

Meadche (2002) defined ontology formally as containing classes, relations and axioms, whilst also allowing for lexical entities referring to multiple concepts and relationships (homonym). It also refers to the concepts and relations through several lexical entries (synonym). In 1993 Gruber defined ontology as:

"An ontology is a specification of a conceptualization." (Gruber, 1993b)

His definition has been developed to be more accurate for defining ontology which is:

"Formal explicit specification of shared conceptualization"

Ontology makes the term clearer and indicates in which context the term can be used. The definition consists mainly of:

A formal: ontology should be machine readable and processed by AI systems. We do not need it to be a communication device between people and people, or even people and machine. Ontology should be formally defined as a formal language. (Morbach et al., 2009)

Specification: means written specifications of language syntax to satisfy certain criteria such as precise, unambiguous, consistent, complete and implementation independent statements (Turner and T.L, 1994). It should offer a communication tool whereby users can share knowledge in consensual ways.

Shared: ontology represents consensual knowledge that, has been arranged and agreed on by group of people as result of social networks rather than an individual's view.

Conceptualisation: this is an abstract model of a domain that is driven by user application, and represents concepts and relationships to be shared and reused. Conceptualisation is based on objects, concepts and other entities already in existence in the area of interest.

Based on this, ontology should be formally defined as being processed by a machine. The ontology is a specific type of information object or artifact. The way the ontology is constructed refers to classes, relations and their instances, all of which play explicitly specified roles in the conceptualisation. Otherwise, the backbone of the ontology consists of specification or generalisation hierarchy of concepts. However, Ontology is not software, though, so whilst it can be used by programs, it cannot run as a program

A far more interesting question is what information systems could learn from philosophical ontology. It is a shared belief that there is a similarity inherent in ontology from philosophical and applied scientific perspectives. Philosophical ontology is describing the real world as it exists, while computational ontology is describing the world as it should be (Kabilan, 2007).

2.1.2 Ontology Theoretic

2.1.2.1 Category Theory

A number of thinkers and pioneers as Aristotle, Hartmann and Husserl (Bello, 2010, Hartmann, 1952), point out that ontology is adopted as a categorical framework that means it seeks for what is universal (Poli, 2010). Husserl's emphasis on the premise of the category theory could be reflected in many ways according to different viewpoints The precise meaning of ontology relies on the theory of category as a grounding in contemporary mathematics (Lawvere, 1969, Krötzsch et al., 2005, Johnson and Dampney, 2001, Awodey, 2006, Hu and Weng, 2010).

Similarities in the relationship between category theory and ontological representation technique are summarised in Table 2-1

Table 2-1 similarity between ontology and category theory

similarity	Ontology	Category theory
classification	as Tree	grammars using tree or TAGS
Defining language	present language by defining term	Mathematical concepts
node	Has node of tree	Has node of tree
relations	Interrelations	Close relations between formal linguistic presentation of domain & tree base representation.

However, categories appear in different ways such as taxonomy (is-a superclass, subclass), to group the domain in classical taxonomical categories according to Aristotle perspective. Recently Aristotle framework becomes matter particularly with time. Theories can help to define formal ontological properties that contribute to characterising the concepts. Husserl introduced the theory of Mereology as basic for formal ontology, and it is an alternative of set theory described by Tennant (2007).

2.1.2.2 Mereotopolgy Theory

Mereology is a formal theory concerned with wholes and parts structures (Husserl, 1970), whereas topology is a theory of wholeness that defines the relations connected to its properties, and how to be represent these components within the system (Varzi, 1996).

The basic metrological system is M= (E, ≤) in which E is domain entities, and ≤ is binary relations. The E, ≤ binary relation is denoted; M can be considered as ground Mereology. The ground Mereology is the first order partial ordering theory as reflexive, antisymmetric, transitive relations; some relations can be axiomatised as follows:

$$(M1) \; \forall x \; (x \leq x), \; \text{(reflexive)}$$

$$(M2) \; \forall xy \; (x \leq y \wedge y \leq x \rightarrow x = y \;), \text{(anti-symmetry)}$$

$$(M3) \; \forall x \, y \, z \; (x \leq y \wedge y \leq z \rightarrow \leq z \;), \; \text{(transitivity)}.$$

More precisely, the general framework Mereology system is defined to the level of granularity and predicate:

$$M(D) = (E, wh(x, l), P(x,y))$$

Any domain is introduced M(D), and where/why(x, l) is the level of granularity and predicate , expressing that x is entity of the level of granularity L.

But with the weakness of this theory it requires more axioms to recomplete the functions (Varzi, 1996, Herre, 2010) The formal precise theory identifies and describes the classical first order logic using variables Y, X, Z etc. For the theory to be semantically and ontologically adequate it is required.

The axioms in Mereotopolgy are designed to serve a formal ontological system. The primitive relations of parthood or constituency are as follows: if says x is a part of y 'x P y' then y will be consisted with x's being identical to y:

$$x \text{ overlaps } y \quad xOy: = \exists z \, (zPx \wedge zPy)$$
$$x \text{ is discrete from } y: xDy: = \neg \, xOy$$
$$x \text{ is a point } Pt(x): = \forall y \, (yPx \rightarrow y = x)$$

While, Boundaries defined as follows:

$$xBy: = \forall z \, (zPx \rightarrow z \backslash sty)$$
$$\text{If X is tangent y then} \quad x \, T \, y := \exists z(zPx \rightarrow zTy)$$
$$\text{If X cross y then} \quad xXy := xPy \wedge -xDy \quad \text{(Barry, 1996)}$$

This research is based on (Herre, 2010)'s view about constricting a domain which is:

$$D = (obj(D), V(D), CP(D).$$

D is a domain that is determined by set of objects obj(D) connected to it. These objects rely on a set of views V(D), and a set of classification principles (CP) for objects obj(D). To make the components highly formal it is necessary to use categories and relations between them. In this case, the domain should be represent as:

$$\text{Concepts } (D) = Cat(D), Rel(D), Obj(D).$$

It is based on (Gurbe, 1993)'s approach of specification of conceptualization. The domain components are supported by relationships Rel(D), classification principle- taxonomy CP(D), additionally the concepts of the domain will be determined by adding axioms, these axioms are presented by interrelations between categories and its properties.

2.1.3 Referencing and meaning in the ontology

Human communication theory is expressed in a general communication context using the triangle of meaning. As depicted by Ogden et.al (1949) this contains three relationships between words, thoughts and things. This describes the real world interaction between thoughts (concepts), words (terms) and things (objects), as depicted in Figure 2-1.

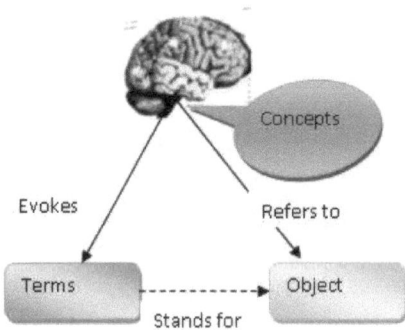

Figure 2-1 the meaning triangle

The diagram shows the relationship between objects and concepts, and an indirect relationship between terms and objects, meaning there is no matching between words and things. In natural languages such as Spanish or English, each concept has a meaning. To explain further, a concept often carries more than one meaning, based on the knowledge background and historical structure in an individual's mind; for example, if someone talks about "AAAE5", the person listening to them won't understand them because there's no matching image in his mind to interpret this or connect it to the real world. However, when the conversation is about a specific concept, for example "jaguar", everyone will interpret or imagine it, based on their background knowledge. One will think it is an expensive car that has an engine, four tyres and needs oil to move, and so on. The other thinks it is a big cat. In this way, one concept can have different meanings.

Concepts are a basic part of the proposition. They can express a certain meaning. The conceptual model helps to abstract models of parts of reality, by describing the key concepts and their relations.

More interesting than this, however, is what ontology can do in this case as a type of conceptual modelling method. Ontology attempts to represent the meaning of concepts, their properties, values and attributes. It provides a clear definition by stimulating a particular meaning, in this case that a jaguar is a big cat with four legs which lives in America. Ontology helps to avoid confusion and supports effective communication.

2.1.4 Ontology spectrum

The first task in the ontology of IS is to control the vocabulary being used. The intention of ontology is to capture and reuse knowledge on a particular subject between software applications and groups of people (Gómez-Pérez et al., 2003). In reality, the nature of ontology has many aspects – some people consider it a thesaurus, some a data dictionary, and others a representation of concepts, classifications or taxonomy.

2.1.4.1 Thesaurus

However, the most popular way of controlling vocabulary is the thesaurus, which is a list of words grouped together, based on their meaning. Librarians in libraries and information centres use it as a tool to categorise information for the purpose of information retrieval. A thesaurus is similar to ontology in some aspects:
- Organizing terminologies in consistent ways.
- Using hierarchy structure as category and subcategory.
- Using terms in a particular domain.
- Providing information as synonym relation.

A thesaurus differs from ontology because a thesaurus provides ambiguity in relationships and offers alternative words and meanings. (Broader then BT, Narrow then NT, Related to RT). These relations are offered but they are unclear and aren't formally defined, unlike ontological relations. The relations should relate to a specific term rather than a range of terms and should also indicate that this term is a part of another term, e.g. (A) is subclass of (B) and (D) is a superclass of (A). Furthermore, the relationships in ontology indicate classes, subclasses, relations and properties, axioms. Ontology therefore provides far more than relationships. Relating to this Daconta (2003) pointed out other relations that had parallels with terms in the thesaurus, such as:

- *Equivalence; if term (A) has a synonym then term (B) is equivalent.*

- *Homographic; when term (Y) is spelled as (F) but has different meaning.*

- *Hierarchical; the term could be narrower than and broader than, e.g.*

    If (A) is broader than (B); then (A) is superclass of (B).

    If (C) is narrower than (D); then (C) is subclass of (D).

- Associative: this means that when (Z) is associated with (Y), there are non-specified relationships between the two terms.(Daconta Michael C. et al., 2003) Figure 2-2 displays some of these relations.

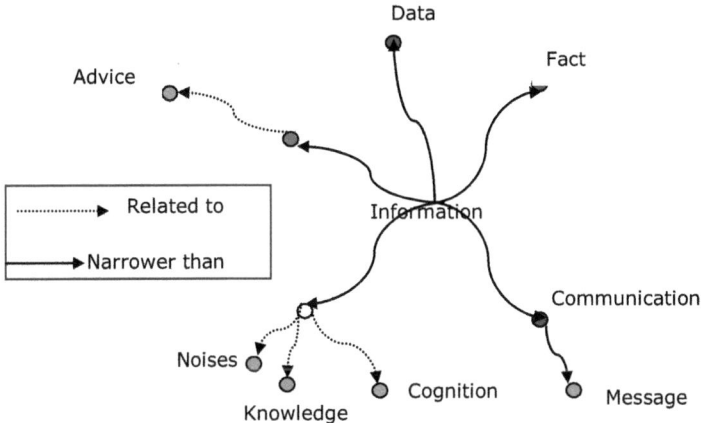

Figure 2-2 Relations between terms in Thesaurus

Ontology's aim is different from that of a thesaurus. The former defines concepts in a structure by revealing the relationships between them, whilst a thesaurus merely illustrates the relations between terms, rather than presenting any defining terms. The thesaurus works to navigate between terms and for information retrieval. The thesaurus is weak in providing strong and rich relations amongst concepts, without taxonomy using narrow and broad relations.

It is more interesting, however, to use ontology in practical applications. This could be better than using a thesaurus, particularly when using searching and query processes for specific information. This is because ontology has machine-interpretable concept definitions, so it can infer precise concepts from information resources.

2.1.4.2 Taxonomy

Ontology is a table of categories. Each entity is tied and captured in some nodes in the form of the hierarchy tree, which basically lays Aristotle's roots of thinking on categories, as well as his medieval successors. Taxonomy classifies entities in a hierarchical configuration – this offers concepts and relations in a domain, which are labelled child and parent. For example, taxonomy supports users in searching and browsing online. (Tsui et al., 2009) The following Figure 2-3 shows a simple example of categories.

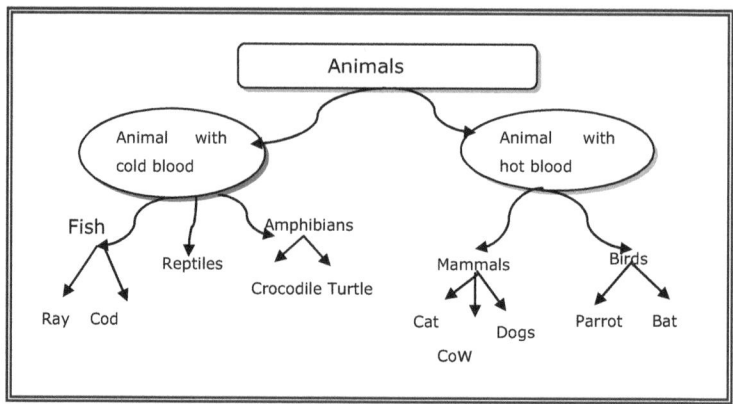

Figure 2-3 Simple Taxonomy

For the sake of clarity, we can say that ontology is similar to taxonomy in its use of classes and subclasses, but ontology provides more conclusions than taxonomy, not just things and parts. It has Classes C, Individuals I, Relations R and Axioms AX, and is formulated by a formal modelling language L. Besides providing a semantic link between classes such as (is –a) relations and synonyms and antonyms.

Furthermore, ontology could shift the semantic web from a weak to a strong tool for information retrieval. So before using ontology, the semantic web is based on a taxonomy, thesaurus and conceptual model. Taxonomy offers and supplies the main structure of information, with ontology adding details to it, whereas the semantic web is a machine that formulates data to enable computers' applications to understand it Daconta et al.,(2003). For instance, Yahoo provides top-level taxonomy as a basic notion of generalisation and specification of concepts. Yet it does not provides Is-A relation.

However, the semantic web can infer any documents on the web, such as an XML document, XML taxonomy and XML ontology, but the differences appear here in information retrieval. The XML taxonomy gives mixed information from the web while the XML ontology gives information in more detail in a logical way Figure 2-4 illustrates the range of ontology.

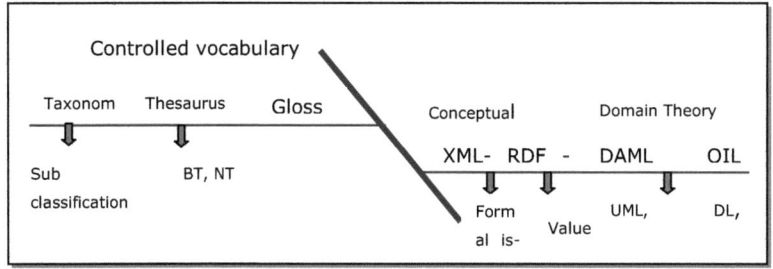

Figure 2-4 spectrum of ontology.

(Daconta et al., 2003)

Based on the above, the Table 2-2 therefore shows which differentiates ontology from similar concepts.

Table 2-2 Differences between taxonomy and ontology

Element	Taxonomy	Thesaurus	Conceptual model	Semantic web	Ontology
Synonym	Tree	Control vocabulary	-	-	model
Presenting	Classification of concept, terms, things	List of words and synonyms organised in a specific order. Connecting the meaning of the term	a mental model about area of knowledge	Describing information on the www	Represents complex semantic of concepts & relations
structure	Hierarchy, tree	By standards of relationships as: Equivalence, Homographic, Hierarchical	Hierarchy in complicated way of knowledge	tree	Relationships between categories
Links of concept	Parent & child	BT, NT, RT relations	Entity, relationships, values, rules	Hierarchy	Classes, instances, relations, properties, constrains.
Based on	Glossary, Thesaurus	Glossary	Taxonomy	Taxonomy	Taxonomy
Purpose	Classify things	Conceptual navigation, research & information retrieval	Represents primary entities in a domain	Automation, integration, reuse information cross applications	To capture and represent the meaning of a domain
Retrieval information	Weak	Weak	Weak	Weak	Strong

To sum up, the synonym of taxonomy is a tree; things are arranged in a hierarchical structure as sub-type, super-type relations; a tiger is subtype of cats, for instance. Whereas, the synonym of ontology is model - that means a formal method for organising knowledge; by putting entities in categories and linking these categories with relations. E.g. ontology describes a tiger that has four legs and has a relation to Asia, the continent where it lives.

In the knowledge representation field, object-oriented software engineering and database development all employ ontology that is conceived as taxonomy. The Table 2-2 highlights the differences between ontology and taxonomy. Taxonomy has a hierarchy structure to arrange terms, classes and relations as 'child' and 'parent'. They cannot therefore present an explicit hierarchy – for instance, the taxonomy of data concept is a subclass of information, whilst in ontology a piece of data can be organised so it classes as information. Ontology could develop from taxonomy – from the knowledge of hierarchy structure, to the thesaurus, to a conceptual model written in unified modelling language (UML), and on to logical theory, arranging knowledge to be rich, complex, consistent and to have meaning.

2.1.5 Approaches for modelling ontology:

The approaches of software designing and developing - top-down, bottom up and middle-out - are well established in computer science.

2.1.5.1 Top-down approach

Emphasises the planning and complete understanding of domain modelling which starts with modelling concepts and relationships in every generic level of knowledge, to classifying into specific concepts. The IBM researchers Mills et al., (1995) initially promoted this approach. The main feature of top—down strategy is control over the level of details.

2.1.5.2 Bottom–up approach

In 1980 a bottom–up approach became popular when object oriented programming emerged. The strategy is identifying the specific concepts to be generalised into abstract concepts, to compose a whole system.

Prieto-Diaz (2003) used the literary warrant technique to categorise keyword and phrases to build the domain ontology automatically.

This approach is an insufficient strategy because it increases the risk of inconsistencies which require reworking and extra effort. (Sure et al., 2008)

2.1.5.3 Middle out approach

This approach is the most popular approach. It starts by reusing pre-existing knowledge to define the upper level of concepts, and sequencing of the upper level arises naturally.

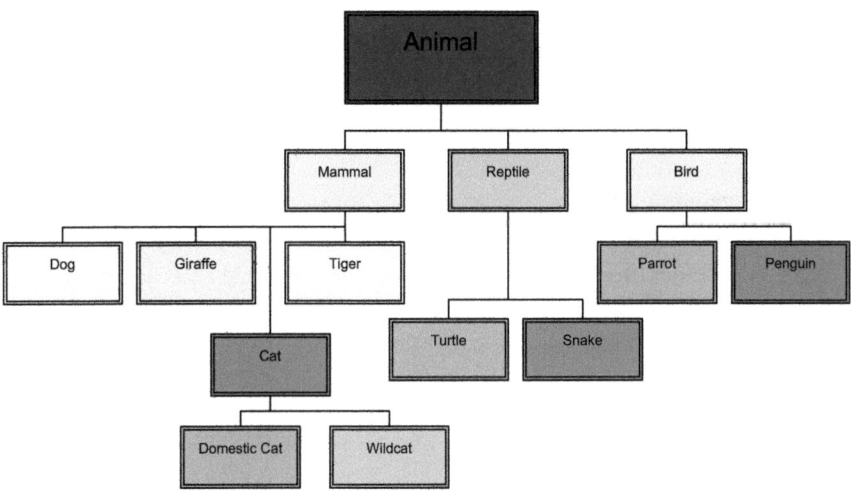

Figure 2-5 Illustration of middle-out approach

Figure 2-6 shows an example of using the middle-out approach effectively. In the example of an animal, the concepts of mammal, reptile and bird are the most important for us. The higher level will be generated as seen in the example at the top, which is animal, and the bottom concepts for bird are parrot and penguin.

In the context of ontology development, a top down approach as Uschold & Gruninger (1996) argued results in a good control of the details. Though it starts at the top level of knowledge it involves some random concepts that are pre-determined at the high level, which leads to less stability in the ontology. A bottom-up approach, on the other hand, requires investing a high degree of effort, and it is hard to stop commonality among the terms. Hence, the risk of inconsistency will be increased during the developing process, therefore requiring more reworking.

Thus, the middle out approach according to Uschold & Gruninger (1996) identifies the most important concepts and the higher category rises naturally with more stability, with less overall effort and reworking.

In this study we adopt and recommend the top-down, and bottom-up approaches in OIS ontology development. This will be introduced in Section 4.1.1.5.

2.1.6 Structure of ontology

Ontology structure has many definitions widely accepted, such as ISO standards 407 2009 of terminology work and principles and methods, and OKBC model (Chaudhri et al., 1998). Ontology structure is introduced in the literature as explicit sign level, based on semiotics, the study of signs. In semiotics theory there are three interlinked parts, namely:

- **Syntax**: the study of relations among signs
- **Semantics**: analysing the relationships between signs in reality.
- **Pragmatics:** searching for how signs are used and analysing the relations between a specific agent and sign (Maedche, 2003). Links between different levels are shown in the triangle of meaning above.

However, construction ontology involves the concepts/classes to be put together with instances, relationships and attributes. So, ontology components are:

1. Entities (Classes): things that can be clearly identified and that represent concepts.
2. Instances (Individuals): are used to present elements in the ontology.
3. Properties: are used to link relationships between instances or from instance to data value, such as has-A, Is-a, hasChild. They can be symmetric, transitive or functional. The standard ANSI/NISOZ39.19.2005(Standards, 2005) indicates the types of semantic relationships in the ontology that links between entities, namely;
    - Hierarchy relation - type of superclass and subclass.
    - Equivalency relation - is like synonym of terms
4. Associative relation - covers associations between concepts such as; cause / effect / accident / injury
5. Restrictions: is information about entities. This information indicates how properties can be used by instances of a class, such as (someValuesFrom, allValuesFrom, cardinality restriction).

6. Axioms: used to represent a sentence that is true. These are very useful to infer new knowledge.

Noy and McGuinness (2001) clarified that there is confusion when using classes and concepts. Classes are concepts and properties are slots. They give each class features and attributes. Additionally, the restrictions on properties are called fact or roles. Hence, the Reasoning task (classification, subsumption) is used to make sure this ontology is built for a specific purpose.

2.1.7 Ontology Categorization

In general, ontologies are categorised from different approaches and have many classifications based on their structure. Ontologies are different from each other. Their different roles and features make them unique. The differences can be as follows:

Ontology scope and purpose: each ontology has a conceptual scope based on the description of its content, in specific domains such as biomedical-information science. This sort of ontology describes the key concepts and relationships.

Ontology describes levels of knowledge from simple lexicons through to taxonomy, where terms are hierarchically related to distinguish between properties.

Ontology has a historical part consisting of terminological and sectional components. The former is about the terms and structure of the ontology domain, while the latter is about populating the ontology with the instances that manifest the terminological definitions. Ontology can be built in different languages such as Open Knowledge Base Connectivity (OKBC), DAML+OIL, or Web Ontology Language (OWL) Dmterie and Verbeek (2008).

Generally speaking, types of ontology vary from heavyweight, lightweight, formal and informal, and upper or top ontology. The light weight ontology contains topic hierarchy and use is-, a relation to search the concepts on the web engine, while the heavy one includes ontologies that have very precise definitions of concepts, and have rigorous relationships between them. This kind of ontology is modelling the targeted conceptualisation of the world to guarantee the consistency. Another type of ontology is top-level or upper-level ontology; this has a level of category to describe general concepts and presents indications about the root concepts, linking them to existing ontology.

Philosophers have attempted to carry this out in their work, for example Guarino (1998) who divides the level of dependence of particular task into four parts. These parts provide structural design for domain ontology modelling. His proposal is influential in research methodology. His suggestion is dependent on identifying the main specific concepts required in application ontology, and then creating the domain and task ontologies which will be abstracted into top level ontology. These contain the general concepts to link with top level ontologies among different domains. His idea is suitable for designing ontology from scratch. However, we focus on Guarino's classification in more details. Guarino has classified the ontology based on their generality, Figure 2-6 illustrates ontology classification in more detail.

- **Top level ontology**: alternatively, called top, generic or upper ontology represents general concepts independent of the domain, such as matter, kinds, even time and space. The most likely purpose is to unify criteria among different users.
- **Domain ontology**: describes concepts related to the generic domain such as biomedical, electronic engineering, information systems. Also, domain ontology specifies the domain concepts that are present in the generic model.
- **Task and problem solving ontology**: describes ontology relating to a specific task or problem
- **Application ontology:** describes concepts related to specific applications.

Figure 2-6 Guarino's proposal for ontology Modularization

28

Broadly, Aristotle's ontology has ten categories including matter, relation, quantity, time, location, etc. Also, Sowa presents four categories; continuant, occurrent, concrete and abstract (Sowa, 2005). Some pioneers show negative attitudes to generic models of ontologies due to the fact that they believe there is on -independent use of ontology; on the other hand, some have justified using upper ontology as a good way to organize the domain knowledge. In this interim, Sowa (2000) has categorized ontology into:

2.1.7.1 *Informal ontology*

Informal ontology could be specified by a catalogue of types - these are either undefined or defined only by statements in a natural language. It contains all the terminology of a domain, classifying the concepts and the relations. More precisely, informal ontology is specified by a collection of names for concepts and relation types organized in a partial ordering by the type-subtype relation.

2.1.7.2 *Formal ontology*

Formal ontology is processed by machine and usually uses ontological languages to encode ontology, e.g. DAML+ OIL and OWL (Sowa, 2000).

Both formal and informal ontologies are fundamental components of knowledge about a domain.

2.1.7.3 *Domain ontology*

The domain ontology is a specific area of knowledge, containing the main concepts and their relations. Gomez-Perez asserted that this kind of ontology has weaknesses including emerging upper-level ontology. It classifies its concepts according to different criteria, which leads to heterogeneity in knowledge. The domain ontology is the solution of specific concepts in each domain. e.g. medical, knowledge, economic, (Gòmez-Pérez et al., 2004, Sowa, 2012). To sum up, we compared between these approaches in Table 2-3.

Table 2-3 ontology categories

Approaches	Categorizations of ontologies
Mizoguchi & colleagues 1995	o Content ontology o Communication ontology for sharing knowledge o Indexing ontology o Meta-ontology
Van Heijst & colleagues1997	Classify ontologies into two diminutions: 1. **It has three categories**: o Terminological ontologies as lexicons. o Information ontologies as database schemata o Knowledge modelling 2. **It has four categories**: o Representation o Generic o Domain Application ontology
Guarino 1998	Ontology is also categorised based on its level of dependency in a particular task: • Top level ontology • Domain ontology • Task ontology • Application ontology
Sowa 2000	1. Informal ontology 2. Formal ontology 3. Domain ontology
Lassila and McGuinness2001	Based on the ontology needs and the richness of its structure • Controlled vocabularies • Glossaries • Thesaurus • Informal is-a relations. • Formal is-a hierarchy • Formal instance • Frames, value restriction • General logical constraints.

2.1.8 Related Research

The number of studies on ontologies has been growing rapidly recently in the knowledge engineering area. Most of the studies in this area are focused on ontology construction. Gartner indicated that the semantic web integration will have a big impact on technologies in the next few years. Ontologies are used as a foundation to enable interoperability through the semantic web (Gartner, 2006). Bhatt provided an approach of sub-ontology extraction to fulfil users' needs based on unified medical language system (UMLS); he designed ontoMove to develop the semantic web. It used RDF, RDFs schema and OWL languages (Bhatt et al., 2009). OntoCAPE is large scale ontology for Chemical process to be used in the industrial field. His proposed ontoSpider which is a novel ontology extractor to extract ontology from HTML web. Nevertheless, the lexical semantic and natural languages have a negative effect on the result because the complicated knowledge and difference of outcome when a word or link is missing (Du et al., 2009).

Ontologies play a fundamental role in defining terms that can be used as metadata. Sabou's project is to develop ontology from OWL-s files in order to describe the web services (Sabou 2005), particularly in a specific domain such as biomedical ontologies - which play a fundamental role in accessing the heterogeneous sources of medical information - and using and sharing patients' data. Many studies on developing domain ontology are proposed, for instance those mentioned below.

The Budgetary domain to analysis budget concepts of expenses followed Methontology; it was designed for the public sector to organise an organisation's knowledge (Brusa et al., 2006).

Domain ontology of e-learning in educational systems aims to describe the learning material (Gascueña et al., 2006, Hong-Yan et al., 2009).

Chi et al., (2006) study described a framework of ontological techniques for reusing and sharing knowledge in natural science museums. This study developed two ontologies of vascular plant and herbal drugs.

Elena (2006) study was about developing historical archive ontology where users are centre of the methodology for extracting the ontology. The ontology expanded mainly to these classes; time instants and time periods, and university things such as students and personnel.

Ontology of the legal domain in Spain was developed by domain experts. The study shows how domain experts can develop domain ontology by themselves, and how Methontology methods and WebODE software can help them (Corcho et al., 2002).

Cooking ontology is for the cooking domain; it described the building process that followed the Methontology. The results was four models, namely; utensils, food, recipes, and action (Batista et al., 2006).

Furthermore, Geoinformatics ontology was proposed as a domain ontology that consists of a semantic layer and a syntactic layer. The knowledge acquiring process was based on a corpus of multilingual dictionaries of the geographical information system GIS (Deliiska, 2007).

GALEN (Generalised Architecture for Languages Encyclopaedias and Nomenclatures) provides reusable terminology resources for clinical systems. It contains 25,000 concepts used to represent a complex structure that describes a medical procedure (Trombert-Paviot et al., 2002). Furthermore, commerce ontologies facilitate exchange of information between suppliers and customers and offer a framework to identify the services and products in the markets.

GENE ontology (GO) was developed by the National Human Genome Research Institute in 1998. It presents a control vocabulary of gene and gene products attributes. It contains (30,000) concepts and is organized as follows; cellular component, molecular function, and biological process. It is regularly updated and is available in several formats (Gasevic et al., 2006, GeneOntology, 2009, Jepsen, 2009).

Standardized Nomenclature for Medicine - clinical terminology (SNOMED) is an ontology containing health care terminology. It contains 350,000 terms that represent clinical meaning. Each concept has a number, ID and full specific name (FSN). SNOMED has the ability to automate functions related to medical record administration and facilitate data collection for research purposes (Jepsen, 2009).

Enterprise ontology is developed to define and arrange company knowledge. The knowledge is included in the processes, activities, strategies and organizations. TOVE (Toronto Virtual Enterprise) is developed in the Integration Laboratory at the University of Toronto. It provides a shared terminology to be understood and shared between commercial and public enterprise. TOVE was implemented in C++ and Prolog for axioms. It covers activities, time , parts and resources (Laboratory, 2011).

Economic ontology is constructed to define the economic domain from economic documents. It uses OntGen tool to semi-automatically construe ontology. The ontology is based on machine learning methods (Vogrincic and Bosnic, 2011).

The ontology of the International Council of Museums- Conceptual Reference Model (CIDOC-CRM) is intended to represent a formal structure to describe concepts with its definitions in the area of cultural heritage documentation. It encodes in RDFs to describe classes and properties. They had created their own properties because RDF does not support properties. Its classes and properties are defined by their initial codes such as E1 entity, P4 property (Group, 2008).

The concept model of Bibliographical records developed by IFLA is called Functional Requirements for Bibliographic Records (FRBR). It was created to develop an entity relationships model to view the bibliographic universe; it aimed to develop OCLC's catalogue and to be implemented in large catalogue databases. It includes four levels of representation; work, expression, item and manifestation (Tillett, 2004).

The ontology for cultural heritage resources was developed to facilitates access to collection of digital material. This study developed by library of the University of North Carolina by involving the social studies teachers in designing and evaluation the ontology. The study focused on modelling prototypes, and its scope covered the collection of Tobacco Bag Stringing (TBS). The TBS ontology is an indexing tool that supports semantic annotations of the TBS collection (Pattuelli, 2011). Table 2-4 summarises some of the domain ontologies.

Table 2-4 Domain ontologies

Domain Ontologies	Aim	Concepts	Relations	Assertions.
Open GALEN ,2002clinical medicine	supporting terminology services	25,000	594	216,000
SNOMED CT ,2004	Acquiring and capturing information to be shared and aggregated for health care information	350,00	50	1.5
UMLS semantic etwork,2004	Bio-medicine ontology to offer a consistent classification of the concepts	135	54	6,864
GENE ontology (GO) 1998	a control vocabulary of gene and gene products attributes	30,000	-	-
CIDO-CRM Conceptual Reference Model 2000	Cultural heritage documentation ontology	90	194	-
FRBR concept model for Bibliographic Records	Intended to develop relation model to bibliographic universe/	9	12	-

In summary, comparison of these studies with this research will be original because:

In this study we consider the development of an ontology of Information science OIS for defining its boundaries and avoiding ambiguities in the concepts. Furthermore, the OIS ontology will be coded by OWL language. It will be metadata for knowledge base systems in a specific domain and improve the retrieval information process on the World Wide Web in the domain of Information Science. This work has never previously been done.

Significantly, however, the domain ontologies contain concepts in a specific subject that provide control vocabulary to control the domain concepts and to construct the relationships between them in a consistent manner. In addition, domain ontologies offer clear boundaries and theories through these definitions. Consequently, domain ontology offers connections between the concepts and their meaning. In natural languages there are different meanings for one concept e.g., "Data". In a dictionary a user might find many definitions of it, whereas ontologies specifying a formal definition avoid vagueness and ambiguity, to be able to choose the accurate meaning. Looking at meaning of data in the Oxford Dictionary, for example, the user will discover many definitions. Ontologies therefore provide single definitions, as revealed in Figure 2-7.

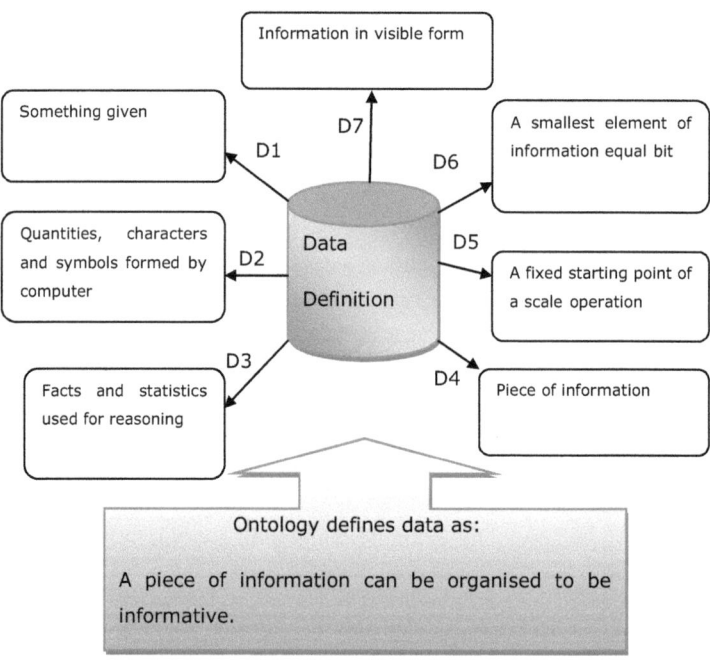

Figure 2-7 an Example of ontology role

On the other hand, the confusion between data and information terms is still a big problem, especially between the domain specialists and users of the libraries and information sciences community. Processing data both manually and by computer produces information. This outcome has a specific context and a high degree of reliability. The information has the effect of changing situations through its reception to become knowledge. Furthermore, information differs from data due to the fact that information provides opportunities to make decision after analysing the data. However, the data remains fuzzy and it cannot be used until it is fully processed to become information (Stonier, 1990).

2.1.9 Designing Criteria for ontology

Gruber has proposed initial sets of designing criteria for ontologies. These designing criteria are as follows (Gruber, 1993, Burtonjones et al., 2005, Fluit et al., 2002):

1. **Clarity**: the ontology concepts should be defined in formal and complete mode, which can be defined according to specific purposes of the design. It helps the communication to be effective and efficient. Consequently, most of the definitions are derived from the social contexts; however, they should be independent of social contexts documented in natural language (NL).

2. **Extendibility**: designing ontologies is used for shared concepts. It should provide a conceptual foundation for a diversity of expected tasks whose outcome can be predicted.

3. **Coherence**: is a vital criterion in evaluating ontologies for ensuring the consistence of concepts which are defined formally. It should permit inference that is consistent with logical definitions

4. **Encoding bias**: it applies when a representation alternative has been made only for ease of implementation.

5. **Minimal ontological commitment:** ontologies need a sufficient ontological commitment to maintain the predictable knowledge sharing tasks ahead.

As you can see the above criteria play a crucial role for designing and developing ontology. It is through defining the requirements for ontology artifact to ensure the ontology is correct, true, and consistent, that it can be evaluated.

2.1.10 Ontology evaluation approaches

The evaluation is still a key problem in ontology development; formal ontologies need to be guided and evaluated and also require objective criteria. The predefined criteria help ontologists to evaluate ontologies. In the literature different approaches have been considered to evaluate ontologies (Brewster et al., 2004, Lozano-Tello and Gomez-Perez, 2004, Maedche and Staab, 2002b, Porzel and Malaka, 2004). Despite this, there is no preferred approach to ontology evaluation. The approach depends on the purpose and kind of ontology being developed. The evaluation process is necessary even when building an ontology for a particular domain from the beginning or modifying an existing one(Gòmez-Pérez et al., 2004, Cristani and Cuel, 2005) .

Additionally, evaluation is required to check the quality of the ontology during the engineering process to ensure it fulfils the requirements. Also, it is useful to be applied in applications. However, there are many approaches, as shown in Table 2-5. Some of them can be done through developing a process to fix errors early, which also ensures they contain the correct data and information to be selected by the knowledge engineers and end users for applications. Ontology can be evaluated by comparing two ontologies, O_1, and O_2. Using specific tools that facilitate knowledge, engineers work to select the most suitable ontology for applications, such as Onto metric.

Table 2-5 Approaches of ontology evaluation

References	Approaches
(Gòmez-Pérez et al., 2004)	-ontology verification - ontology validation
(Yao et al., 2005)	Ontology cohesion metrics: - Number of Root Class: (NoR) - Number of Leaf Classes: (NoL) - Average Depth of Inheritance Tree of Leaf Nodes (ADIT-LN)
(Maedche and Staab, 2002a, Porzel and Malaka, 2004, Brewster et al., 2004, Lozano-Tello and Gomez-Perez, 2004)	Ontology evaluation can be classified into these categories: -Compressing with other ontologies(Golden-Standard) - Using ontology application to evaluate the results. - Compressing with source data of the domain Knowledge. - Assessment ontology by experts in the specific area based on predefined criteria.
(Vrandecic, 2010)	Ontology can be evaluated : - By them selves - With some context - Within an application - In the context of an application and task

Gòmez-Pérez et al., (2004) indicates a different approach which involves dividing the ontology evaluation into ontology validation and ontology verification. The verification assesses the ontology to be built correctly and implements its definitions correctly. The validation indicates whether ontology definitions represent the real world or not, according to the purpose of its creation. Her emphasis on the aim of evaluating ontologies is to ensure whether the concepts are defined correctly or not. The verification of ontology relates to these criteria:

- **Consistency** which means the class will not obtain a contradictory conclusion, which is called Consistency error.
- **Completeness** is about in which level the ontology represents the real world. If it does not cover the whole domain, for instance, that is called Completeness error.

The Conciseness criteria are concerned with the consistency of all the information that is available in the ontology, which are called redundancy errors.

The validation approach is important to assess ontology quality. It can be performed automatically by the DL reasoner. The DL reasoner performs range of inference types, because most of the results are unpredictable, Baader and Nutt provide example of:

Child ≡ ∩ Person ∃ hasParent. Mother ∩

∃ hasParent.Father

Child ⊆ 2 = hasChild

Child ≡ Person ∩ ∃ hasParent.Mother ∩

∃ hasParent.Father ∩ 2= hasChild   (Baader and Nutt, 2003)

To define format semantic of concepts, we suppose that child is person and has parent mother and father that mean child ≡ equivalent to a person.

Based on the validation approach the quality criteria are discussed. The domain experts can evaluate the ontologies according to quality criteria such as:

1. **Consistency:** means there is no contradiction between the concepts of the ontology. So, inconsistency manifests itself by:
    - Circularity
    - Disjoint partition error
    - Incorrect classification

2. **Completeness:** means how the ontology covers the ontology subjects. The incompleteness can be indicated by:
   - concepts are imprecisely defined
   - Missing some concepts.
   - Some concepts are partially defined
   - Disjoin properties
   - Redundancy of classes, relationships, or instances.
3. **Conciseness**: means that needless information is present in the ontology,.
4. **Clarity**: is how the ontology presents concepts in effective meaning.
5. **Generality**: is how the ontology will be used for a variety of purposes in the same domain.
6. **Robustness:** means how the ontology has the ability to support any future changes.
7. **Semantic data richness**: identify the richness and diversity of the ontology conceptualisation.
8. **Subject coverage** of a particular domain and its richness:
   - Determine which Level the ontology will cover exact subject

The OIS ontology evaluation will be based on Gòmez- Pérez' approach. The OIS ontology has been revised by domain experts filling out a quality evaluation report, see in Appendix A, which consisted of several question related to the criteria.

However, it is clear that the domain's experts can assess ontology at various levels, such as; lexical, vocabulary, concept, data to ensure the ontology meets the scope and components required. The context application level is useful for evaluating ontology if it is a part of large ontology. Also, the Syntactic Structure/architecture/design is useful if the ontology is manually structured or if it needs a certain structure, whereas other approaches cannot cover this as well, for example, application based, data driven and level golden standard. Table 2-6 summarises these approaches.

Table 2-6 an overview of levels of ontology evaluation

Evaluation levels	Approaches			
Complexity Level	Level Golden standard	Application based	Data driven	Assessment by humans
Data, Lexical, concept, vocabulary.	+	+	+	+
The hierarchal taxonomy	+	+	+	+
Other semantic relations	+	+	+	+
Context, application	+	+	+	+
Syntactic	+	-	-	+
Ontology designing, architecture, Structure.	-	-	-	+

2.1.11 Ontology Engineering Methodologies

Since ontology is the backbone of the semantic web and the semantic web is a conscious version of the WWW, methodologies support the crucial process of creating ontologies. Methodology offers guidelines for developing ontologies, choosing suitable techniques for each activity of the building process. Since the 1990s many methodologies have been proposed to build ontologies. Most of these have different approaches; some methods are designed for creating ontology from scratch and others reuse existing ontologies.

The ontology building process as widely known in the ontological engineering community is more of a craft than engineering activities. Furthermore, each method of creating ontology follows its own principle of activity and design even if it is not clear whether their contribution is successful or not. In fact, it is the absence of agreed guidelines and methodologies that hinders ontology development (Gasevic et al., 2006).

Methodology of developing ontology can be classified into three categories; the methodology approach for building ontology from scratch, for example Cyc methods were created in the 1990s by Lenat and Guha. In 1995 Uschold & King proposed developing ontology enterprise modelling (TOVE), followed by Grüninger & Fox's methods in 1995 in the same field of ontology enterprise. In 1996 Uschold and Grüninger proposed outlines of developing ontology. Methontology emerged in 1996, as one of the methods used to build ontology using tools such as OntoEdit and Protégé. It provides a general framework defining designing criteria for ontology criteria. (Noy and Musen, 2000, Sure et al., 2002, Pattuelli, 2011). In 1997 SENSUS methodology was extended to Methontology, which proposed creating SENSUS, a huge ontology. But it still represents methodology for creating ontologies from scratch. The next section presents and analyses some prominent methodologies against the IEEE 1074- 2006 standards for developing the software Life Cycle.

2.1.11.1 CYC Method

The Cyc method was created in the 1980s by Microelectronics and Computer Technology Corporation (MCC) (Lenat, 1990). Cyc encompasses a knowledge base of more than 1,000,000 hand defined assertions. Each assertion is presented in a Microtheory. The Microtheory organises the knowledge hierarchy to facilitate inferential focus and knowledge reuse. The Cyc knowledge is separated into collections of 164.000 concepts and 3,300,000 facts, in a specific area of knowledge. Cyc uses the Cyc language (CycL) for implementation. CycL is a hybrid language that combines predicate calculus with frames. (Curtis et al., 2005).

- Lenat 1990, proposed three stages for the ontology design process, as follows:
  - Articles and pieces of knowledge could be manual coding. This stage of knowledge is acquired by hand since learning machines and natural language systems do not have a common specific knowledge, hence in search knowledge is acquired as follows:
  - The encoding of knowledge requires the knowledge that is already in books and articles. This is searching and representing the fundamental knowledge that is already assumed to belong to the readers.
  - The assessment and examination of the contents of articles that is incorrect. This examination is finding out where those articles are incorrect.
  - Question identification for users, to be able to answer their questions by reading the text.
- The coding supported by using tools based on the knowledge stored in the Cyc Knowledge base.

2.1.11.2 Uschold & King Method.

The first method of creating ontologies was presented by Uschold & King in 1995. It was extended in 1996 by Uschold & Gruninger. They point out this method is insufficient and the relationships are unspecified between the stages. As a result they proposed guidelines of ontology designing and developing. (Uschold and Grüninger M., 1996) The methodology is summarized as follows:

- Stage1. Identifying the purpose of creating the ontology, its scope and which domain it will cover, besides determining the users and developers.
- Stage 2. Building the ontology: building the ontology starts with the following phases:
  - Ontology capture: this phase is capturing the knowledge of the ontology such as:
    - Identifying the domain concepts and relationships.
    - Generating accurate definitions for the concepts and relationships within the domain.
  - Identifying each term that indicates to identified concepts and its relationships for consensus on the concepts.
  - Coding: capturing the knowledge to represent it explicitly. Uschold & Gruninger recommend committing general terms to be used to specify the ontology, and choosing formal languages to write its codes.
  - Integrating existing ontologies: refers to using existing ontologies in capturing ontology or even in coding it.

- Stage3. Evaluating the ontology: Uschold & Gruninger assert that evaluation of the ontology is very important to be able to make a technical judgment.

- Stage 4. Documentation: documenting the ontology process, which means guidelines are established (Fernández-López, 1999).

2.1.11.3 Gruninger& Fox Method.

Gruninger & Fox (1995) provide a formal design approach for creating and evaluating ontology, compared with Uschold & Gruninger's methods. This method based on the first order logic and extensive ontology such as Toronto Virtual Enterprise (TOVE). TOVE is a set of ontologies for different features of the business projects. Gruninger & Fox's method consists of these steps:

1. Identify motivation scenarios: the motivated scenario is a problem that has not been addressed in existing ontology. These scenarios have a vital impact on guiding the ontology design and providing a possible solution to the problem. The provided solution offers informal semantics of the objects and their relationships.

2. Elaborate some informal competency questions from the specified scenario. The ontology represents these questions using formal terminology. The competency questions support the evaluation of ontological commitment for developing the ontology.
3. Using a formal language to specify the ontology terminology: using informal competency questions for the purpose of extracting ontology content and specifying terminology in a formal language. This means to formally represent the concepts, attributes and relationships through ontology language. Actually this step corresponds to the coding stage in Uschold & King's method, discussed previously.
4. Write formal competency questions to define the competency questions formally.
5. Using the first order logic to specify axioms: Gruninger & Fox (1992) declare that axioms should be specifying the definitions of concepts and constraints by using first order logic.
6. Specification of completeness theorem: the establishing of conditions characterises completeness of developing ontology, so defining the conditions under which solutions to the question are completed (Gòmez-Pérez et al., 2004).

2.1.11.4 SENSUS Methodology

The SENSUS methodology is designed to assist in the creation of new domain ontologies from a large ontology, to generate its skeleton (Swartout 1997). The main process in this ontology is linking domain concepts to the SENSUS ontology. The main processes of it are as follows:

> **Process 1 Identifying the seed terms:** the key terms relevant to a specific domain are identified.
> **Process 2 linking the seed terms manually to SENSUS**: thereafter, the terms are linked by using OntoSarus to broaden the coverage of the ontology.
> **Process 3 Adding paths to the roots:** requires collecting all concepts to be linked to roots of SUESUS.
> **Process 4 adding new domain terms** that have not yet been included which are relevant to the domain.
> **Process 5 adding complete sub trees:** sub trees should be added to the final ontology, if nodes of a sub tree are relevant. (Gòmez-Pérez et al., 2004)

2.1.11.5 Methontology

Methontology was developed at the Polytechnic University of Madrid in a Artificial Intelligence laboratory (Fernadez-Lopez et al., 1999). Methontology is used for creating ontologies from scratch or to reuse ontology. Its framework facilitates the construction of ontology at the knowledge levels. Fernandez (1997) proposed several steps that are similar to Gurninger and Fox (1995), and Uschold and Gruninger (1996). But it differs by emphasizing the evaluation and documentation steps. Furthermore, it supports the ontology life cycle based on evolving a prototype which makes changing and adding easier at each new phase, contrasting with others that support top down, middle out, or bottom-up approaches (Fernández-López et al., 1997).

Gòmez-Pérez, et al. (2004) indicates that the framework of methodology includes the following phases:

Phase 1 Specification: the ontology specification step starts with several activities, such as; *identifying goals, scope, strategy and boundary.* It must specify the purpose of building and designing the ontology, and its scope.

Within the specifications phase, questions should be answered about the main reason for developing ontology, as proposed by (Fernández-López et al., 1997) questions and answers (both formal and informal) are written down to establish the purpose and scope; these questions are similar to the competency questions recommended by Uschold & Gruninger (1996).

This phase aims to assemble the resources covering the ontology's objects, purposes, scope and granularity. This includes:

Knowledge acquisition: building the conceptual model needs acquisition knowledge. It is an essential activity to start with because the concepts must be assessed to ensure their currency, which helps to reduce many errors in future stages.

Phase 2 Conceptualisation: provides a conceptual model in the ontology to be created, whose purpose is integrating the domain knowledge in a way that arranges and structures knowledge through the knowledge acquisition phase, which will impact on the rest of the ontology construction.

Following knowledge capture and acquisition, the knowledge needs to be conceptualised. The ontology's designer needs to use the conceptual model technique as proposed by (Gòmez-Pérez et al., 2004). The conceptual model contains tasks of knowledge construction in formal models.

Creating a conceptual model is to determine the ontology construction, also, to present the preliminary designing activity. Its intent is to organise the acquisition of domain knowledge. There is a very strong relationship between conceptual modelling and knowledge acquisition, as illustrated in Blum's model tree of fundamental software process. Figure2-9 consists of three activities described as:

1. (T_1: N _____ C) this is for the transfer of domain concepts to the conceptual model and describing users' needs.

2. (T_2: C _____ F) transfers the conceptual model to a formal model that describes essential properties in the produced software.

3. (T_3: F _____ I) transfers the formal model to software that is correct in respect of the formal model. (Blum, 1996).

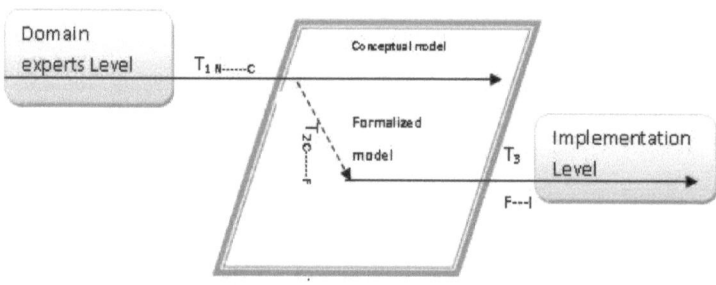

Figure 2-8 conceptual modelling

The activity of building the conceptual model is as follows:

- Building Glossary of terms to identify which terms need to be included in the ontology; the glossary includes the term name, Synonym, Acronyms, and a description of it.
- Identify the binary relations between concepts of the ontology.
- Build concept classification.
- Build the data dictionary to identify the concepts with their meaning, instance, class attributes, and their relations.
- In the data dictionary the instances attribute should be described in more detail, and class attributes also needs to be described.
- Describe the formal axioms and the rules (Gòmez-Pérez et al., 2004). In Methontology the rule of conceptual modelling is introduced in ontology designing.

Phase 3 Formalisation: conceptual model needs to transform into a formal or semi-computable model. The formalisation of ontology needs to be represented by using representation languages.

Phase 4 Integration: Methontology supports the integration of existing ontologies. Much research has been done in semantic integration ontology and ontology mapping such as (Noy, 2004).

Phase 5 Coding: in this stage the computable model has been created in computational language to be machine readable.

Phase 6 Evaluation: Gómez-Pérez (1995) emphasises the necessity of evaluating the ontology to guarantee that the information that is attached to each concept is completed and to ensure all descriptions and instance attributes are correctly defined, thus minimising errors. Furthermore, ensuring both the class attributes and instance attributes are consistent and makes sense with each concept.

Step 7 Documentation: the documentation is a very important phase, which helps to facilitate the reusability of the ontology designed as with any software developing project.

Step 8 Maintenance: Gómez-Pérez recommended that ontology needs to be updated and maintained once it is designed.

Methontology has been adopted to develop ontologies and implemented in many applications such as a chemical ontology Fernández López et al. (1999), and legal ontology Corcho et al. (2002), as shown in Table 2-7

Table 2-7 implementation of Methontology

	Ontologies developed with it	Applications using it
Methontology	Chemical ontology(Fernández López et al., 1999)	Onto Agent (Arpirez et al., 1998)http://delicias.dia.fi.upm.es/OntoAgent.
	Environmental pollutants ontologies (Gòmez-Pérez and Rojas, 1999)	Chemical OntoAgent(Arpirez et al., 1998)
	The reference ontology(Arpirez et al., 1998)	Ontogeneration (Aguado et al., 1998)
	Knowledge acquisition ontology (KA)(Blazquez et al., 1998)	

Ontology development is an area of knowledge engineering, whose purpose is to enable the control of knowledge within software applications and projects in a domain. Our approach visualises IS knowledge in this context, as depicted in Section 4.1

2.1.11.6 Comparison of Methodology

Roughly speaking, the majority of methodologies are based on the experience of developing enterprise ontologies. These methods propose common development stages to ontology engineers. The main phases are: identifying the purpose, knowledge capture, codifying the concepts and their relations. There is no specific agreement on the best methodology for designing and building ontology, because decisions are based on application and purpose (Noy and McGuinness, 2001). Purpose and need must be the starting points for the construction of a new ontology or the reuse of an existing one. (Pinto and Martins, 2001).

The study conducts a contrasting of the previous methodologies based on ontology dependency level with respect to its application. According to these criteria methodologies could be categorised as:

- Application independent: the ontology process is independent from users, such as Cyc, Methontology, and Uschold & King methodology.
- Application dependent; scenarios of ontologies are identified in a specification process.
- Application semi-dependent; this type of ontology is based on applications that use them, such as Gruninger & Fox, SENSUS methodology. (Fernandez-Lopez and Gomez-Perez, 2002).

Methods used for different ontology projects have been used as a way of justifying why Methontology was selected as a mature methodology.(Fernadez-Lopez and Gomez - Perez, 2002). "Methontology is a framework that enables the construction of ontologies at the knowledge level" (Calero et al., 2006 p.18). Methontology is the methodology of creating ontologies both from scratch or reusing an existing one. Its stages are conceptualisation, requirements analysis, formalisation, implementation, maintaining and evaluating. Methontology is involved in re-engineering methods for the purpose of creating a conceptual model. On one hand, re-engineering methods are considered an extension of the Methontology framework. On the other hand, Methontology emphasises the possibility of return to the previous activity if limitations are found later. SENSUS methodology does not evolve a life cycle model. There is a similarity between constricting ontologies. In Uscholdard in Gòmez-Pérez and colleagues' method 1996, the first stage of building chemical ontology is to acquire knowledge while the second phase is building a requirements specification document. First stage in constructing chemical ontology is to gather knowledge, and then a requirements specification document must be built. A Cyc method was created in the 1980s; it does not code the contents of books and articles in its codification process, but instead looks at knowledge available to readers, and seeks to represent it. Languages such as ODE and WebODE both support Methontology. Table 2-8 summarises differences between methodologies.

Table 2-8 comparison between methodologies

ontology	Cyc	Uschold & King's	Gruninger & Fox's	SENSUS	ONION	Methontology
Purpose of designing	To capture what consensus knowledge that people have about the world	To provide guidelines for developing ontologies	To develop knowledge base system by using first logic order	Building the skeleton of domain ontology starting from huge one.	Integration of terminology in medical domain	-Enabling the construction of ontology at the knowledge level
Advantage	Ability to use it for building Cyc knowledge base about the world	The methodology process clearly defines acquisition, coding, evaluation	It can be used as direct to convert informal scenarios in quantifiable models	Linking two independent developed ontologies	Integration many sub-domain ontologies in medicine domain. - has an ontology open to revisions without giving maintenance trouble. - support creating, integration, updating and maintenance ontology.	-It has its root in activities that identified in software development process & knowledge engineering methodologies – Live cycle based on prototype to enabling adding and moving terms. – possibility of return to any process to amending or modifying
Based on ontology	Yes	No	TOVO project of business process	Yes	Yes	Depends ontologuia
Tools	Cyc tools	Not – specific	Not – specific	OntoSaurus	Not – specific	Portage , WebODE, OntoEdit
Details of methodology	Little	Very little	Little	Little	Medium	A lot
Strategy of building application	Application-independent	Application-independent	Application-independent	Application-independent	Application- dependent	Application- independent
Strategy of identifying concepts	Not specified	Middle-out	Middle-out	Not specified	Not specified	Middle-out

2.1.11.7 Evaluation of ontology methodologies

Evaluation methodologies of building ontology are compliant with IEEE 1074–1995 standards. IEEE 1074–1995 describes the process of software development.

> *"According to the IEEE definition, software is "computer programs, procedures, and possibly associated documentation and data pertaining to the operation of a computer system"; ontologies are part (sometimes only potentially) of software products. Therefore, ontologies should be developed according to the standards proposed for software generally, which should be adapted to the special characteristics of Ontologies".(Fernández-López, 1999p.4-2)*

Fernandez Lopez (1999) points out the framework bases on IEEE 1074-1995 to evaluate different ontologies' development process, which is:

1. Project management process; includes the creation framework for ontology life cycle.
2. Ontology development process that is divided into three parts:
    a. Pre-development that is related to feasibility study.
    b. Development of the ontology designing and implementation.
3. Post-developing ontologies includes all operations, and maintaining processes.
4. Integral process means the completion of the project successfully. It starts with capturing knowledge, configuration, evaluation, and documentation (Fernadez-Lopez and Gomez-Perez, 2002, Hong-Yan et al., 2009). In Table 2-9 summarises this analysis.

Table 2-9 Methodology Standards

Methodology Standards		Cyc	Uschold and King	Grüninger and Fox	SENSUS	Methondology
Project management processes		No	No	No	No	partially
Project development-oriented processes	Predevelopment Processes	No	No	No	No	No
	Development process	No	Yes	Yes	Yes	Yes
	Post development processes	No	No	No	No	partially
Integral processes		partially	partially	partially	No	partially

No-not support / Yes-support/ partially support

Generally speaking, "most of the methodologies focus on development activities, especially on the codification of the ontology, and they do not pay attention to other important aspects related to management. This is because ontological engineering is relatively new" (Fernadez-Lopez and Gomez-Perez, 2002). There are several methods for corporate Knowledge Management, to design and implement an intensive information system. Some of them focus on initial stages of developing a knowledge management application. Other methodologies support application scenarios.

2.1.12 Techniques Involved

Ontology is a key part of the semantic web for capturing knowledge and translating it into a machine-readable form. The web ontology language (OWL) formalises knowledge in a semantic framework (Horridge, 2009). When a new ontology is to be built, several questions must be asked: which tools are needed? Which language will be used in importing knowledge? This section explains the tools and languages of ontology, to show their differences, similarities, and development, so we can determine which tool to implement.

2.1.12.1 Ontology languages

There are several ontology languages discussed in literature, all of which have been created in order to represent knowledge and implementation of ontologies. These languages enable us to access web content and also present extra semantic information, so that it can be shared, processed and understood by computers as a way of exchanging and processing data rather than just presenting information.

Tim Berners-Lee's (2000) analysis supports the notion that more mark-up languages are needed for the web to be able to display information and resources. An ongoing effort is therefore taking place to represent logical knowledge in web language. Primary approaches work at Extensible Mark-up Language (XML) level, but different languages must be used to explain information in a logical way – for this, Resource Description Framework (RDF), (RDFs) schema level and ontology language (OWL) are used.(Antoniou and Harmelen, 2004) The next graph 2-9 is a widely-cited in the literature that shows some information about semantic web languages.

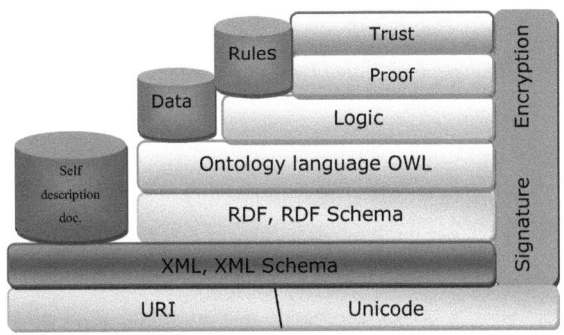

Figure 2-9 Semantic web languages

As well as being called semantic web languages, these are also called mark up languages. Semantic web technologies contain many layers, as asserted by the W3C Consortium, so these languages will require re-evaluation in future. Furthermore, these layers are built on the basic of URLs, and XML, XML schema, followed by RDF and RDFs. OWL and its rules sit at the top of the pyramid, created through logic, proof and trust. XML data can be defined as a nest of elements for building a data model. The model originates from the precursor of XML, called SGML. SGML is used as the mark up languages for describing text.

2.1.12.2 Resource Description Framework RDF, and RDFs

XML language has a standard syntax specifically for meta language, which allows user to mark up documents by using some tags. XML does not, however, provide any semantic meaning for data. There is, for instance, no meaning associated with nesting tags. Below is an example of a sentence written using XML, showing how tags are used:

Melvil Dewey is a developer of Dewey Decimal class (DDC)

Illustrating the sentence can be done in various ways, such as:

< developer name="Melvil Dewey">

<system> DDC</system>

</developer>

Or

<system name="DDC">

<developedby> Melvil Dewey</developedby>

</system>

The above example shows nesting that provides the same information. It illustrates that there is no consistency to assigning meanings in tag nesting.

RDF language represents relationships between things. In RDF statements is an object, attribute, or value, for instance. Alexander Maedche is an author of an ontology learning publication, as shown in the example below:

RDF syntax is given in XML. When RDFs provide definitions, users are able to define terminology in schema language, as used in the RDF data model. As shown above, the relationships between objects can be shown as:

Information retrieval is a subclass of information system

Classification schema is a subclass of classification

In this sentence DDC is a classification system. (subClassof) shows us that there is associated meaning, which allows us to illustrate why RDFs based on XML tags are important.

<Classification > DDC</classification>

<Developed by>Melvil Dewey</developed by>

<subject "Geography">

<content> 10 Categories</content>

</subject>

This illustration shows that this information makes the semantic model possible in a specific domain, but not in XML or RDF. If we use RDFs we get semantic data, which can be machine-processed. RDFs also organises vocabulary in hierarchical ways, for instance classes, sub-classesOf, properties, sub-propertiesOf , resources and domain – all arranged through using formal language. Figure 2-10 shows the semantic net using RDFs.

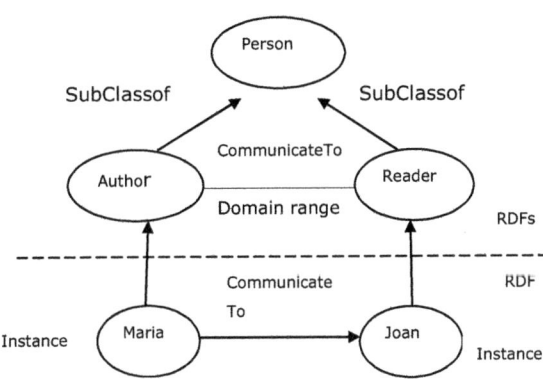

Figure 2-10 semantic net in RDF, RDFs

The XML schema describes how XML documents are constructed. In RDF sentences will always contain (object, attribute and value), called statements, as RDF is a data model showing relations between things.

Table 2-10 shows differences and similarities between the main semantic languages XML, RDFs, OWL.

Table 2-10 Comparison between semantic languages

Languages	contexts		Object class & properties		Inheritance / concept of inheritance	Property/ element Range	Property element domain	Property element cardinality restrictions	Basic data Type			Enumeration of property value	Order data set	Bounded List	Transitive properties	Negation	Necessary & sufficient
	Depending	Type	Class	property					numerical	string	literals						
XML schema	✗	xmlns	✗	✗	✗	✗	✗	✗	✓	✓	✗	✗	Defult	✗	✗	✗	✗
RDF schema	✓	xml	✓	✗	✓	✓	✓	✗	✗	✗	✓	✗	<rdf:seq...> tag	✗	✗	✗	✗
OWL	✓	xml+rdfs	✓	✓	✓	✓	✓	✓	✓	✓	✓	✓	<owl:list>tag	✓	✓	✓	✓

2.1.12.3 Web Ontology Language (OWL)

This section explains the motivation behind choosing Web Ontology Language (OWL) as the language for building the OIS ontology research tool.

The designing of OWL is focused on representing information about objects, and in which way the objects are interrelated and organised within a specific category (Krivov et al., 2007a). OWL is derived from description logic that aimed to bring reasoning and expressive power to the semantic web. OWL sits on top of RDFs to describe classes and subclasses. It also provides definitions of vocabulary. OWL is a W3C standard; this is as important for building and developing ontologies as any other applications or tools that share information to make it readable and understandable. It is designed to be well-matched with existing web standards such as XML, RDF and DARPA Agent Mark-up Language (DAML); it has been built on DAML+OIL. It differs from RDF in machine interpretability, as it has a large vocabulary and a strong syntax.

Furthermore, it is uses a language construct called Restrictions class. Restrictions define members of a class by existing properties and classes. These restrictions are namely; owl: someValueFromand owl: allValueFrom, owl: hasValue (Allemang and Hendler, 2008)

OWL Layers

OWL is one of the knowledge representation languages. It has a history and evaluation affects its design, which comes in three layers (Horrocks et al., 2003). OWL is built on RDF schema (RDFs), to develop ontologies. Its purpose is just like RDFs, to define ontologies in classes, properties and relations. Yet it describes relationships in more richness and capability. Liyang Yu (2011) defined OWL language:

"OWL = RDF Schema + new constructs for better expressiveness".

1. OWL Lite (light): provides simple classification and enabling to defined ontology classes and properties but it is more expressive than RDFs
2. OWL DL (description logic): is more expressive than owl Lite - by allowing cardinality restrictions, DL enables creation of class expressions using Boolean combinatory such as, intersectionOf, UnionOf
3. OWL Full: gives clear expressiveness and the syntax is self modifying. which means it is free from RDFs(Jepsen, 2009).

Although there are some differences between OWL full and OWL DL, they use the same set of modelling constructs. OWL lite has limitations in cardinality restrictions and does not have any hasValue restriction. (Allemang and Hendler, 2008)

OWL Semantic

The semantic structure of OWL is designed to complete the description logic system. Both OWL Lite and DL have a clean DL semantic. DL language is built on two primal symbols; concepts and roles. The concepts are interpreted as unary predicate symbols. The roles are interpreted as binary predicate symbols which are used for expressing the relations between concepts. One type of concept is concept expression which is formed based on Boolean operations and role restrictions (Krivov et al., 2007a, Krivov et al., 2007b). OWL has many role restrictions, as shown in the example:

- *($\exists P, C$) $\exists hasChild, male$* the written concept indicates that all individuals have at least one male child.

- ($\forall P.\ C$) $\forall$ *hasChild. Female* the written concept indicates that all individuals whose children are all female.
- ($\geq nP$) ≥ 2 *hasChild* this concept is denotes to a set of individuals who have at least two children.

As Modelling motivates a logical definition of OWL, OWL statements are constructed on formal logic. The specific logical system of OWL is Description Logic (DL), which is a logic based knowledge representation formalism - it can be represented as statements in formal descriptions of class and individuals, and can make relations among them; for example, in this example the letter C refers to the concept (class). (C1⊆ C2) means concept C1 is a subclass of concept C2, and (C1⊑ C2) man ⊑ male the class man is equivalent to class male. Some of the OWL constructors are shown in Table 2-11. The DL system has different sets of class constructors and axioms for building complex classes and roles. OWL consists of classes and axioms that offer semantics by inferring information based on the explicit data. These axioms interpretation and facts are illustrated in Table 2-12.

Table 2-11 OWL constructors

Constructor	DL syntax	Example
intersectionOf	$C1\pi....\pi Cn$	*Human ∧ male*
UnionOf	$C1\mu....\mu Cn$	*Doctor ∨ Lawyer*
ComplementOf	$-C$	*- male*
OneOf	$\{X1........Xn\}$	*{John, Mary}*
toClass	$\forall P.\ C$	*∀ hasChild. female*
hasClass	$\exists P, C$	*∃ hasChild, male*
hasValue	$\exists P.\{X\}$	*∃ citizenOf.{USA}*
Max Cardinality	$\leq nP$	*≤1 hasChild*
minCardinalityQ	$\geq nP$	*≥ 2 hasChild.*

(Baader and Nutt, 2003)

Table 2-12 OWL axioms interpretation and fact

Axiom	DL syntax	Examples
subClassOf	$C1 \sqsubseteq C2$	$Human \sqsubseteq Animal$
equivalentClass	$C1 \equiv C2$	$Man \equiv male$
disjointWith	$C1 \cap C2$	$Female \cap male$
sameIndividualAs	$\{x1\} \equiv (Alani\ et\ al.)$	$President\ Obama \equiv Barack\ Obama$
SubPropertyOf	$P1 \sqsubseteq P2$	$hasSon \sqsubseteq hasChild$
equivalentProperty	$P1 \equiv P2$	$Price \equiv Cost$

(Horridge and Patel-Schneider, 2009)

2.1.12.4 Comparison of ontology languages

The Table 2-13 compares the most relevant ontology languages, with the aim of illustrating differences and similarities between them. For each cell in the table we put symbol ☑, to indicate that this element supported in the language, while ☒ is used for "does not support it".

From the table we can reveal that there are some differences between traditional languages and ontology mark up languages. Also, some of them represent heavyweight and lightweight ontologies; the heavyweight ontology language represents formal axioms rules, functions and other components, while the lightweight ontology language represents concepts, concepts taxonomy and their relations. Obviously, the components of representation knowledge can be modelled in traditional language such as Ontolingua LOOM, and OCML. Most ontology languages permit representation of concepts and define them by their attributes except RDFs and SHOE. In fact, the disjoint, conjunction, and disjunction axiom is provided by most languages such as Ontologuia, OCML, IL, DAML+Oil and OWL. The binary relation between concepts can be represented in all languages, while hierarchy semantic relations cannot be represented in OKBC, FLogic, SHOW and XOL. Moreover, OWL has the ability to define restriction class. The anonymous classes can be defined based on the restrictions of the value for a specific property of the class.

Table 2-13 comparison between ontology languages

Elements	Concept		Attribute				Instance			Axioms				Semantic Relations			
Languages	Definition	Name	Definition	Name	Basic Type	Instance Attribute	Name	Concept instance	Relation	Conjunction	Disjunction	Disjoint	Covering	Binary relation	n-ray	IS-a	Hierarchies
KIF	✓	✓	✓	✓	✓	✓	✓	✓	✓	✗	✓	✓	✓	✓	✓	✓	✓
Ontolingua	✓	✓	✓	✓	✓	✓	✓	✓	✓	✓	✓	✓	✓	✓	✓	✓	✓
LOOM	✓	✓	✓	✓	✓	✓	✓	✓	✓	✓	✓	✓	✗	✓	✓	✓	✓
OKBC	✓	✓	✓	✓	✓	✓	✓	✓	✓	✗	✗	✗	✗	✓	✗	✗	✗
OCML	✓	✓	✓	✓	✓	✓	✓	✓	✓	✓	✓	✓	✗	✓	✓	✗	✓
FLogic	✓	✓	✓	✓	✓	✓	✓	✗	✓	✗	✗	✗	✗	✓	✗	✗	✗
SHOE	✓	✓	✗	✓	✓	✓	✓	✗	✓	✗	✗	✗	✓	✓	✓	✗	✗
XOL	✓	✓	✓	✓	✓	✓	✓	✓	✓	✗	✗	✓	✗	✓	✗	✗	✗
RDFs	✓	✓	✗	✗	✓	✓	✓	✓	✓	✗	✗	✓	✓	✓	✗	✗	✓
OIL	✓	✓	✓	✓	✓	✓	✗	✓	✓	✓	✓	✓	✓	✓	✗	✗	✓
DAML+OIL	✓	✓	✓	✓	✓	✓	✓	✓	✓	✓	✓	✓	✗	✓	✗	✗	✓
OWL	✓	✓	✓	✓	✓	✓	✓	✓	✓	✓	✓	✓	✓	✓	✗	✗	✓

2.1.12.5 Ontology Tools

The aim of using a tool for building ontologies is providing sustainability for the ontology life cycle and ontology reuse. Constructing ontology can be a very challenging task, made easier by using ontology tools. many of these tools were created in 1990s, supporting users by offering interfaces. Many have appeared recently, with rise of the semantic web. Gòmez-Pérez, (2004) distinguishes between them by dividing them into groups, see Table 2-14. Some of these tools are presented below:

Table 2-14 Groups of Ontologies Tools

Ontology Tools	Purpose of using	Types
Ontology development	Building new ontology from scratch	-Ontolingua Server, OntoSaurus, WebOnto, OilEd, Protégé, WebODE, OntoEdit, KAON
Ontology evaluation	Evaluating the content of ontology, to reduce problems	
Ontology merge and alignment	Solving problems that emerge from different ontologies in a specific domain	Protégé & Chimaera
Ontology – based annotation tools	Use for insert new instance and relations (semi-automatically)	GATE & Cmap
Ontology querying & inference engines	Using to implement ontology	____

2.1.12.6 Ontologua server

This was the first ontology tool developed at Stanford University in the Knowledge System Laboratory in the mid 1990s. Ontologua is an easy tool for developing, evaluating and maintaining ontologies. The ontology editor is the main application inside Ontologua server works with a form-based web interface (Farquhar et al., 1996). The Ontologua server enables access to an ontology library for the creation of new ontologies and even for modifying existing ontology. Interacting with the server could be in different ways:

- Remote application: ontology could be modified and browsed over the internet because it is stored at the server.
- Remote disseminated groups enable multiple users to work simultaneously on the ontology.
- Translating the ontology into specific format, to use in several applications such as, LOOM, CLIPS or Prolog.

2.1.12.7 OntoSaurus

OntoSaurus was created at the University of South Carolina in the Information Science Institution. It was implemented for browsing and editing on LOOM ontologies. Moreover, it consists of two modules; web browser and ontology server, to use the system of representing knowledge attached with LOOM language (Swartout 1997, Gòmez-Pérez et al., 2004)

2.1.12.8 WebOnto

WebOnto was developed to be a tool to edit and browse ontologies collaboratively, which supports cooperation ontology edition synchronously and asynchronously. It was designed at the Open University at the Knowledge Media Institute in 1997. It is an ontology editor using OCML language to represent expressions. WebOnto's editor is based on Java applets rather than HTML forms (Domingue, 1998).

2.1.12.9 OilEd:

In 2001 OilEd was developed at the University of Manchester by Sean Bechhofer as an editor for developing ontologies using ontology interchange language (OIL). OilEd was adopted to export ontology in OWL or DAML +OIL format. It is a tool for helping users to model ontology, and checks its consistency using the reasoner Fast Classification of Terminologies (FaCT) (Bechhofer et al., 2001).

2.1.12.10   Cmap tools

Concept Map (Cmap) was developed at Florida Institute of Technology and it is an application to encourage and facilitate collaboration between creation knowledge models. It also, allows members to modify and add to the knowledge model. Furthermore, users can edit and save the Cmaps automatically, updating the website without the need for any technical involvement.

2.1.12.11   Protégé

Protégé was developed at Stanford University by Stanford Medical Informatics. It is open source, and as an ontology editor, it provides a suite of tools to construct the domain model using various formats. Also, using plug-ins for adding further functions makes it flexible. These plug-ins such as importing and exporting ontology language (XML, OIL, FLogic) and a reasoner, for instance. The platform of Protégé supports two ways of modelling ontologies:

- Protégé frame editors, which enable users to create and populate ontology support by Open Knowledge Base Connectivity protocol (OKBC).

- Protégé OWL editor, which enables users to create and develop ontologies using web ontology language (protégé, 2011b, Noy and McGuinness, 2001).

2.1.12.12   Web Protégé

WebProtégé is a web interface which provides a flexible environment for experts to work collaboratively. It is a tool to develop ontologies processes and make the ontology accessible from any web browser. There is a difference between WebProtégé and other tools such as Wikis. It supports OWL 2.0 which is compatible with Protégé 4.(Tudorache et al., 2011, Tania Tudorache et al., 2010)

2.1.12.13   General Architecture for text engineering (GATE)

In the field of language engineering GATE is one of the most used tools. It has plug-ins such as part of speech (POS) taggers, Named Entity Recognizers, and sentence splitters. Using natural language processing (NLP) includes information extracting tools.

GATE was developed by a team at the University of Sheffield in the early 1990s as a free open source tool. It runs on any platform and supports JAVA 5 .0 . It has a user interface to enable user editing, visualisation and quick application development, and, in addition to ontology management, it supports manual annotation, semi-automatic and semantic (Moens, 2006).

The automatic and semi-automatic semantic annotation and manual annotation features help users to create own annotation; the GATE developer is used for extracting terms and concepts from specific texts for this purpose. It will be also speed up the ontology process of building a conceptual model as an ontology of IS. GATE supports many languages such as XHTML, XML, HTML, PDF, Emails., MS word, plain text, etc. (Cunningham and Tablan, 2000)

2.1.12.14 *Comparison of ontology tools*

These tools are compared using different criteria that are summarised in the above table. Clearly, it can help to provide interoperability solutions among tools and languages. Table 2-15 shows ontology tools that was researched and evaluated. These contain criteria of formal axiom languages which are the most functional features to be used when developing ontologies with them. Another criterion is architecture of ontology tools (client server, standalone). Concerning ease of use, Protégé and WebOnto offer graphical vision to present a data overview. The table shows that most tools are based on first order logic. The lexical capability of tools such as OntoSaurus and WebOnto does not support it, whereas Protégé provides query searching in the ontology. Overall, the most important tool selected is Protégé, which has many features such as; allowing representing class, partitions, relations, attributes and axioms. It has a graphical interface that makes it easy to use. It also supports several languages that can be exported in RDFs, XML, FLogic, Java and ClIPS. It is standalone, free, open source as well being built on a reasoner that helps to infer answers. Furthermore, it has extensible plug-ins, it is powerful and it has easy to use such as features as the DL query tab that allows ontology to be searched (Protégé, 2011a).

Table 2-15 Comparison between ontology tools

Ontology Editor	Designed	Base language	Import from language	Export to language	Usage (web support)	View Graphic Text	Architecture	Lexical capability
Ontolingua Server	1990	Ontolingua	KIF,CML, IDL,	. Export, KIF, LOOM, Epikit, IDL	Web access to services	NO	Client /server	Search for terms in loaded ontologies
OntoSaurus	2002	LOOM	Loom IDL onto C++ KIF:Loom	Loom IDL onto C++ KIF:Loom	No HPPT browser	Yes hierarchy	Client /server	No
WebOnto	1997	OCML	OCML	RDF,export:RDFs, GXL, Ontolingua, OIL	Web service deployment site	YES	Client /server	No
OilEd	2002	DAML+OIL	RDFs, OIL, DAML+OIL,SHIQ	:RDFs,OIL, DAML+OIL, OWL	RDF URI's; limited namespaces; limited XML Schema; exportHTML.	YES	standalone	synonyms
Cmap tools	2004	Java		None	URL references	Yes	standalone	Syntax,speil check,word net
Protégé	2000	OWL	xmlrdfS, OWL, XMLS	XML,RDFs, OWL,XMLS, FLogic, Java.	Reference ontologies by URL	Yes	standalone	Query tab allows searching
OntoGen	2007	Natural language	-	-	URL documents	yes	standalone	Querying for particular concepts

(Corcho et al, 2003)

2.2 Information Science (IS)

2.2.1 Overview

Information science (IS) has a comprehensive history. It needs to determine the interdisciplinary relationships with other fields, to clarify the confusion surrounding its specialisation to identity and define its position among other sciences. IS acquires and collects, organises, retrieves the information resources that contain information held by libraries and information centres. IS faces a big problem of how to be defined. A number of researchers have dealt with its historical perspective, such as Buckland and Liu (1995), Cleverdon (1987), Shera and Cleveland (1977) Bourne (1980) Farkas-Conn (1990).

The IS is concerned with studying properties and behaviours of information, and creating, using, controlling the flow for it to be accessed and used. This includes processes of production and dissemination of information. Hence, IS is derived from mathematics and logic, linguistics, psychology, information technology, computer and operation research, communication and library science, for instance. It also has a strong relationship with social science and humanities. It provides a service to all members of the community through libraries and information centres. These libraries and documentation centres play an important role in collecting human intellectual heritage and preserving it for the benefit of future generations.

2.2.2 Definitions

The term IS began to be used in 1958 (Hanson, 1968), and developed over time. The first formal usage of the term of IS dates back to 1959, when it was presented by Moore School of Electrical Engineering at the University of Pennsylvania. But by 1962 in the USA this term was still not use in titles of books or even conferences held in that period. But the terms information retrieval and scientific information were used instead, and sometimes the term documentation was used to refer to any recorded information.

The first significant definition of IS was published in October 1962 at the Georgia Institute of Technology conference (USA):

"Information Science is a science that investigates the properties and the behaviour of information, and the means of processing information for optimum accessibility and usability. The processes include the organization, dissemination, collection, storage, retrieval, interpretation and use of information." (Nicolae, 1961p.1)

In spite of this the following early pioneers in the IS field, such as:

- Cyril Cleverdon
- Robert Fairthorne
- Derek De Solla
- Eugene Garfield
- Manfred Kochen
- Frederick Wilfrid Lancaster
- Brian Vickery
- B. C. Brooke

Were interested in finding a proper definition of IS as unitary discipline. There is a lack of unanimity on what constitutes IS.

Although using the same information technology in the document preparation process and providing information for users, however, the separation between concepts of libraries and information continued until the period after World War II in many countries. The impact of this separation can easily note from the title Library and information science.

Shera's (1983) theory indicates that library science is an alternative term for information science. He emphasises that information transmission by the library cannot be done without transfer of information itself. Also, he indicates that the concept of IS is derived from Shannon's theory of information. Information theory focused on the word information to coin the term; it can be quantified, analyzed, and coded.

$$H(X) = \mathbb{E}_X[I(x)] = -\sum_{x \in X} p(x) \log p(x).$$

(CHEUNG et al., 1984)

The information quantity is entropy H indicates how easily message can be compressed whereas X can measure the information amount to get the communication rate. Also, Brookes defined aspects of the information science through the basic equation;

$$K(S) + I = K(S + S_1)$$

(Bawden, 2011)

This equation clarifies in general the aspects of the IS science, which indicates the change in the cognitive structures $K(S)$ to a new case of the knowledge to become $K(S + S_1)$ by adding more information (I) where (S) Q refers to the change in the situation.

2.2.3 Relationship of information science with other sciences

IS is a science without identity, due to the fact that it is intended to develop the foundations of the theory among other fields. It was a theoretical stalemate and the lack of scientific methodologies and philosophy led to a big problem, particularly when information scientists tried to establish the main basic areas of the science and identify its boundaries against other fields. The pioneers of information science emphasise that IS, as any natural science, has its basic roles and foundations (Machlup and Mansfield, 1983).

At that time IS began to establish IS theories, but most of them are relative to other fields, such as applications of computer technology in the fields of medicine and chemistry. It was a clear trend to attach it to communication science or to computer science as Informatics, although there were attempts to establish it as an independent science with its own identity and boundaries.

The main characters of IS are:

- The nature of IS is interdisciplinary and its relations with other fields are changing over time
- IS is connected to information technology.

IS has deep human and social dimensions. In fact, information science consists of a set of sciences, such as:

- Library science, which concerns transferring information and recorded knowledge.
- Communication science, which deals with the principles, roles and theories governing the transfer of messages and signals.

If we study some of these fields to highlight the relations between them, we find that:

- Computer science plays a great role in information systems, in particular the processes that are related to storage and retrieval of information.
- Communication science has the role of transferring information by different methods.
- Psychology is related to the study of reading and using information. There is a lot of research in psychology-oriented studies relating to the process of storage, search and retrieval of information in the human memory, as illustrated in Figure 2-11

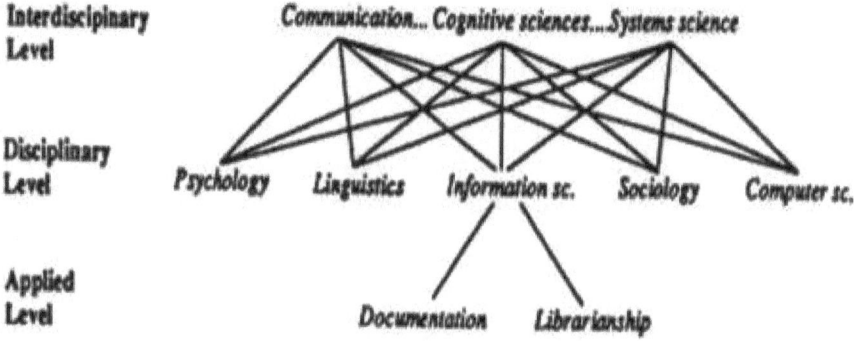

Figure 2-11 Information Science relations with other sciences

(Ingwersen, 1992 p.103)

Any self-discipline or field of knowledge is based primarily on the challenge of its relations with other disciplines, to find out the degree of overlap with them. However, IS has been affected by a large number of other disciplines which still need to be identified. Buckland said:

"[we] should now make more of a distinction between the Information Science, or overlaps with, Library and Information Science and the formal, quantitative Information Science associated with cybernetics and general systems theory."(Zins, 2007a).

A lot of work has been done to organise knowledge of the IS field. Zins developed four articles from a critical Delphi study which used questionnaires to explore the foundation of Information Science. The international panel contained 57 leading scholars from 16 countries, representing important aspects of the field. This study has mapped 10 basic categories of information science: *Foundations, Resources, Knowledge Workers, Contents, Applications, Operations and Processes, Technologies, Environments, Organizations, and Users.* See Figure 2-12 (Zins, 2007d).

Domain	Foci	Main Categories (1st division)	Sub-Categories (2nd division)	Sub-Categories*/Examples & Explanations** (3rd division)	Exemplary Fields
Meta-Knowledge	Knowledge on the field of IS itself	1. Foundations	Theory	A. Conceptions B. Disciplines (e.g., Anthropology (e.g., "culture"), Arts (e.g., "design"), Communication (e.g., "communication", "media", "message"), Computer science (e.g., "computer language"), Economics (e.g., "information economics"), Education (e.g., "learning"), Engineering (e.g., "information technology"), History (e.g., "primary source", "secondary sources", "tertiary source"), Law (e.g., "intellectual property", "copyright"), Linguistics (e.g., "language"), Philosophy (Epistemology (e.g., "knowledge"), Ethics (e.g., "information ethics", "professional ethics"), Political Science (e.g., "democracy"), Psychology (e.g., "cognition"), Research Methodology (e.g., "evaluation", "research", "research methodology"), Semiotics (e.g., "sign"), Sociology ("e.g., "society") C. Theories	Theory of IS
			Research	A. Theoretical B. Empirical 1. Quantitative 2. Qualitative	Research Methodology
			Education	academic education and to professional training: theoretical knowledge and practical knowledge.	LIS Education
			History	Historical accounts of the field.	History of IS
Subject-based knowledge	Knowledge on the explored phenomena (i.e., the mediating aspects & conditions of human knowledge)	2. Resources	Issues	quality information (resources), information (resources) quality	Information Quality Information Systems
			Types	Primary resources (i.e., the human originators), secondary resources, tertiary resources	
		3. Knowledge Workers (Who? mediators)	Issues	A. Personality traits B. Theoretical knowledge C. Applied knowledge and practice	Information Ethics LIS Education
			Types	Taxonomies of professional workers by fields of expertise (e.g., medical informatics), and organizational sector (e.g., librarians, archivists)	
		4. Contents (What? matters)	Issues	Content related issues (e.g., What is a subject?)	
			Types	Taxonomies of structures (e.g., knowledge maps, subject classifications schemes, thesauri), classification systems (e.g., LCC, DDC, UDC, CC, BC), subjects (i.e., Archeology, biology, Computer Science) and the like.	
		5. Applications (Why? Motives)	Issues	issues related to the development of application oriented systems.	
			Types	Taxonomy of applications (e.g., (information) searching, shopping, socialization and socializing).	
		6. Operations & Processes (How? methods)	Issues	Issues related to the various operations and processes involved in mediating human knowledge.	
			Types	Taxonomy of operations and processes: documentation, representation, organization, processing, dissemination, publication, storage, manipulation, evaluation, measurement, searching, and retrieving knowledge.	
		7. Technologies (means (mode))	Issues	Technological related issues (e.g., user-interface design).	
			Types	Taxonomy of knowledge technologies and media: electronic-based technologies (e.g., computer-based information systems, Internet), paper-based and printing-based technologies (e.g., books), communication-based technologies and media (e.g., cellular phones, MP3).	
		8. Environments (Where and when? milieus)	Issues	Social issues (e.g., Information policy, information accessibility), including ethnic and cultural issues, professional issues related to the settings, as well as legal issues (e.g., Intellectual property, privacy), and ethical issues (e.g., privacy vs. public interests).	Information Ethics Social Informatics
			Types	A. Ethnic & Cultural environments B. Settings (e.g., Education, Health)	
		9. Organizations	Issues	Issues related to the organizational settings (e.g., managing knowledge in business organizations)	
			Types	A. Organizational Type: 1. Governmental Sector 2. Public sector 3. Private sector B. Functional type 1. Memory organizations 2. Information services	
		10. Users	Issues	User related issues (e.g., user information needs, user behavior, user search strategies)	User Studies Information Behavior
			Types	A. Individuals B. Groups and Communities 1. Gender-based 2. Age-based 3. Culture & ethnicity-based 4. Need & interest based (e.g., division by profession)	

* The words in **bold** are categories. ** The other terms are exemplary terms (entries).

Figure 2-12 knowledge map of Information Science

(Zins, 2007c)

2.2.4 Information Science Taxonomy

In the past, ever since people started to record and collect information, there has been an urgent need to organize this information. Recently there has been a growth in using computers and search engines to search for information, which requires organisation of the information. These demands increased particularly with growing knowledge in different fields, which causes the knowledge heterogeneity. The search engine is based on the traditional role of classification schemes to retrieve information.

Classification is recognised as an electronic information retrieval tool. Also, classification schemes have been used to arrange library items to be available for users to access these items physically. We need to explore several classification methods including their disadvantages, to show the feasibility of our methodology.

In the history of classification systems there are several universal classification schemes such as **Dewey Decimal Classification (DDC)** which is still used in most libraries around the world - there are 200,000 libraries in 35 countries still using it as the main tool to physically arrange the resources. DDC divides knowledge into 10 categories, and each category is dividing into 10 sub-categories (OCLC, 2010).

In DDC structure there is a general class such as 000 - computer science, information and general works. This class is broad and is not limited to a specific work or discipline. However, this class deals with any subject under computers and information in general.

Within this specification 001 is knowledge, 002 any books in this area, 003 systems, 004 data processing and computer science and 005 computer programming and data. The DDC divisions are based on categorising the subjects for physically putting books on the shelves.

In this system computer science is compressed into the low-level class which has 001.64 numbers. On the other hand, in the 20th edition of Dewey classification, computer science is promoted into three levels of his divisions to be in 004 Data processing and computer science, and 006 special computer methods (Broughton, 1999).

Although, DDC is still widely used today, it makes communication poor. If you are looking for a book on human computer interaction, for instance, in Dewey classification you will find it under 004, which includes all computer science found under 004 in the section of general works. Computer human interaction is classified under 600: technology and applied science. **004.019 advances in human –computer interaction**. Is another example for a book entitled **3D sound for virtual reality and multimedia.**

The subjects of the book are virtual, human-computer interaction and computer processing, classified under 600 Technology, then under 621.3893. As a result users will miss a large section of information contained in different resources, which are physically classified under different numbers and locations. The shortcomings of the DDC classification system are widely acknowledged amongst the scientific community.

2.2.4.1 Universal decimal classification (UDC)

The first edition was published in 1905. It is a system of library classification for information retrieval. UDC develops Dewey classification by adding auxiliary signs to the hierarchy division for Dewey, to specify a variety of special aspects of subject and the relationships between subjects. Additionally, it improves the process of information retrieval. The difference between UDC and DDC is that it facilitates the identification process on the substantive divisions, which reflect on the nature of classification and its motives as a tool of information retrieval (McIlwaine, 1997).

2.2.4.2 Library of Congress Classification (LCC)

LCC is developed by specialists in various sciences for special needs and purposes to arrange books in the congress Library. LCC divides subjects into broad divisions consisting of letters and numbers. An advantage of LCC classification is that it provides accurate details of many of the topics that are not available in other classifications because it covers various topics. Also, a disadvantage it has specifying books in the library rather than universally (Miksa, 1998).

2.2.4.3 Colon Classification Scheme (CCS)

This is also called Facet classification, which was developed by Ranganthan in 1933. Facet classification is an appropriate method for knowledge organising (Wang and Jhuo, 2009). Ranganthan pioneered an alternative dynamic and multidimensional view for universal knowledge organisation, by analysing and representing things in a scheme of classification.

Ranganathan's contribution was delivered in facet analysis. His approach was the creation of five categories, namely: personality, matter, energy, space and time. These are called PMEST.

These categories could analyse any component of any subject and his approach builds classes from the bottom up rather than the top down. Comparing with the earliest universal classification schemes, today CCS is not widely used. These categories as analytic synthetic analysis derive from two main processes, namely:

- Analysis: this means breaking down the subject into element concepts
- Synthetics, which is recombining these concepts into subject strings or a descriptor.

A far more interesting case, however, is that of Ranganthan, whose approach was more broad than Dewey's. He catalyzed that classification scheme for change; any item could be classified under five classes rather just one topic. He expressed the idea that any topic had various angles and it could seen from different perspectives.

For example, the book titled: **A history of photograph and computer art**. In Dewey classification this will be into 770 from Art division 700. According to Ranganthan classification, this subject is analysed from different angles, such as photography, electronic art and history. It could be under History 900, technology 600, computer 400 and Art 700 as illustrated in Figure 2-13.

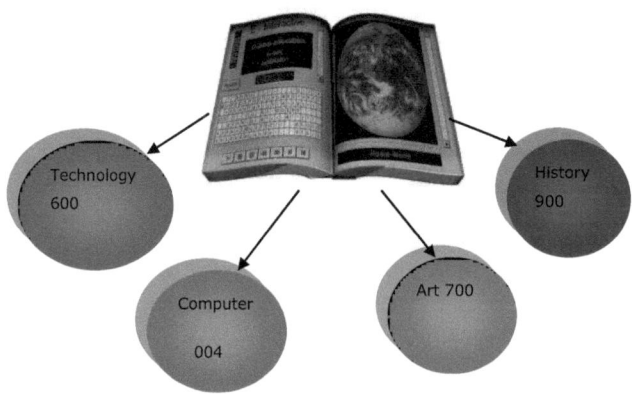

Figure 2-13 Differences between Dewey & Ranganthan classification

2.2.4.4 *The advantages of Facet analysis system (FAS)*

The Facet analysis system (FAS) is relevant to an electronic context. In fact, it provides flexible methods for organizing digital materials in the electronic environment.

A number of research studies have shown that classification information in a multidimensional hierarchy is more easily reached than a one-dimensional classification. The notation of a facet classification system may be useful for the researchers to compound concepts. The combination of analysis concepts can be extended to provide hierarchy structure.(Broughton, 2001)

For example: the heading of (Library) could be extended to offer the following list of headings:

Library
Library – Academic
Library – Academic – University library
Library – Academic – College library
Library – Academic – Higher education institution
Library – Academic – Department library
Library – International
Library – Public
Library – School - Multimedia Centre
Library – School- Learning Centre
Library – School - Resource Centre
Library – School- Learning Resource Centre
Library – School - Audio-Visual Centre
Library – School- Library Media Centre
Library – School - Instructional Materials Centre
Library – School - Comprehensive Library
Library – School - service
Library – School – service - Loan
Library – School – service- Loan - Internal
Library – School – service- Loan - External
Library - Special
Library - Special – Scientific research centre
Library - Special – Library of institutions of commerce and industry
Library - Special – Library of organisations and non-profit organisations
Library - Special – specialized libraries in institutions

The structure in this way could be predictable visible and logical to retrieve easily. A far more interesting case, however, is facet analysis principle, which offers a wide range of standard categories that could be extended to include additional properties of digital materials. Thus, the rule of combination in IS is more complex than in physical collections. However, FAS provides the ability to express a complex subject through electronic documents. It ensures the system syntax is managed in a consistent manner.

2.2.4.5 Classification Research group (CRG)

In 1955 British experts were influenced by Ranganthan's approach and they pronounced that facet classification should be followed as the basic method for information retrieval by filling the gap between theory and practice. CRG adopted Ranganthan's theory in which they analysed the subject based on the five categories but they had extended it to a thirteen-faceted approach; things, kind, part, property, material, process, operation, agent, patient, product, by space and time. (McIlwaine and Broughton, 2000).

Broughton (2001) points out that the five categories could be extended as much as the subject's requirements and needs.

"..... *fundamental thirteen categories have been found to be sufficient for the analysis of vocabulary in almost all areas on knowledge. It is however quite likely that other general categories exist; it is certainly the case that there are some domain specific categories, such as those of form and genre in the field of literature*" (Broughton, 2001. pp 79 - 80)

His suggestions had catalysed to create the facet classification that is needed. Also, Vickery's soil classification in 1960 has 18 eighteen categories. Broadly, there are many attempts at developing classification schemes after the (FAS) became more popular in the www for information retrieval.

Petersen (1994) created a small facet classification for the Art and Architecture Thesaurus (AAT) for the Getty Research Institute, as followed: Associated Concepts, Physical Attributes, Styles and Periods (as Space and Time), Agents (Organisations or People), Activities (Energy) ,Materials (Matter), and Objects (Personality).

Social care taxonomy is a hierarchy arrangement in free database that covers the material of social care; includes over 100,000 records such as documents of the government policy and research report. Yet this taxonomy is similar to the structure of a thesaurus, using terms like RT related to (NT) Narrow than (T) Top term, (GO) go term, (S) stop term and so on (SCIE, 2010). Also, mathematical science education is classified basic on dividing the subject into 9 categories - each category has many categories (MSEB, 2010). Based on the above classification schemes our approach will be discussed in Section 3.1.1

2.2.5 Why Information Science Taxonomy:

Taxonomy of Information science is providing a control vocabulary and hierarchical arrangement of IS topics for browsing, searching and indexing material on an IS subject.

In contrast to this, the frame system and subsumption in OWL means necessary implication, so the hierarchy means that:

"All Librarians is Employee"

"All Employees is person"

Does it mean that Employees and users, are different, and can there be anything that is both Employee and users? We assume that they were different unless they had an explicit common child. Likewise, they are to be used as sharing terminology in an area to improve the exchange of information between professionals and organisations in the field of IS.

Taxonomy of IS allows the building of complex topic-based search string algorithms to find a word where one or many strings or patterns are found within a text. IS taxonomy is developed to covers a broad range of IS issues and is created to improve and enable browsing for research results in a database that amplifies in size.

2.3 Knowledge management (KM) and Virtual communities of Practice (VCops).

Whilst a lot of literature covers the use of communities of practice as a part of knowledge management strategy, no formal academic research has been identified that relates specifically to the context of supporting ontology development via virtual communities of practice (VCops) in the Information Science domain. This section provides an overview of some perspectives from knowledge management (KM) and (VCops). It provides a background of the key literature relevant to this research, giving the reader a comprehensive overview. First, however, it starts with some basic definitions. The next section need to establish what is meant by data, information and knowledge.

2.3.1 The Main components of knowledge management.

This section will begin with discussion of the concepts of data, information, and knowledge that have been discussed in the literature. Many of the pioneers used these terms interchangeably (Huber and Daft, 1987). Davenport and Prusak (1998) emphasised the relationship between data, information and knowledge, but highlighted they are have different definitions. To define knowledge clearly should distinguish between these terms, because the fundamental problem behind the failure of defining knowledge management is lack of understanding of the meaning of knowledge itself. It is often confused with information and data (Senge, 2003).

Marco(2003) asserted that the former terms are central to knowledge management. However, misunderstanding and confusion between these terms can lead to a problem in information systems design and knowledge representation (Davenport, 1998). Hence, discussing them has important implications for developing ontology of information science.

2.3.1.1 Data

Many researchers have defined data as the raw material of information, and it is a set of symbols which have not been interpreted. Davenport (2000) defined data as

> "*a set of discrete, objective facts about events*" (Davenport, 2000, p.2).

Furthermore, Dalkir (2005) provided a comprehensive definition of data which is

"Data are necessary inputs into information and knowledge, and are defined as a series of observations, measurements, or facts in the form of numbers, words, sounds, and/or images. Data have no meaning, but provide the raw material from which information is produced". (Dalkir, 2005p. 430),

2.3.1.2 Information

Information is data which has been processed and organized to become a useful and meaningful. Thus, information describes particular conditions and situations.(Zins, 2007b, Feather and Sturges, 2003, Tuomi, 2000). Roberts (2000), briefly defined information as:

> *"analyzed data – facts that have been organized in order to impart meaning"*
> *(Roberts, 2000 p. 335)*

2.3.1.3 Knowledge

We assess and order information in order to turn it into knowledge that can be used appropriately (Feather and Sturges, 2003). This means knowledge is a combination of meanings, concepts, and beliefs composed in the human mind as we observe, assess and understand phenomena around us, whilst also solving complex problems. Knowledge is defined by Nonaka (1995) as,

" *A dynamic human process of justifying personal belief toward the truth."* (Nonaka I., 1995, P58).

Knowledge is defined in Webster (2011) as certain and clear insight into something.

> *" the fact or condition of knowing something with familiarity gained through experience or association". (Webster, 2011)*

Furthermore, knowledge has four types:

- Know- what: including knowledge of facts which are close to traditional knowledge such as doctors knowing medical facts.
- Know- why: including knowledge of the reasons that lie behind natural phenomena, and its ability to serve human beings and scientific and technological processes.
- Know- who: this knowledge refers to the experience of doing and executing objects, whether these objects are individual management or operation of processes. This knowledge is usually owned by the company or institution.

- Know- how: the importance of this knowledge has increased as it improves business performance and most projects need this knowledge to speed up implementations and ensure success.

Learning how to gain these four types of knowledge ensures improvement in organisational performance. The Know-what and Know-why type of knowledge can be acquired from books, and databases; they can be accessed from different sources, but Know–how and know–who are only gained from practice and experience, which is important in learning and managing. (Polanyi, 1974).

It is widely agreed that data, which is simple facts, becomes information in a meaningful form. Subsequently, information becomes knowledge when people have the ability to add information and organise it in the right context.

2.3.2 Knowledge Management

Knowledge management has become a significant development over the last twenty years, capturing the attention of organizations (Davenport and Prusak, 1998).

Knowledge is an essential part of both the management process and the performance of organisations. There are innumerable books and articles on virtually every aspect of knowledge management (Leonard, 1995; Nonaka, 1991; Nonaka and Takeuchi, 1995; Stewart, 1997).

The subject area has attracted many perspectives (BSI, 2003; SAI, 2001; Polanyi, 1974).

Knowledge sharing between individuals, groups and organisations, using efficient tools of knowledge management systems technology (KMS) is a particularly interesting aspect (Davenport and Prusak, 1998; Wenger, 1998; Dixon, 2002; Nonaka and Konno, 1998; Wasko and Faraj, 2000). Knowledge can be shared and created in an organisation at individual or group levels. The author has selected the SECI model of knowledge creation, which places tacit knowledge at the heart of capturing and communicating knowledge. If we consider Nonaka's approach of tacit knowledge, and its transformation to explicit knowledge, his research considers knowledge as simply a presentation of real life, in a representational approach (Nonaka, 1991; Nonaka and Takeuchi, 1995), for which it is necessary to obtain a clear understanding of how knowledge sharing and creation work in practice. Despite numerous studies in the area, there is still only a small amount of attention paid to how knowledge is created, because knowledge is created by individuals and not by organisations – to do anything else is impossible..

The Ontological Diagram of Organisational Knowledge illustrates the fundamental elements of knowledge (Vasconcelos, J, Kimble, C., & Gouveia, F. R. (2000). See Figure 2-14

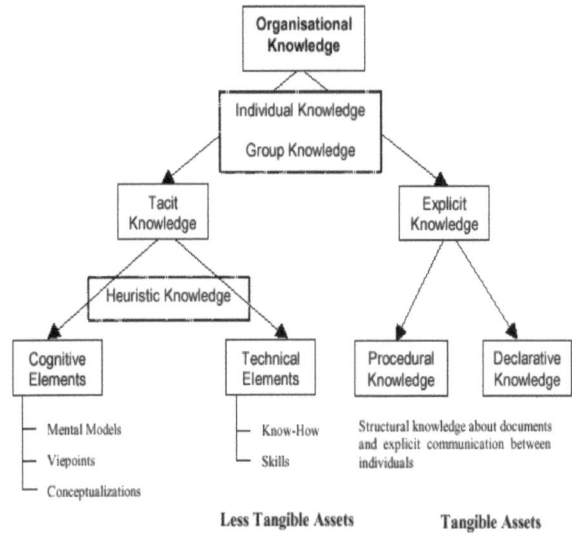

Figure 2-14 classification of knowledge in ontological diagram

(Vasconcelos et al., 2000)

In fact, knowledge exists at two levels, which are individual and group, in both tacit and explicit forms. This dichotomy between explicit and tacit knowledge is vital, and is essential in understanding the challenges in the KM discipline. Tacit knowledge is known as individual knowledge that results from interaction between individuals or groups of people (Mohamed et al., 2006). On the other hand, explicit knowledge is viewed as being procedural or declarative knowledge (Anderson, 1983).

> "The procedural knowledge is describing the action for the subsequent step and responds the question of How?". (Perez-Soltero et al., 2006p. 44)

The declarative knowledge is interrelated to the physical aspect of the knowledge and answers the questions of What- Who- Where- and When. It describes specific actions to perform certain tasks.

Human knowledge has previously been classified into many types of knowledge, for instance, explicit and tacit; hard and soft; implicit and formal (Nonaka, 1991; Kimble and Hildereth, 2005). However, knowledge takes many forms – it can be tacit or explicit, individual or collective knowledge. Social activity, discussion, and problem solving enables tacit knowledge to be converted to become numerical, linguistic and transmitted (Nonaka, 1991; Nonaka and Takeuchi, 1995; Rangachari, 2009).

Nonaka and Takeuchi (1995) defined explicit knowledge as:

> "Explicit knowledge can easily be processed by a computer, transmitted electronically, or stored in a data base", whereas, "tacit knowledge is not easily visible and expressible." (Nonaka and Takeuchi 1995: P.8, 9)

Nonaka and Takeuchi believe that tacit knowledge contains technical skills – informal, individual experience, beliefs, values that can be captured in the term 'know how'.

Nonaka & Konno (1998) Say that tacit knowledge is intertwined with the notion of creativity which consists of using digital and numerical language to express oneself and share thoughts. This connects with the second aspect of this research (Gourlay, 2002).

In the interim, "knowledge is unstructured and understood, but not clearly expressed as implicit knowledge. If knowledge is organized and easy to share it is called structured knowledge. To convert implicit knowledge into explicit knowledge, it must be extracted and formatted."(Power, 2000 p.9)

Ontology is intended to make tacit domain knowledge explicit and it has been widely applied in the context of knowledge representation (Berners-Lee et al., 2001). In this respect, we see that ontologies are a knowledge representation of specific domains. Thus, ontologies are a form of knowledge base comparative with meta-data, thesaurus, taxonomy and knowledge base, according to Victor Lombardi's definition (2003):

> " An Ontology populated with data" (Lombardi, 2003).

It focuses on the important aspect of this research, Knowledge Representation (KR). Thus, the scope of KR and its roles in AI can be explored, as well as the role of ontology in knowledge management as a whole.

2.3.3 Knowledge Engineering (KE)

Sowa (2000) defines Knowledge Engineering as "an application of logic and ontology to the task of building computable models of some domain for some purpose". (Sowa, 2000, p. 132) Knowledge Engineering is the process of creating an expert system that is a form of Artificial Intelligence system (AI). AI has a long history in dealing with knowledge from both practical and theoretical perspectives, which is a major requirement. Furthermore, knowledge engineering has a strong connection with conceptual analysis and formal ontology that can establish the foundations of the ontological engineering field (Guarino, 1997). In the meantime, ontological engineering is a subfield of knowledge engineering concerned with controlling explicit knowledge using software applications (Shadbolt and Milton, 1999).

Knowledge Engineering is composed of many principal stages, namely:

Knowledge Acquisition is related to knowledge collection approaches and mechanisms.

Knowledge Representation is related to the method of analysis and represents the gathered information.

Knowledge Validation is related to validation of knowledge representation.

Knowledge inference, explanation and justification are related to the model that has been identified to be explained and justified.

Ontology is an emerging meaning of knowledge representation. It can develop information management and organization in many applications. This research concentrates on knowledge representation as the focus of research on domain ontology representation, as ontology of Information Science OIS.

2.3.4 Knowledge Representation (KR)

Knowledge Representation looks at how to use symbols that represent a set of facts inside a knowledge domain, to facilitate inferring facts to create a new element of knowledge (Markman, 1999). Knowledge representation plays a crucial role in the AI field as described by (Davis et al., 1993), namely:

Role 1 : Knowledge Representation is a surrogate:

In the real world things such as physical objects and relationships need to be represented in a model to describe them, to be stored in a computer which is essential for AI agents to be readable, understandable and computable. The symbols serve as surrogates for the external world. Inference in KR made by the artificial agents can make the model of the real world that is based on logical facts.

Role 2: Knowledge Representation is a set of ontological commitments:

Sowa (2000) indicates that ontological commitment is determined by a variety of variables in the knowledge representation. As ontology is a study of existence, so it determines whether or not the categories of things are existing. Then ontological commitment makes conscious choices about aspects and boundaries of the real world. Furthermore, ontology is an appropriate form of knowledge representation. Ontology can be represented by using specific languages such as Frame-Logic(F-Logic), Ontology Conceptual Modelling Language(OCML), Web Ontology Language(OWL); Davis and his colleagues point out that "the essential information is not the form of this language but the content, that is the set of concepts offered as a way of thinking about the world" (Davis et al., 1993p. 20).

Role 3: Knowledge Representation is a sub- theory of intelligent reasoning:

It is the key role in knowledge representation, especially for AI applications. This is often implicit, but is evident by studying its components:

"(1) the representation's fundamental conception of intelligent inference, (2) the set of inferences that the representation sanctions, (3) the set of inferences that the representation recommends".(Davis et al., 1993p. 21)

Hence, ontology as defined inside the AI scope sticks to this role. This the reason behind choosing the formal logic based on the language rather than frame based language for knowledge representation.

Role 4 : Knowledge Representation is a medium for efficient computation:

Knowledge should be encoded within the AI system to be processed by the computer efficiently. Any problem can be represented easily, yet solving it may need time and effort to compute. The design and use of knowledge representation languages has been influenced by the development of software and hardware theory.

Role 5: Knowledge Representation is a medium of human expression:

Finally, the main role of representation language facilitates communication between domain experts and knowledge engineers. The knowledge engineer writes the rules and definitions and the experts read them (Sowa, 2000).

In brief, knowledge representation means expressing things in the real world through the medium of communication and expression that informs the machine about the real world. It aims to facilitate efficient communication between humans and machines, and express things in the real world to be understandable for both. In the interim, ontology becomes inevitable.

2.3.5 Virtual Communities of practice (VCops).

2.3.6 Communities of Practice (Cops)

The Community of Practice (Cop) is not just a process of obtaining learning as social structure, but also a way of gathering knowledge that could be developed regarding Mayo's theory of human relations knowledge. It can be formed and shaped at team levels through negotiations, discussion and conversation. This study has adopted Mayo's theory, takes an approach regarding knowledge as a product of discussion and resulting social processes. (Mayo, 1975). Mizoguchi argues that ontology should be developed by many people or a community. This way supports the ontology construction by people with the same interest and subject area rather than knowledge engineers (Mizoguchi, 2003).

Cops is introduced by Lave and (Wenger, 1998) as a learning process within Legitimate Peripheral Participation (LPP). LPP, in his perspective, is an important aspect of effective social learning. LPP is based on the idea that members of the community with less experience will learn from social interaction with experts in a specific domain. This initial definition is related to the theory of situativity: situated learning in ethnographic study (Andrew et al., 2008).

Cops developed more extensively when it was redefined by(Wenger, 1998). It has been used in business environments, but could be used in knowledge management as a tool for successful knowledge sharing processes, as it has received a lot of interest from both scholars and participants in the knowledge management area. A Cop is defined as:

".. *group that coheres through mutual engagement on an indigenous (or appropriated) enterprise, creating a common repertoire. The tight knit nature of relation is created by sustained mutual engagement". (Cox, 2005 p.531)*

"*A system of relationships between people, activities, and the world; developing with time, and in relation to other tangential and overlapping communities of practice 'is an intrinsic condition of the existence of knowledge" (Roberts, 2006 p.624).*

The above definitions refer to the idea of information exchange, knowledge and sharing concerns within groups of people.

Cops is not a formal structure for knowledge generation. The generation of knowledge accrues when people co-operate and communicate to seek resolutions of problems or to develop a new product. Many studies conducted show that the community of practice is the best and strongest way to unite a team.(Nirenberg, 1995, Stewart, 1997).

Wenger (2008) declared that a Cop consists of a small group who participate in the community regularly with their own leadership. We cannot call any group of individuals working together a Cop unless the characteristics of Cops are present, which are: mutual engagement, learning or identity acquisition, a sense of joint enterprise, and a shared set of communal resources. Wenger stated that a Community of Practice requires individuals to do things together to create a source of learning and knowing. Also, they can bring benefits for learning and competency (Coakes and Clarke, 2008, Thrysoe et al., 2010).

Group members are more likely to share commonalities with volunteers than a group of employees at a company. (Wenger 2002).

Cops have been investigated in knowledge management literature taking several approaches, which have highlighted several different sorts: e.g. physical Cops, social groups, network Cops, and online Cops, which might take names like: community of commitment (COC) community of interest (COI), network of practice (NOP), virtual cops, Networks Cop (Malhotra, 2002, Nolan et al., 2007).

Cops can take many forms, for instance study groups or informal discussion groups; many Cops also exist online (Murillo-othon., 2006, Noriko H., 2007, Porra and Parks, 2006). The rise of the internet as a communication tool has influenced the formation of Cops to a significant extent. Cops function as a mediated tool in computers to improve communication between people; these may take the form of websites, electronic bulletin boards, emails, blogs and forums. (Hildreth et al., 1998).

Wenger (2005) says that Cops are mediated by technology that has been developed by interaction, discussion, and the exchange of views in order to solve problems and generate artefacts.(Wenger, 2005).

Furthermore, McDermott (1999) has indicated that are points to take into account when building communities, depending on the area of interest:

1. Gather as a group of specialists, using informal discussion to exchange knowledge.
2. Some communities make attempts to gather knowledge from group members.

3. Members of the group contact one another irregularly to exchange advice and solutions.
4. The use of information technology keeps members connected.
5. Members of the group identify themselves as a Community of practice
6. Some communities attempt to capture knowledge from members.
7. Many communities are keeping people involved by using information technology (McDermott, 1999).

However, widespread development of the organisations, around the world led to challenges in accessing knowledge that resides in a specific context.

2.3.7 Virtual communities of practice (VCops)

Virtual communities have emerged from technological development. People are able to connect and share conversation, play games or build relationships, as well as sharing knowledge across the world (Jansen W 2002, Wenger 2002).

'Virtual community' was coined by J.C.R Licklider as computer network. This term can be used as:

- Group of people using computers as a social network to communicate.
- Online group using chat rooms and listing services and activities online(Gourlay, 2001).

A virtual community has been defined as:

"*A group that shares knowledge and meets through networks as internet, they are separated by time and place*".(Catherine et al., 2000p. 229)

"*Are social aggregations that emerge from the net where enough people carrying on those public discussions long enough, with sufficient human feeling, form webs of personal relationships in cyberspace?*" (Gomez, 1998p.218)

"*Virtual teams are composed of geographically dispersed individuals who interact through interdependent tasks guided by a common purpose with links strengthened by web of communication technologies.*" (Panteli and Duncan, 2004p.424)

VCops are a crucial tool for knowledge acquisition. The reason behind that is tacit knowledge is embedded in people's minds and storytelling and conversation take place between experts when they talk about their experience to gain skills. Since the world become a small village and face-to face communication is limited to exchange ideas, and with the rise of websites on the internet, virtual communities have become an alternative to a physical community of practice with dispersed multinational organisations.(Araujo, 1998, Ardichvili et al., 2003).

There is no single agreement on what constitutes VCops of Practice, when looking at literature on the subject; this study defines some of the key features from the literature review; these features are:

1. The ability to meet in a virtual space and communicate via the Internet
2. people who might never meet face-to-face are brought together by means of a technical platform
3. VCops facilitate activities by using Information Technology (IT).
4. The existence of the virtual community can help to identify of an idea or task
5. Groups can self-select
6. That members' interests are usually related to a specific Knowledge Domain.
7. Community members can establish social relationship and a sense of belonging to the groups.
8. Building trust

VCop is team of individuals who communicate and meet virtually; they are linked by a specific interest and social relationship. Their key tool is a technical infrastructure to enable knowledge exchange within virtual communities, and using it allows the transfer of tacit knowledge which is difficult to articulate.

Also, trust is a crucial feature of the success of VCops in bonding member together to develop the quality of conversation and discussion (Usoro, 2003, Fang and Chiu, 2010). In the meantime, distrust is a common element related to internet relationships - it really is a threat to the success of virtual communities(VCs), due to the fact that anonymity is easy; joining web groups and pretending to be a member of the community who has the same interest is easy, and even though people in Cops are connected to each other by their interest. they need trust to communicate efficiently (Leimeister et al., 2008, Schwen and Hara, 2003).

Recently, many VCs are based on social networks on the internet, for instance, YouTube, news groups, wiki, Facebook, Twitter and LinkedIn. All of them focus on working as virtual groups, whereas not all VCs are VCops; in the former, knowledge can be transferred from expert to inexpert, but later on knowledge can be exchanged between peers whether they are professionals or experts in a specific domain. (Lu and Yang, 2011). There are more than 800 million active users on Facebook (Facebook, 2011). Also professionals using Cops possess skills to codify tacit knowledge, which decreases vagueness in coding and analysis.

This research gives a clear explanation to distinguish between VCs and VCops; it also provides some empirical insights into the application of the concept of VCops (Lin et al., 2008, Dube et al., 2006, Llum et al., 2010). VCs are social aggregations that come from the internet, in which people can interact and exchange information.(Chan and Li, 2010)

In terms of classifying VCs many studies have been investigated. Herring, (2008) clustered VCs on the internet into five groups:

- Support groups like Health groups.
- Interest groups such as Soap opera fans.
- Task- related such groups as Cops.
- Groups based on geographical distances like community networks.
- Commercial groups such as product websites.

He point out that Cops are one of the type of VCs called Task-related groups, whereas Cops could be physical or virtual. (Herring, 2008).

Members of VCoPs should be professionals in a specific domain to ensure an accurate representational approach to knowledge sharing. Professionals should be those who hold knowledge in a particular domain, who have the ability to solve problems and who are committed to efficient working. This means VCops should be groups of experts who are able to represent the knowledge used in the knowledge base (KB). In real life there are many VCops in existence, for instance, VCops in the educational domain such as Tapped In htpp://www.tappedin.org.(TappedIn, 2010).

Not all VCs are VCops, as Zhang (2008) reminds us (Zhang and Watts, 2008) – many types of group work collaboratively. Roberts (2008) reviewed different types of collaborative working: task-based work, epistemic collaboration, professional practice, virtual collaboration. This study concentrates solely on professional practice in virtual collaborative environments in the IS domain. Our review of available literature highlighted several characteristics common to communities where knowledge is obtained, aggregated and dispersed by professionals. Opportunities to improve competency is vital in tacit and explicit knowledge sharing so that newcomers can move from peripheral participation to full involvement. Creativity is a way of connecting these various groups exchanging knowledge and facilitating interaction by using the same language; These people are specialists in its language (Roberts, 2008, Gervassis, 2004, Walsh and Crumbie, 2011).

According to Wenger's characterisation of Cops, there are many ways in which virtual professional Communities of Practice (VCops) are different from virtual communities. These characteristics include:

- Topics of discussion in VCops are driven by participants or users under control of a moderator.
- The moderator of a VCop plays an important role in keeping the discussion focussed on the main issues.
- Participants' activities develop through a website.
- Participants of VCops have shared norms and values.
- Mutual engagement: widely distributed user interactions
- Communities: participants build strong personal relationships despite having no face-to-face contact.
- Learning or identity acquisition: members are valued by participants within the learning environment
- Joint enterprise: members sustain focused negotiations.
- Shared repertoire and development of knowledge repository. These characteristics will be considered in designing the ontocop website.

Many studies and projects are relevant to this research, and are inspired by various perspectives to combine to form a new framework to create IS Ontology, these include previous work in the area of ontologies and communities of practice which are briefly presented and discussed. Several pieces of research have illustrated how ontology can serve as a symbolic tool within a community of practice (Domingue et al., 2001). Ankolekar, Sycara's work presents a semantic web system for open resources software communities relying on a specific ontology (Ankolekar et al., 2006). This study, which is titled "an ontology for supporting Cop" presents an ontology built from an analysis of information sources about eleven Cops available in Palette project. It is aimed both at modelling the members of the Cop and at annotating the Cop's knowledge resources (Tifous et al., 2007)

Ontocopi (2003) is a project based on a community of practice identified through ontology network analysis (ONA). Ontocopi used a spreading activation algorithm to crawl through the knowledge network to identify similar objects and the relations between them. This study does not follow standard methodology to integrate Ontocopi because the community of practice lacks establishing methodology. Ontocopi plugs-in protégé and uses AKT ontology which provides opportunities for users to select the class and the class instance display on the panel, and select the relation based on its importance. (O'Hara et al., 2002, Alani et al., 2003)

As you can see the author reviews the literature to discover the basic features of Cops, Vcos and VCops to explain our virtual community of professional practice. Table 2-16 summarises the differences between communities of practice.

Table 2-16 comparison between communities of practice

Category	Traditional Cop	Virtual Cos	Virtual VCops
Communication via the internet	☒	☑	☑
Existence for an identification of an idea or task	☒	☑	☑
Existence according to a place based	☑	☒	☒
Norms	☑	☒	☑
Groups self-selected	☒	☑	☑
Groups emerge through task	☑	☒	☑
leadership	☑	☒	☑
boundaries	Evolving	Fluid	fluid
Transparency	Low	High	High
Knowledge Domain	Interest –related work	Interest – related knowledge	Interest –related knowledge
Trust	☑	☒	☑
Membership criteria	☑	☒	☑
Level of member participation	Limited	Widely	widely

2.3.8 Summary

This chapter investigated and discussed the related subjects to be considered as theoretical framework for this study in three sections. Ontology in philosophy is dealing with being or realty. It is logical semantic built on the theory of meaning, that mean ontology is an important part on semantic web. The ontology concept was discussed, and its development from the philosophical approach to the Computer science approach.

In addition, it conducted numerous comparisons between theories and methodologies of ontology building and designing. It also investigated designing criteria and the tools used for that purpose in order to stand on and follow the proper way in this study. All of these issues were taken into consideration for design OIS ontology information.

In the second section were analyzed characteristics of information science which need to be considered as a science still needs identification and there are many problems need to be solved. Although, there are many studies have been done to identify this science. In addition, reviewing and analyzing classifications systems that used in library science such as UDC, LCC, CCS, and CRG to identify their advantages and disadvantages in order to find the appropriate classification, which is FAS classification system. The FAS is multidimensional hierarchy and more easily reached than a one-dimensional classification. The notation of FAS may be useful for the researchers to compound concepts

While, in the final section has been dealt with knowledge management to identify the role of VCops. The VCops are teams of individuals who meet and communicate virtually with others; they are linked by a specific interest. VCops has an enormous affect in transferring tacit knowledge which is difficult to articulate. It support acquiring and representing domain knowledge and how they are employed for the purpose of this research.

Meanwhile, Ontological engineering is subfield of knowledge engineering concerned with controlling knowledge using software application, and how to systemizing knowledge to fill the semantic gap between metadata. It is a set of activities that concern the ontology development process, the ontology life cycle, as well as the methodologies, tools and languages required for building ontologies.

Part 2: Methodology of Creating Ontology of Information Science (OIS)

3 Chapter 3: Methodology Employed

In the previous chapter we have discussed the main fields related to the research: ontological engineering, knowledge management, and Virtual communities of practice. As stated before, our concern is representing domain knowledge by creating OIS ontology.

After reviewing the ontology literature to find an appropriate theoretical perspective focusing on the content-related variables for theoretical model construction, we found that theories can help to define formal ontological properties that contribute to characterising the concepts. Meanwhile, ontologists nowadays have a choice of formal frameworks which derive from formal logic, algebra, category theory, set theory and Mereotopology.

However, to gain a better understand of OIS ontology development and its role in semantic web, the framework is established to describe the main theoretical base. The theoretical base of our framework is based on ontology theoretic in Section 2.1.2.

3.1 Theoretical Approaches

Ontology theoretic is about concepts classification which based on faceted classification system, and ontology algebra which is based on Mereotopology theory.

Ontology is usually organized in taxonomy which contains a primitive model such as classes, relations, instances and axioms. This chapter presents the main theory of ontology developing from information science by organizing IS classification. To achieve the research objectives in Section 1.4, based on category theory in Section 2.1.2.1 the OIS ontology will defined as follows:

The Definition of OIS=

C : is concepts of information science objects
R: is the relationship of the concepts
A: is the attributes of information science object
X: is axioms of the concepts
I: is instances

3.1.1 Taxonomy of OIS ontology approach

In the ontological engineering area attention has been given to the content of information rather than just the formats and languages used to represent information. The research approach consisted of constructing the contents of OIS ontology based on faceted classification system Section 2.2.4.3 as a solid theoretical and philosophical foundation. The approach emerged from both ideas:

First idea; Information science is multidisciplinary, as noted in the literature, it overlaps with other sciences, and it has been changed dramatically over time, Section 2.2.3. This change needs logical ontology to clarify the science boundaries among others. Ontology of Information Science draws a number of disciplines in several sciences, including archive science, library science, and computer science as shown diagrammatically in Figure 3-1

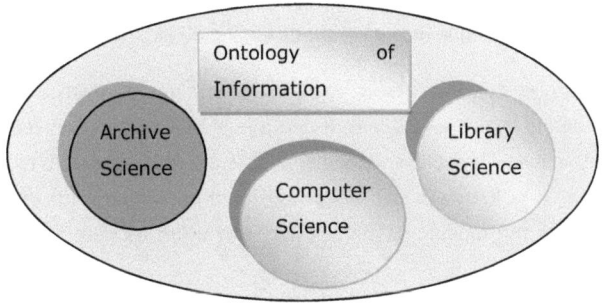

Figure 3-1 the main components of OIS ontology

The initial idea was to analyse each of these branches separately, based on the main categories of each one. It could be divided into two main parts; practical and theoretical, as illustrated in Figure 3-2

The practical part of library science is composing from collection, organisation, preservation, information retrieval, information service, for instance. Research in these fields includes a variety of specialised terminology. To get actionable results, some of the connections between different fields should be made in a systematic way. Yet the complexity of these fields makes it hard to track what of the information in each field is relevant to another field. For this purpose the modularisation is supposed to be contained in three single models: archive science, library science, computer science. Creating small ontologies for each with a specific domain (sub-ontology model) to be integrated has advantages and disadvantages, such as that the building process could be more flexible and manageable, and helps to increase efficient use of the ontology during its usage within the application, even minimising the needs of the whole ontology, in terms of being used when it is not necessary. Also, different domain views can be presented within single overall domain ontology to introduce clear and flexible design.

On the other hand, it is supposed to be partitioned into many separate modules, which require much more consideration. In this case, each aspect of ontology modelling should be designed independently from the perspective of usability, although it is difficult to make them completely independent. Yet it could be possible to determine that each module has different concepts and it is easy to define them. In the obvious example it is reasonably indubitable that the concept *information retrieval* would be defined in the computer science model.

In certain cases it is could be unclear as it can be under the *Library science* class or a subclass of the main functions of the library science module.

In this case, for clarity, there is a need to determine in which module it will be appropriate to define the concepts, e.g. if one thinks that information retrieval would be determined in the computer science module, so it is also quite possible to be defined in a different module. It is impossible to keep both of the modules with concepts that are incompatible unless the module supports their view when its relations are defended to avoid conflict.

But this view is limited and inflexible in creating many of the relations between these entities that are inconsistent with the notion of ontology. For this reason we adopt Facet Classification (FAS) to design taxonomy of IS to express domain knowledge accurately and readably see Section 2.2.4.3.

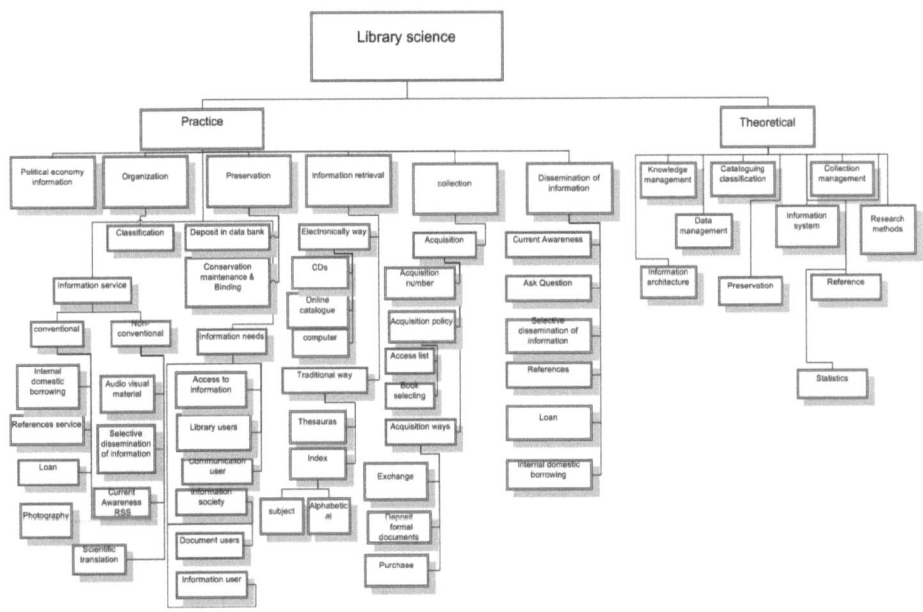

Figure 3-2 taxonomy of Library Science module

Second idea; (IS) is a science as is any science. We must make clear the comprehensive concept of the word science itself, where the word science comes from, even what the nature of science is. The definition of the word science indicates that it contains every type of knowledge, theoretical and practical. For instance the Webster dictionary defines science as follows:

> "Knowledge attained through study or practice".
>
> (Webster,2011)

From this definition we can interpret the aim of science to be acquiring knowledge according to specific methods and techniques applied by scientists, controlled by law, regulations, and ethics. Operations and the outcome of the science are based on the studies and theories, applying methods and techniques processed by actors. So the study interprets this view to categorise the high level of the OIS ontology.

Based on this explanation the OIS ontology has been developed by identifying the entities representing the key objects to meet multiple requirements. This approach has been influenced by the Aristotelian perspective of categorising the higher levels of the universe.

The classification of OIS ontology is basically based on a faceted analytic-synthetic system (Ranganathan, 1962). As well as this, our approach is corresponding to Research group classification (CRG) which has extended these categories into 14 facets.

Based on above, we analyse IS as a domain split into 14 extensions; these categories are the upper level of classes of ontology that are as follows:

Actors, Method, Practice, Studies, Mediator, Kinds, Domains, Resources, Legislation, Philosophy & theories, Societal, Tool, Time, Space.

These classes are identified and structured in a hierarchy connected by relationships, in Section 4.1.2 and the taxonomy schema of the IS domain is shown in Appendix B.

The IS terms for this study were identified to provide clear definitions for classes that would be of interest to the domain users and developers. The associated attributes and characteristics of the objects with their relations were also identified.

Each entity has attributes and type of relations for operating between these entities. The study intends to provide a conceptual model in Section 4.1.1.14 to serve as a base for related specific relations and attributes. Furthermore, the research is focusing on analysis of IS data to define in a systematic way in which ways the information will be used.

3.2 The methodology to be adopted

The choice of method relies on the research motivations and aims, and analyses some development ontology methodologies and IEEE 1074-2006 standards for developing a software project life cycle process as criteria. This methodology uses an iterative approach, allowing us to create ontologies in an accurate manner for the Information Science domain. This research adopts the Methontology methodology to develop ontology of Information Science OIS.

Methontology is the most representative of methods. It also fared quite well against other methodologies in comparison – see Section 2.1.11.6.

3.3 Techniques and Tools to be employed

Several questions need to be answered when building a new ontology, such as: Which tools do we need and which language should we use for implanting it? For this part we present tools and languages of ontology to understand the differences and similarities are between them, and to demonstrate their development through time.

The landscape of the study tools that support different stages of ontology creation and development comprises of;

- Knowledge management tool Community of practice (Ontocop). Tools such as this are used when feedback is needed.
- General Architecture for Text Engineering (GATE) see Section 2.1.12.13.
- Ontology language (Web Ontology Language (OWL)) for coding the ontology, which formalises knowledge in a semantic model, see Section 2.1.12.3
- Ontology editing (Protégé Editor) used to edit the ontology. See Section 2.1.12.11
- Ontology publishing (WebProtégé) is an ontology library for ontology browsing, used when the stable version of the ontology was created to get feedback, see Section 2.1.12.12

3.4 Establishing the ontology model

In general, creating ontology requires design to be applied through the development process. The designing process consists of the *conceptual aspect* and the *computational aspect:*

3.4.1 Conceptual aspect

The principle in the conceptual aspect is to represent the domain clearly and accurately and to be easy for users to use. Ontology in conceptual aspect should be created based on

- **Represent accurately as possible:** it is difficult to represent the whole domain in a complete and accurate manner. Describing the domain needs firstly full agreement between experts in the domain and knowledge engineers. Recognising this is crucial for capturing the knowledge, particularly when there is not full agreement, to avoid ambiguous concepts or when the concepts are equally valid for representing in the ontology. There is an important consideration over describing the concepts in a domain in detail, to ensure the concept is captured within the context of the domain. Also, some concepts are more important than other concepts.

- **Reusing the ontology:** the domain ontology as reference for building other ontology should be designed to be reused; Whether the whole ontology or some element of it requires a hierarchical taxonomy to cover the domain and use inheritance when it is needed. The hierarchy taxonomy should not be deep, to facilitate use of concepts at the bottom to avoid conflict between the relations and between structures of ontology. These relations should be expressed within the domain correctly and accurately to describe the whole domain.

3.4.2 Computational aspect

The computational aspect interprets the conceptual model by the machine, to be machine readable as accurately as possible. Ontologies are represented by the machine using OWL language, to describe it in a logical manner. Still there is debate whether or not OWL is expressive enough. On one hand, some people say OWL is not enough to represent the whole domain. On other hand, we believe that it is a more expressive language than other languages due to the fact that it expresses difficult relations in logical description.

3.5 Introducing OIS design methodology

This section presents our proposed methodology for ontology conceptualisation, designing and development. The proposed approach is targeted to answering the aim of the research, namely how the OIS ontology has been created to model the domain knowledge and how the Ontocop community can assess the developing process. Methodology of creating OIS ontology mainly consists of two phases, namely:

- Designing ontology of Information Science model.
- Designing ontocop website tool

3.5.1 Designing ontology model

The ontology moves slowly from knowledge level to implementation level to be machine understandable. Firstly, we begin by introducing a method for constructing OIS ontology, which comprises two stages; building the conceptual model and converting it to a logical model. Development of the OIS ontology starts from identifying the specific purpose and scope that is included in specification.

1. Specifications

Identify goals, scope, strategy and boundary of the domain: to identify the domain interest to be captured and scope of the domain - this refers to the limitations or boundaries for constraining the conceptualisation of the domain. In this stage there are many questions that need to be answered as recommended by Uschold and Grüninger, which are similar to the competency questions. These questions put together the resources that cover the ontology's objects, purposes, scope and granularity

- What are the general characteristics of ontology of information science? To answer this question the content of the ontology should be described which include: taxonomic organisation, the kind of concepts it will cover at top-level division, internal structure of the concept.
- What is the scope of the domain - will it cover the general domain or be specific?
- What is the purpose of ontology of IS?
- Identify targeted users, applications and functional requirement.
- Choose knowledge acquisition method and tool
- Choose tool to create the ontology.
- Choose modelling approaches of ontology that will be used. In this stage, the designer should make decisions about how to start the analysis and design the domain ontology.
- Choose level of ontology representation; it is necessary to decide what level of ontology will be represented; informal or formal, as discussed in Section 2.1.7.
- To evaluate the OIS ontology, the consistency checking and domain experts evaluation suggested by (Guruninger and Fox, 1995) has been chosen.
- Using and maintaining the ontology - in this step we follow Methontology to model, develop, maintain and document the ontology. Ontologies need to be maintained particularly for adding new concepts to update them, removing redundant concepts.

Knowledge acquisition: in this study the acquisition method and tool for collecting domain knowledge have been chosen.

2. Conceptualisation:

After gathering the knowledge it needs to be conceptualised. The activity of building the conceptual model is:

- Building Glossary of terms to identify which terms need to be included in the ontology; the glossary includes the term names, synonyms, acronyms, and descriptions of each term.
- Identify the binary relations between concepts of the ontology.
- Building concept classification.
- Building the data dictionary to identify the concepts with their meaning, instance, class attributes, and their relations.
- In the data dictionary the instances attributes should be described in more detail, and class attributes also need to be described.

Computational model starts from

3 - Formalising Ontology by transferring the conceptual model into a formal model. Ontology needs to be coded using the chosen knowledge representation languages and tools, such as Protégé and OWL.

4 - Evaluation: ontology needs to be assessed. So, its contents need to tested and verified to satisfy the real world that need to be modelled.

- Documentation facilitates the reusability of the ontology design.

- Refinement and maintenance: ontology never completes its need to be updated and maintained over time, as revealed by the development process in Figure 3-3.

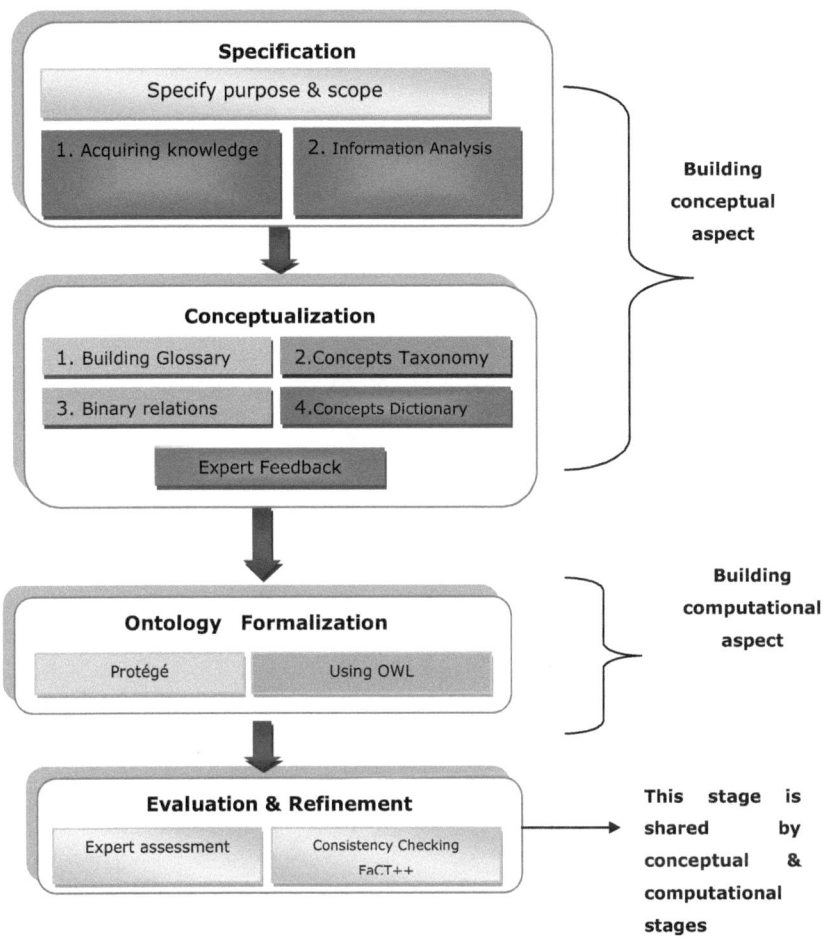

Figure 3-3 Domain ontology of OIS developing process

3.5.2 Designing ontocop website tool

The website designing stage requires us to ask many questions in order to start, to identify the aim and needs for the VCops before starting this stage – see Section 4.2.

- What I do need from the website?
- What technology do I need in the website to make it more attractive?
- How can I attract members of the community to make them come back?
- What are the needs of members in this community?

These questions would be helpful in clarifying what exactly should be the purpose and aims of the website.

3.5.3 Summary

In this chapter the theoretical foundation of developing domain ontologies was addressed. The theoretical base of the OIS emerged from analysing archive science, library science, and computer science. It resulted OIS ontology classification which basically based on a faceted analytic-synthetic system. Also, this approach is corresponded to CRG Research group classification which has extended these categories into 14 facets that will be formalized. Furthermore, methodology for ontology conceptualization, designing and development was proposed. The methodology mainly consists of two phases, namely: designing ontology of Information Science model and designing ontocop website tool.

Part 3: Implementation

4 Chapter 4: Modelling Design of OIS ontology

This chapter presents the development of OIS ontology and the main elements that formalised in OWL-DL. The OIS ontology followed Methontology as a general framework of methodology as discussed in Section 2.1.15.5. The main result will be introduced, namely, the modelling design of OIS ontology which follows the description of the activities involved in designing the OIS ontology model. The OIS ontology model identifies the terms and definitions in the IS domain. Also, designing the ontocop system and how it can be a useful platform for supporting and assessing the OIS ontology. It starts by introducing OIS designing methodology. At the end of this chapter we will discuss how this tool will help to develop the OIS ontology to be modelled in a comprehensive and consistent manner.

4.1 Building Conceptual Model

4.1.1 Specifications

Ontology specification comprises of several activities. It needs to specify the goal of building and designing the ontology, and the scope of the domain that will be captured in the ontology, as well as whether it will be one domain or more than one domain. Identifying the scope indicates the level of detail that is required. This stage aims to put together the resources that cover the ontology's objects, purposes, scope and granularity. This activity includes:

4.1.1.1 Identifying the purpose and the scope

In software design methodology, the designer needs to establish the domain scope to be captured and described in the proposed ontology, even whether the domain is a single domain or a combination of domains. Prescribing the ontology is important in identifying the domain boundaries to be investigated. In the specification phase we answer questions about the main purpose for building the ontology: why is the ontology of information science (OIS) being built? What are its planned uses? Who are the end users? It is necessary to identify the boundaries of the domain that the ontology will cover.

The process in this stage is to start by identifying the domain ontology that the ontology will be used for and where it will be implemented, by identifying the main features to gain an understanding how the ontology is related to other domains. As shown in Table 4-1. In Figure 4-1 we illustrate the domain scope of the proposed ontology of IS.

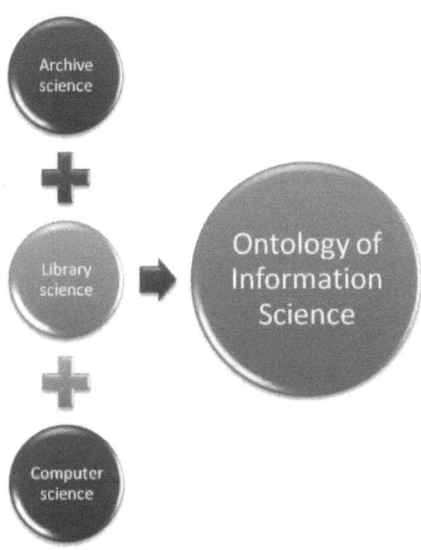

Figure 4-1 the main component of IS domain

Table 4-1 the scope of IS domain

Domain ontology	Information science
Date	2009- 2012
Built by	Research student at Informatics department in School of Computing and Engineering – University of Huddersfield.
Purposes	Providing consensual knowledge modeling of IS domain. It is to be accessible and usable by scholars and ultimately users of IS domain. The OIS ontology will be used when the information about the domain is required in technique, process, analysis. Also, it could be applied in other applications for shared knowledge as an index tool for supporting semantic web mark-up of IS knowledge.
Scope	The scope reflects the domain knowledge in semantic model. The OIS ontology is domain specific. It covers each of these branches; library science, computer science, archival science..
Level of formality	Formal ontology

Sources of knowledge	Ontocop experts' publications and domain publications in general.
	The following dictionaries: International Conference on Science Abstracting
	http://jpw.umdl.umich.edu/pubs/teixml-lc/sld003.htm
	http://www.thefreedictionary.com/administrative+data+processing
	http://www.fact-index.com/i/in/information_science_glossary_of_terms.html
	http://lu.com/odlis/index.cfm
	Dictionary of information and library management Stevenson, Janet. , ebrary, Inc. London: A. & C. Black, 2006. electronic book http://site.ebrary.com/lib/uoh/docDetail.action?docID=10196635
	Dictionary of ICT
	The Blackwell Encyclopaedic Dictionary

4.1.1.2 Knowledge acquisition

Building a conceptual model requires gaining knowledge that describes the domain. Knowledge needs to be elicited, analysed and interpreted, and transferred into a machine representation.

The purpose of knowledge acquisition is to capture the domain concepts of information science (IS) to be organized into a hierarchical structure-based ontology competence. Furthermore, identifying the main concepts and the necessary information to be described, and discerning the core relationships between these concepts.

As knowledge representation is procedural it is difficult for people to develop ontology. The AI community approach tends to acquire knowledge as preliminary stage by domain experts before coding the knowledge. Our strategy in this study is performing the process manually and semi-automatically because of the large number of literary outputs in the field. The knowledge acquisition helps to frame the ontology structure and provides the main set of concepts. The terms of IS were aggregated through text analysis of domain documents. The concepts are identified either by pattern extraction or from the natural text of domain documentation.

A far more interesting case, however, is the engagement of domain experts in developing the process of the OIS ontology, which supports organising and structuring the domain knowledge. The experts have a deep understanding of the domain construction that offers a very strong foundation of the ontology. The knowledge organisation systems were consulted in the developing process mentioned in Table 4-1 above in the knowledge resources part.

The main technique used to analyse and annotate text was GATE. It starts by creating a list of terms in a Gazetteer list to match, and extracts relevant concepts from text to develop the conceptual model. Figure 4-2 shows a screenshot of the IS Gazetteer in GATE software.

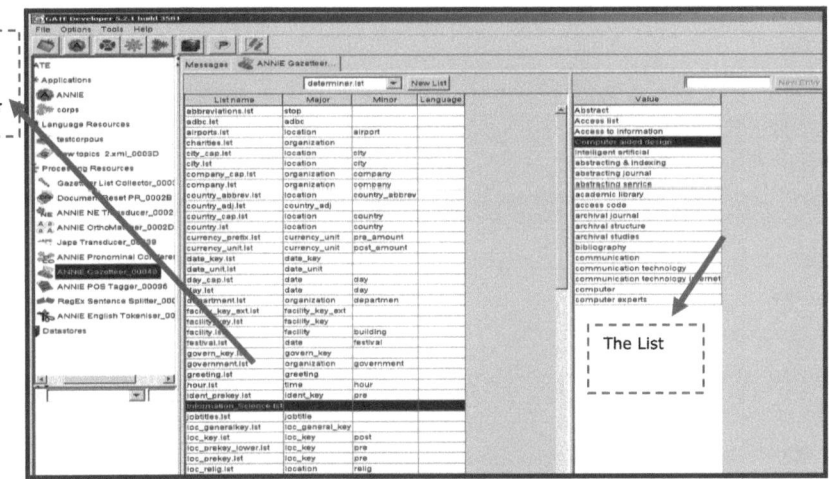

Figure 4-2 screenshot of IS Gazetteer

This research presents the semi-automatic extraction method based on A Nearly New Information Extraction System (ANNE) by creating Java Annotation Patterns Engine (JAPE) grammars that help to extract concepts form different formats - XML, and HTML. The process followed the method presented in IEEE standards (1996) for developing software life cycle process as indicated in Sawsaa and Lu's paper (2011). The paper describes a method of annotation concepts of Information Science, to build domain ontology, using Natural Language programming NLP technology. We used our JAPE grammars (Java Annotation Patterns Engine) to support regular expression matching to annotate IS concepts by using GATE developer tool. This is for speed up the developing ontology process as time consuming and experts in the domain has many barriers as time and loads to do. The following JAPE rules have written to extract concepts.

Phase 1: information

Input: Token Lookup

Options: control = all

Rule: concept1

(

({Token.string == "information"})

{Token.string == "service"}

({Lookup.minorType == region}) : reginName

) : service

-->

: reginName.Location = {},

: Information service.concept = {}

The first entity detected is Information service {Type=Token, start=867, end= 837, id= 4210, majorType=concept} labelled as information service .concept.

Phase: Two

Input: Lookup Token

Options: control = all

Rule: concept2

Priority: 20

(

({Token.string == "information"})

{Token.string == "service"}

({Lookup. major Type == "concept"})

) : information

-->

: Information. concept = {Rule=concept2}

For more precise details we apply regular expressions for matching strings of text, e.g

Phase: Concept

Input: Lookup Token

Options: control = appelt

Rule: Glossary

(

```
({Token.string == "catalog?e"})
): concept
-->
:{} .concept= {Rule= "Glossary"}
```
The rule is specifying a string of the text {Token.string == } string matching to specify the attributes of the annotation by using operators as "==",which provide the whole string matching. Some of these regular expressions in the next example annotate concepts related to (abstract) meta-characters(dot, *, [ ], |),

{Token.string == "abstract(ing)"}

It may be abstract, abstracting, abstractor.

Also, if we want to annotate the acquisition concept followed by another word as:

{Token.string == "acquisition. number"}

It could be annotated thus:

Acquisition. police

Acquisition .service

{Token.string == "archival * "}

It will annotate archival library, archival journal, archival processing, archival software, and archival studies. All these rules are sorted in the INFCO. JAPE file .The result is as shown in Figure 4-3

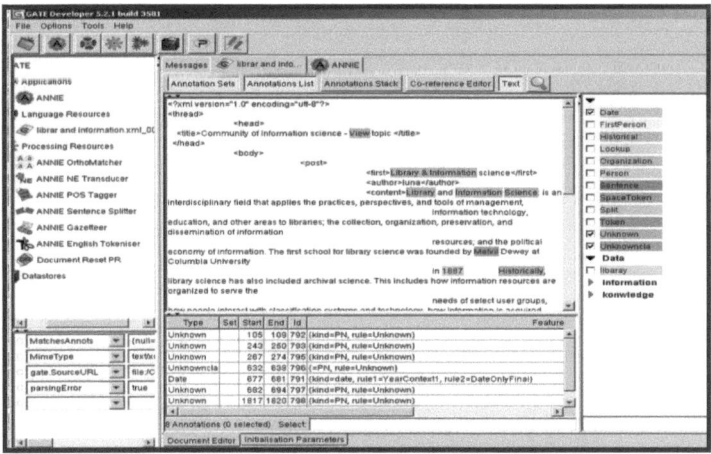

Figure 4-3 annotations of IS terms

Extraction of IS concepts by using JAPE grammar and Regular expression, based on the GATE developer for automated extracting of information, provides a significant output. The main idea of using JAPE and Regular Expression is to identify IS terminology as tokens, for example, Computing, Libraries and Information Technology, from a large text where terms are located. The term 'identification' relies on lookup from the Gazatteer list of IS which could match; for instance, it could be book art, book card, book guidance or book catalogue. Also, it will look up concepts such as computer application, computer science, computer experts, computer file, or computer image. The corpus was used to extract information science concepts contains 300 documents which were obtained. Therefore, the total document is analysed by running the ANNIE application organised as document reset, Tokenizer, Sentence Splitter Gazetteer, POS tagger, JAPE transducer and Orthomatcher. In annotation the set appeared in the display panel and concepts are highlighted in the annotation default.

Figure 4-3 presents the results of annotating the IS concepts after running ANNIE and highlighting the matching concepts. The results show that our approach successfully annotates concepts. We recalled 541 of the *Knowledge* concept, 275 Information concepts and 35 of the *organisation* concept see Figure 4-4. Each annotation starts from a specific point and ends at a different point, based on how many tokens it has. The knowledge concept starts at point 557 and ends at 566, while the organization concept starts at 624 and ends at 636, with its features {major Type=concept}.

Start	End	Key	Features	=?	Start	End	Response	Feature
557	566	knowledge	{majorType=concept, minorType=term}	=	557	566	knowledge	{majorType=concept, n
624	636	organization	{majorType=concept, minorType=term}	=	624	636	organization	{majorType=concept, n
751	760	knowledge	{majorType=concept, minorType=term}	=	751	760	knowledge	{majorType=concept, n
867	879	organization	{majorType=concept, minorType=term}	=	867	879	organization	{majorType=concept, n
896	905	knowledge	{majorType=concept, minorType=term}	=	896	905	knowledge	{majorType=concept, n
1023	1032	knowledge	{majorType=concept, minorType=term}	=	1023	1032	knowledge	{majorType=concept, n
1084	1096	organization	{majorType=concept, minorType=term}	=	1084	1096	organization	{majorType=concept, n
1151	1160	knowledge	{majorType=concept, minorType=term}	=	1151	1160	knowledge	{majorType=concept, n
1280	1289	knowledge	{majorType=concept, minorType=term}	=	1280	1289	knowledge	{majorType=concept, n
1323	1332	knowledge	{majorType=concept, minorType=term}	=	1323	1332	knowledge	{majorType=concept, n
1492	1501	knowledge	{majorType=concept, minorType=term}	=	1492	1501	knowledge	{majorType=concept, n
1876	1885	knowledge	{majorType=concept, minorType=term}	=	1876	1885	knowledge	{majorType=concept, n
1898	1910	organization	{majorType=concept, minorType=term}	=	1898	1910	organization	{majorType=concept, n

Figure 4-4 annotation of IS concepts

We conduct this experiment to achieve accuracy rates that are equal to the manual output by IS experts for the annotating concepts. Statistics of the corpus show pattern matching of IS concepts based on the lookup IS list 402, correct concepts and accuracy were generally higher, with partially correct 0 missing and false positives 0.

However, we use GATE due to its benefits as open source and it contains multi-language NLP models which can be reused for developing other resources.

Correct:	403		Recall	Precision	F-measure
Partially correct:	0	Strict:	1.00	1.00	1.00
Missing:	0	Lenient:	1.00	1.00	1.00
False positives:	0	Average:	1.00	1.00	1.00
Statistics	Adjudication				

Figure 4-5 result accuracy

The primary outcome of this stage is a glossary that contains the list of concepts relevant to domain knowledge. We will present it in the next section.

4.1.2 Conceptualisation of IS entities ontology

According to Methontology, conceptual models contain tasks for constructing information in a logical model. Conceptualisation starts when most of the knowledge has been acquired and it needs to be organised. Furthermore, when the conceptualisation is completed the ontology displays for the experts to evaluate it.

- *Identification of concepts and relations*

This task starts with building glossary terms which emphasises the ontology components that are described above (Concepts, Relationships, Individuals, Attributes, Constants, Formal Axioms and Rules). These components build inside conceptualisation activity as illustrated in Figure 4-6.

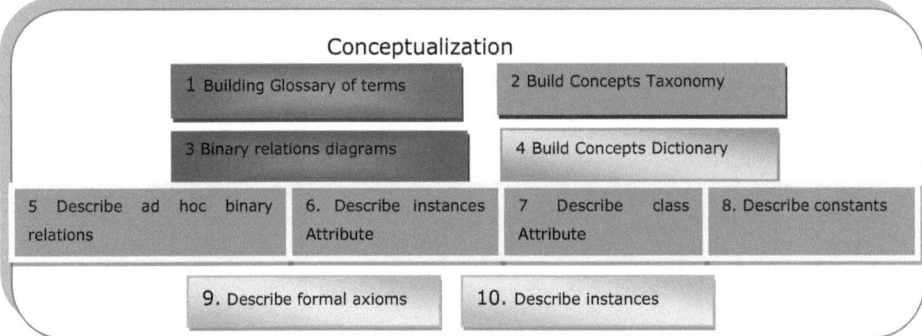

Figure 4-6 Conceptualisation activities

4.1.2.1 Building Glossary of terms of IS

The starting point in creating a glossary of IS is requiring the integration of all relevant terms in the field of IS. Building a conceptual model of ontology is creating the glossary of terms, which includes synonyms, acronyms and a simple description for each term included in the ontology. Table 4-2 shows a section of the glossary of terms of the IS entity ontology. Initially, the glossary contains 650 terms. The glossary shows in the Appendix C.

Table 4-2 part of the glossary of terms of OIS ontology

Concept Name	Synonyms	Acronyms	Description	Type (class, instance)
Abstract	theoretical	-	Summarises ideas of the contents of document, and it is usually accompanied by description bibliography to enable access to the original document[1]	class
Artificial Intelligent	Thinking machines	AI	An area of computer science focusing on mimicking human ability. This device and its applications is used to make decisions	class
abstracting & indexing	-	-	Service provides bibliographic citation and abstract of the literature in a specific subject.	class
abstracting			Process of producing, extracts as much information from the document and expression. This process is complementary to the indexing	class
abstracting journal	Abstracts of articles	-	A journal that specialises in providing summary (is for journal)	subclass

4.1.2.2 Building Concepts taxonomy

Building the concepts taxonomy starts when the glossary of IS contains a sizable number of domain terms. Natural language is used to define unambiguous and precise classes to be structured in semi-formal hierarchy, before creating a computational model of the ontology is really fundamental.

Building a concept taxonomy of the IS domain provides concepts, classifications and descriptions, to be described in a hierarchy. The concepts taxonomy follows ontology construction approaches to develop it. These methods are top-down and bottom-up, which allows identification of the first concept to control the level of details such as (Classes –Subclasses of – Partition-of).

Methods of Information science architecture

The workflow of building OIS ontology is composed from creating taxonomy. Our approach of building OIS ontology is based on a combined method which is:

Top-down

To involve a better understanding of the IS domain, the study defines the high level structure of the ontology based on assumption or what could be postulated. It emerged as result of reinitialise 28 classification schema in Zins' work.

This process postulated and captured, based on Aristotle's view, as mentioned in Section 2.1.5.1, the domain to identify key concepts based on FAS. The reason behind adopting Facet Classification (FAS) to design taxonomy of IS to express domain knowledge accurately and readably, as seen in Figure 4-7

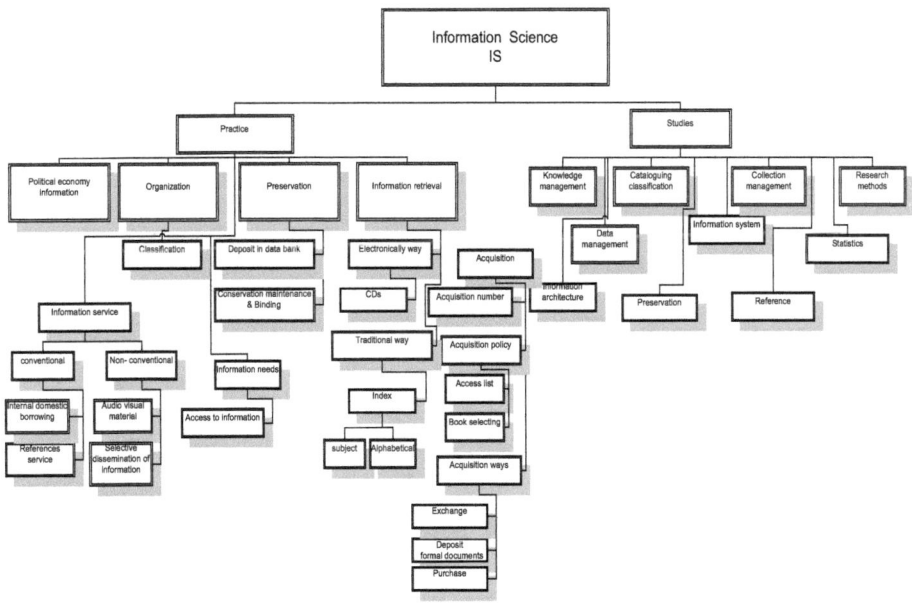

Figure 4-7 shows Top-Down method

Implementation starts with most general concepts in the domain such as: Information services, Users, Foundation. We mentioned it in more detail in Section 3.1.1.

Furthermore, the four taxonomic relations in Methontology are used, such as Subclass-Of, Exhaustive-Decomposition, Disjoint- Decomposition and Partition.

- This can be seen if class C1 is subclass of C2, and an instance of C1 is also an instance of class C1, then C2 is a subclass of class C1, e.g. a library user is a subclass of users, since every library user is users.
- The Exhaustive-Decomposition relation of the class C1 is a set of subclass of C2 that means they have common subclasses and instances e.g. if class American Library association and Canadian Library association are Exhaustive-Decomposition relations of the class Professional association that means these classes have common instances, such as that Library association is Canadian Library association and American Library association.
- If the class C1 is a set of subclass of C2 and there are no common instances between them, then the relation is disjoint-Decomposition e.g. the class funding agents and service provider disjoint–Decomposition of class institution because an institution can be a funding agent and service provider at the same time.
- The Partition relation can be depicted in this example. If a class C1 is a subset of C2 they do not have common instances but if C1 covers part of C2 then the relation is Partition. e.g. Class Library user and Researcher make a Partition relation of class Users because every user is either Library user or Researcher. Figure 4-8 outlines the taxonomy of OIS ontology.

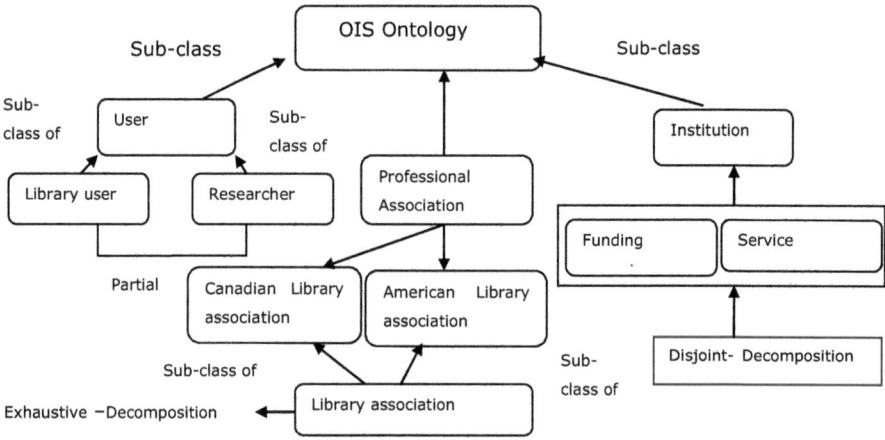

Figure 4-8 concept Taxonomy of OIS ontology

Bottom-up methods:

This involves precise understanding of field details that help users to explore related content, as seen in Figure 4-9. In this process concepts are clustered and categorised, and informed manually. This approach is consistent with Prieto-Diaz's view in Section 2.1.5.2. Our approach differs from his approach due to the fact that human thinking is still better than machine for clustering and representing concepts in a specific domain based on expertise.

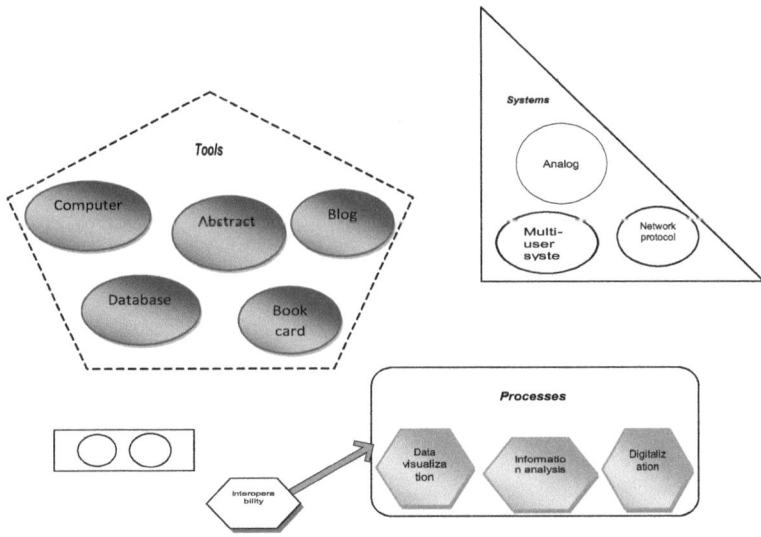

Figure 4-9 Bottom-up methods

The mechanism of Bottom-Up Method

Text annotating assists in creating a list of key words and concepts. Keywords and terms are extracted from the document of the IS domain. This list is the main input in clustering and grouping domain concepts. Annotating text processing is a mature technique which starts with document Reset, Tokenising process and annotated beads on the ANNIE Gazetteer using JAPE Transducer. The resulting key words are annotated in the editor. For more details see Section 4.1.1.2 of thesis. Additional details are contained in (Sawsaa and Lu, 2011).

The concepts are clustered manually, based on grouping, and categorised similar concepts that are related to each other and have things in common under a common classes name, for instance, an operation in library science is collecting, classifying, and dissemination information. So, all of these concepts are clustered under operation or process, to identify facets.

This process provides initial clusters significant to the task of building the taxonomy of IS ontology concept clustering; the Bottom-Up approach provides initial groups of related terms. See Table 4-3.

Tool	Process	Location/ organization	Service	Resource	Midea	Activitie
A programing language	Abstracting	Academic library	Access service	Active database	Compact Disc	Advertising
Abstract	Abstracting and Indexing	Acquisition in archival	Abstract service	Active document	Digital image	Informercial
Abstract Journal	Abstracting service	Alxandrian library	Acquisition service	Archival copy	Digital video disc	
Access	Access charge	Architecture library	Archival reference service	Archival file	Disk	
Access code	Access control	Archival administration	Ask librarian	Archival journal	DVD	
Access point	Access to information	Archival library	Bibliographic service	Archive group	DVD-RAM	
Access policy	Accessiblity	Archival storage	Borrowing library	Archive materials	DVD- ROMDVD-RW	
Access time	Accumulation	Archival	Business information service	Archives	Floppy disc	
Accession	Accuracy	Archive repository	Current Awareness	Art book	Random access memory	
Accession number	Acquisition	Archives	Digital reference	Article	Video	
Acquisition number	Administration	Art library	Dissemination of information	Artificial classification	Video Compact Discs	
Acquisition policy	Administration data process	Bibliotheca / historical library	Document delivery	Audio book		
Administration history	Algorithm design	Bibliotheca Alexandrina	Electronic document delivery	Audio newapaper		
Alphabetization	Archival arrangement	Collection archives	Electronic mail	Book arts		
Alphabtic subject catalouge	Alphabetization	College library	Electronic information retrieval	Audiovisual materials		
Alphabtic subject index	Alphanumeric	Depository	Financial service	Book		
Anglo- American ataloguing rules	Annotation	Descriptive cataloging	Frequent Ask Question	Bulletins		
Aperture card	Annotation computing	Documentation center	Information & referral	Childern book		
Appendix	Archival description	Film archives	Information desk	Classic book		
Archival box	Archival practice	Government library	Information Dissemination	Dictionary		
Archival database	Archival processing	information center	Inter library loan	Dissertation		
Archival quality	Archival preservation	Institutional library	Internet service provider	Document		
Archival standard	Art	International library	Library information service	Documentray		
Archival teaching unit	Availabiltiy	Law library	Library statistics	Documentary drama		
Archival textile box	Batch	Laibrary	Management information system	Electronic journal		
Archive policy	Bach process	Library media center	Non-conventional Inform. Service	Electronic book		
Arificial diget	Bibliographic description	Lbrary of Congress	Online processing	Electronic collection		
Artificial classification	Biblogony	Library school	Q &A fact retrieval system	Electronic magazine		
Attachment	Bibliographic retrieval	Map library	Really Simple Syndication	Electronic newsletter		
Auiovisual	Browse	Mobile library	Reference service	Encyclopaedia		
Authoatic abstract	Communication technology internet	Museum	Traditional Information retreival	Essay		
Author abstract	Clustering	National library	Traditional Information service	Film		
Author bibliography	Collection management	Organization	Web - based service	Full text database		
Author catalouge	Classification	Picture library		General encyclopedia		
Author entry	Communication	public archives		Gazette		

Table 4-3 concepts clustering

Implementation of this approach reduces individuals and instances to general concepts, for example: information scientists, archivists, record managers, and librarians can be classified under the concept Information professional.

114

Information scientists

Archivist

Records manager

Librarian   } Information Professionals

Abstracter

Indexer

Curator

Communication
   Telecommunication
        Cable
        Wireless
        Satellite
        Mobile devices
        Digital camera
        Fax machine
   Radio communication
   Telemetric
   Teletext
   Networks
        Distributed networks
        Internet network
            Invisible Web
            web address
            Web- based service
            Internet protocol
            web server
            search engines

Libraries
        Alexandrian library
   Archival library
   Art library
   Academic library
        university library
        college library
        Department Library
   University Library
   Government library
        Library of Congress
   Library media centre
   School Library   Library media centre

   special library
   National library
   International library
   Map library

   Architecture library

   Picture library

   Public library
   Virtual library
   audiovisual library
   Mobile library
Information centres
   Health information centre
   Military information centre
   International information centre

This approach was based on the idea of archival science as the base of information science, and library science builds on this approach. That IS and computer science emerged at the same time and they have complex relationships cannot be ignored. Each approach is classified on the view of researchers, and it will be reviewed by the members of the ontocop community to evaluate its accuracy and gain full agreement on the ontology's foundation, as mentioned in Section 5.1.

4.1.2.3 Building ad hoc binary relation:

After building the concepts taxonomy the binary relations should be built. In this activity the binary relations aim to establish ad hoc relations between same or different concepts that already included in the concept dictionary. Diagram 4-11 presents the ad hoc binary relations of OIS ontology with the relations Has-A, and Is-A and their inverse relations isPartOf ,and haspartA; these relations connect between these classes Archival Science is part of Information Science in the OIS ontology. Before going further the ad hoc binary relations should be checked to ensure there are no errors, particularly if the domain and ranges axiom is applied.

If the *Information* class has *Fact* as subclass, the relationship will be named Has-A, and the inverse relationship will be is- an elementOf

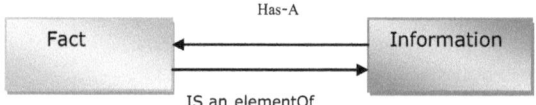

Figure 4-11 ad hoc binary relations

4.1.2.4 Build the concept dictionary

Ontology identifies relationships and instance attributes of each class. The classes should be defined in a dictionary that contains the domain concepts, such as concept name - class attribute - relations.

Table 4-4 concepts dictionary

Concept Name	Instances	Class attribute	Instance attribute	Relations
Library	Public Library , National library, Law library digital library	Library type	Name, size, service, URL	Is part of, has relation with , subclassOf
Classification Rules	Anglo-American Cataloguing Rules	Rules name	standards	Is kind of
Tools	Digital Video Disc	-	size	Has A, Is A

4.1.2.5 Define ad hoc binary relation

This activity aims to explain the binary relationships in the classification tree. The binary relations are sorted in a table to specify each relation name, names of source and target concept, cardinality and inverse relationship for each ad hoc relationship to identify the correct binary relations. Table 4-5 presents section of the ad hoc binary relation of OIS ontology.

Table 4-5 part of the ad hoc binary relation of OIS ontology

Relation Name	Source concept	Cardinality	Target concepts	Inverse relation
accessableBy	Library	N	User	ToAccess
employeeIn	Information Center	N	Staff	worksFor

4.1.2.6 Define instance attributes

The main target of the instance attributes table is to describe them in more detail than are included in the concepts dictionary. The instance attribute is what has been defined in the concept yet it takes a value in this instance. The table includes the following fields; its name, the concept name that belongs to it, value type, value range (numerical value), and cardinality (max, min). Table 4-6 shows part of the instance attributes of OIS ontology.

Table 4-6 shows part of instance attributes of OIS ontology

instance Name	attributes	Concept name	Value type	Value range	Cardinality
Bibliographic classification		Classification Schemes	string	-	(1,1)
American Association	Library	Library association	String	-	(1,1)

4.1.2.7 Create class attributes table

The aim of the class attributes table is to describe class attributes in more detail than is included in the concepts dictionary. The Ontologist should put this information in the class attributes table to include the following fields; name, defined concept name where the attribute is defined, value type, and cardinality (max, min). Table 4-7 shows part of the class attributes of OIS ontology.

Table 4-7 A section of the instance attributes table of OIS ontology

Class Name	attributes	Defined Concept	Value type	Cardinality	value
Publication date		publication	integer	(1,2)	Date
Name of course		Education of computer science	String	(1,1)	string

4.1.2.8 Define constants

In this activity the constants are specified by their names, describing natural language, value type, and value and measurement unit. The attributes can inferred based on constants. Table 4-8 illustrates a fragment of the constants of OIS ontology.

Table 4-8 a section of constants table of OIS ontology

Class Name	attributes	Defined Concept	Value type	Cardinality	value
Academic education	staff	Employee	Cardinal	Min 1 certificate	year
Publication date		Publication	Cardinal	2000	year

4.1.2.9 Define formal axiom

Identifying formal axioms is not an easy task, which requires a precise description. Methontology specifies the following information; Axiom name, description, expression, referred concepts, referred relations and variables.

4.1.2.10 Define instances

Methontology proposes to identify the relevant instance that included in concept dictionary. The following information should define; instance name, concept name, attribute and values. As the OIS is a general model, individuals are not included now. But it provides some of them to explain the individual role in the model for future development, based on specific applications of use. The current version contains only 99 individuals. Table 4-9 illustrates some of them.

Table 4-9 the instance table of the OIS ontology

instance name	concept name	attributes	values
Dewey Decimal classification	Classification Schemes	Number of schedule	30
Digital Video Disk Read only	Compact Disk	Decimal	Max 8 GB

4.1.3 Conceptual Model of OIS Ontology

In this stage, a list of the core basic terms is elaborated according to the Methontology method in Section 2.1.11.5. The outcome of conceptualisation is a conceptual model to visualise and express the theoretical construct that represents the IS domain. Conceptual models reflect on the computational model; it could be a communication device with experts in the domain. The conceptual model was developed using ArgoUML software. It shows the entity classes, attributes and their relationships in OIS ontology. We elaborate the main relationships among the defined classes.

The first entity, *Actors,* endeavours to cover all people and organizations that provide service to everyone who need information, to be used for different purposes, and represents relationships with other subclasses as depicted in Figure 4-12. The study assumes Actors is a person but it could be an individual or group. The individual, such as Researchers, Library users, can access Resources by Mediator such as Libraries, Information Centres etc.

Another example is the *Library* class related to the *Resources* class by hasA Book. The book is createdBy Author and hasA specific Location. The specific location determinedBy, or AccessedBy author Entry, Tilte Entry or Subject Entry. At the same time author Entry, Tilte Entry or Subject Entry part of LibraryCatalogue. It could be a traditional catalogue or digital catalogue. Each user hasA access ID to access the Library Catalogue. This combination lets us express the relationship between these classes. Some of the results are not shown for the reason that the data is too big to present here.

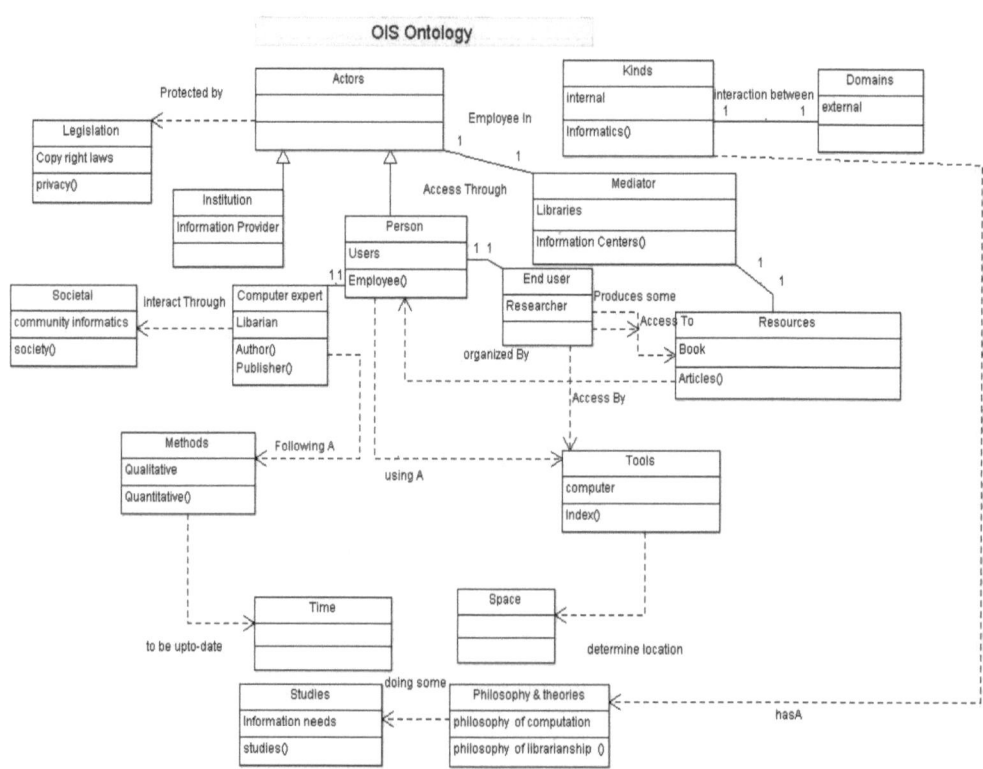

Figure 4-12 part of conceptual model of OIS ontology

4.2 Building Computational Model – Formalization:

Conceptual model of the IS in natural language need to be modelled. The primary output of this stage is OIS ontology, which is structured in the appropriate ontology editor such as Protégé. The OIS ontology is structured in natural language to be suitable for data modelling and knowledge representation.

It indents for expression of unambiguous and complete specification of domain concepts with relations between them, and organises them in super-types and sub-types of hierarchy. Furthermore, ontology in Protégé can be exported to different formats such as RDF and XML, The list 1 shows the ontology in OWL language.

List 1 OIS ontology is written by OWL.

```
<rdf:RDF
xmlns="http://www.semanticweb.org/ontologies/2011/1/Ontology1298894565306.owl#"
xml:base="http://www.semanticweb.org/ontologies/2011/1/Ontology1298894565306.owl"

   xmlns:dc="http://purl.org/dc/elements/1.1/"

   xmlns:rdfs="http://www.w3.org/2000/01/rdf-schema#"

   xmlns:owl2xml="http://www.w3.org/2006/12/owl2-xml#"

   xmlns:owl="http://www.w3.org/2002/07/owl#"

   xmlns:xsd="http://www.w3.org/2001/XMLSchema#"

   xmlns:rdf="http://www.w3.org/1999/02/22-rdf-syntax-ns#"

   xmlns:Philosophy="&Ontology1298894565306;Philosophy&amp;"
xmlns:Ontology1298894565306="http://www.semanticweb.org/ontologies/2011/1/Ontology1298894565306.owl#">
<owl:Ontologyrdf:about="http://www.semanticweb.org/ontologies/2011/1/Ontology1298894565306.owl#">

   <rdfs:comment>Information Science ontology that describes the domain of IS.</rdfs:comment>

   <dc:creator xml:lang="en"

     >Ahlam Sawsaa 2011.</dc:creator>

</owl:Ontology>
```

The OIS ontology allows the users to explore the ontology structure by browsing the upper level of the tree. The upper level provides a general understanding of the IS domain, whereas the deeper levels can be reached when they are navigated to through multiple levels of the tree.

The Upper-level of classes contains abstract entities created based on taxonomy of IS and the philosophical approach of science definition, as discussed in Section 3.1.1. Formally, the OIS model includes fourteen level of representation, which provides the foundation of knowledge framework for the OIS ontology. The OIS ontology root classes are: **Actors, Method, Practice, Studies, Tools, Mediator, Kinds, Domains, Resources, Legislation, Philosophy & theories, Societal, Time, Space**. The root classes are hierarchically specialized, each sub class is grouped under a main class, for instance "Education of Information Science", "Education of Computer Science", "Education of Library Science", were grouped under the Education class, as shown in Figure 4-13. The OIS ontology structure is extendable and flexible.

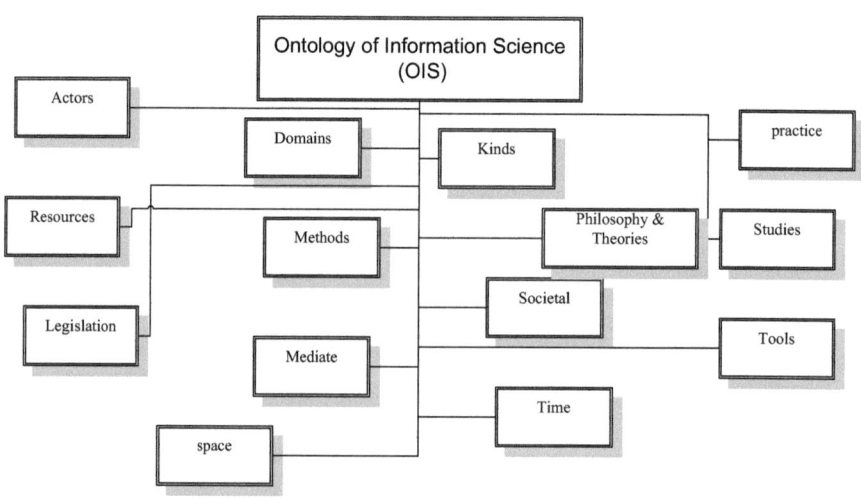

Figure 4-13 Upper-level of OIS ontology

The root class in OWL is thing (owl: Thing) which is the root of all classes such as Resources in RDF (rdfs: resources) The list below displays a simple hierarchy of the main classes of OIS ontology by owl; the upper-classes of our OIS ontology are as shown in list 2 .

List 2 the Upper-classes of OIS ontology

```
<!--    http://www.semanticweb.org/ontologies/2011/1/Ontology1298894565306.owl#Abstract    -->
<owl:Class rdf:about="#Abstract">

    <rdfs:subClassOf rdf:resource="#Tools"/>

    <rdfs:comment >representation of the contents of document.</rdfs:comment>

  </owl:Class>
http://www.semanticweb.org/ontologies/2011/1/Ontology1298894565306.owl#AbstractJournal -->

  <owl:Class rdf:about="#AbstractJournal">

    <rdfs:subClassOf rdf:resource="#Abstract"/>

    <rdfs:comment >Summaries of the articles.</rdfs:comment>

  </owl:Class>
<http://www.semanticweb.org/ontologies/2011/1/Ontology1298894565306.owl#Abstracting -->

  <owl:Class rdf:about="#Abstracting">

    <rdfs:subClassOf rdf:resource="#NonConventional"/>

      <rdfs:comment  >Processing of creating extract as much information from the document and expression. This process is complementary to the indexing.</rdfs:comment>

  </owl:Class>                                                                         <!--
http://www.semanticweb.org/ontologies/2011/1/Ontology1298894565306.owl#AbstractingJournal -->

    </owl:Class>
```

Furthermore, the current version is defined by a large number of classes 706 and consists of approximately 179 assertions, including more than 70 rules and relations, to determine the rich semantic expression capability of the language. The restrictions of classes are defined as Necessary conditions not Sufficient and Necessary conditions for the reason that class inference is not applied at instances levels. The classes' interrelations and characteristics defined through means of OWL property and ontological restriction are presented in the next subsections.

4.2.1 Actors

The *Actors* class is an abstract entity that describes a person or institution's act in the domain. The actor class is identified as the main components of OIS ontology. This upper category is important to stress the personal relationships and their roles in the IS field as human beings. In what concerns the Actors class, two main concepts were used to structure the information, as shown in Figure 4-14.

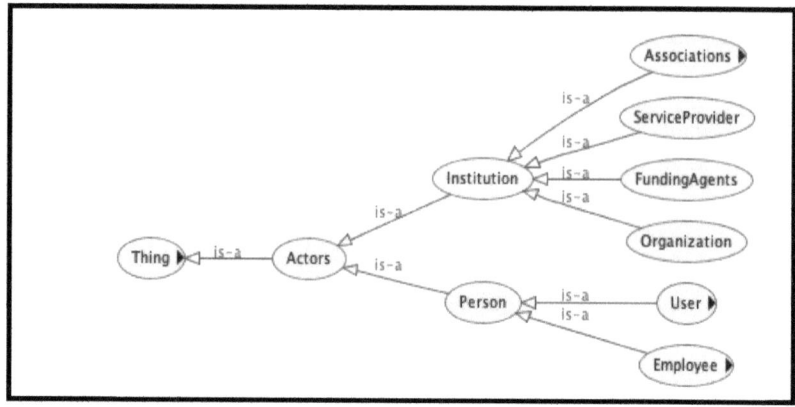

Figure 4-14 Main Actors class

4.2.1.1 Person

The person concept means who is doing activities in the domain, such as the person who works at libraries and information centres to provide service to users, as well as the users of the field. Person conceptualisation is a hierarchy with multiple inheritances of Actors concepts. It consists of two main areas;

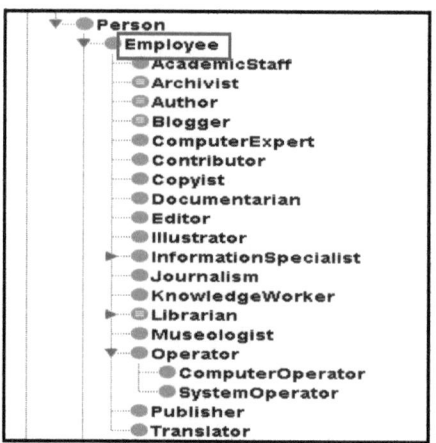
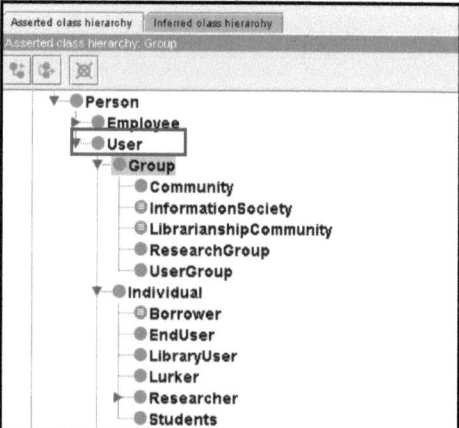

Figure 4-15 Person class

124

Subclasses; *Employee and User*. The User class could be a Group or Individual. The Employee class has sub-classes such as academic staff, archivist, author, Information specialist and librarian. These subclasses correspond to the main people they working at and beneficiary from the domain. Librarian can be: ChildernLibrarian, LibraryDirector, LibrarianManager, SpecialLibrarian, or acadmicLibrarian, all of these subclasses have relationships with the class StudiedLibrarianship by property hasA and studied In. Another example, The Museologist annotation axiom is "specialist provides specific service in museums and historical centres. Museologist is subclass of Employee, who WorksIn Museum, studied Museology.

Also, Library User: is a person who obtain the LibraryService

Library User: is subclassOf AccessTo ∃ some Libraries ∩ and using ∀ only Libraries.The excerpt of Person and Employee class is illustrated in Figure 4-15.

4.2.1.2 Institution

The Institution class structures knowledge about the main institution in the field of information science that provides information service to users, the institution class is specialised into four main subclasses such as:

- Association

- Funding agents

- Organization

- Service providers; see Figure 4-16

Figure 4-16 Institution Class

A relationship defied for Institution subclass is inspired in common IS organization and agents, for example:

- Institution is an Actor

- Institution is not Person. So, it is not joint class Person
- Associations is Subclass of Institution
- Then, CollageLibrary Class is =equivalentTo Institution., which is provide serviceTo ∃ some Institution

Also, FundingAgents and ServiceProvider are subclasses of Institution. The NetworkserviceProvider is type of ServiecProvider , it is annotation axiom is " a body that provides service to others such as, web service, internet access, mobile phone operator and web application hosting".

4.2.2 Domains

The Domains class is a meta-class about areas of knowledge that have interaction with information science and other sciences, such as Chemical domain, Geographical information science and Informatics. All the knowledge required about the relationship between Information Science and other sciences is structured under class domain, which will link with other ontologies of other domains, as illustrated in Figure 4-17.

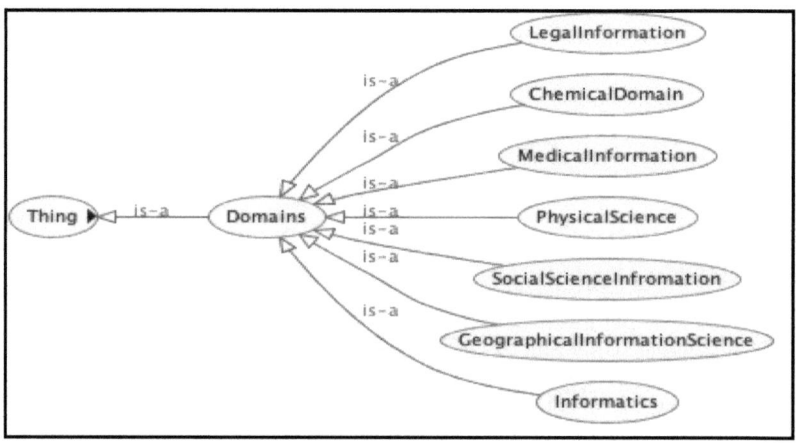

Figure 4-17 Domains Class

4.2.3 Kinds

The kinds class indicates the internal relationships between Information science with other sciences that have had a big effect on its structure, such as Archival science and Information architecture, Museology and computer science, as demonstrated in Figure 4-18.

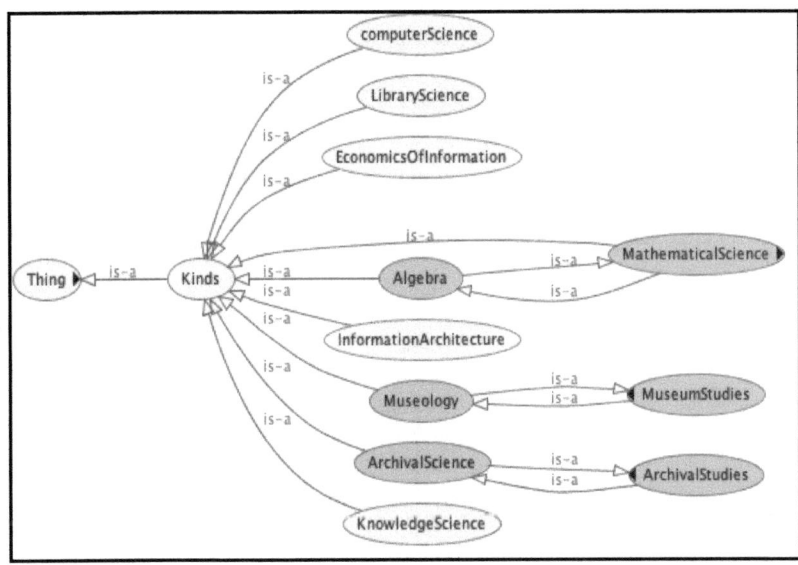

Figure 4-18 Kinds class

4.2.4 Practice

The Practice class consists of (15) concepts for structuring information about the activities that actors do when they prepare information services. Figure 4-19 illustrates them in hierarchy;

Information service	*Visualization*
Acquisition	*Evaluation*
Preservation	*Administration*
Storage	*Access*
Transmission	*Data process*
Publication	*Information process*
Dissemination	*Knowledge process*

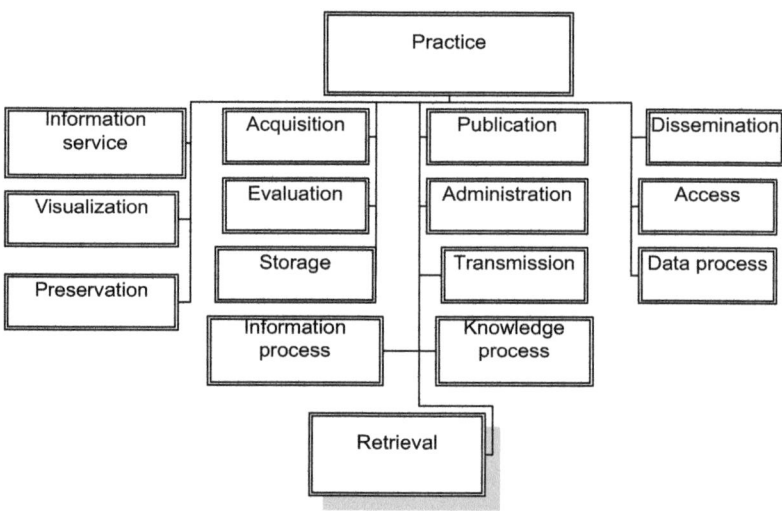

Figure 4-19 Practice concepts

4.2.4.1 Information Service

The Information Service sub-class defines the process of providing useful information for users. The information service is divided into two main parts:

- **Conventional**

The information structured under this class is about all the traditional services that Libraries and Information centres provide, such as; archival reference service, bibliographic service, classification, Loan, and subject analysis.

- **Non- Conventional**

The non-conventional structure is for information that is related to non-traditional services that can be provided to users, such as; Abstracting, Ask librarian, Cataloguing, and current Awareness. As shown in Figure 4-20

Figure 4-20 Information service class

4.2.5 Studies

The studies class is structured around the information that related to applying methods to learning and understanding the subject in the IS domain. The major studies in the field can be archival studies, computer studies, librarianship, information economics studies, usability studies and user studies. The information economics studies class is described next.

4.2.5.1 Information economics studies

The information economics studies sub-class is about the theory in microeconomics that has developed simply because of the unique nature of information, and it has two subclasses, which are: Information economic and microeconomic, see Figure 4-21.

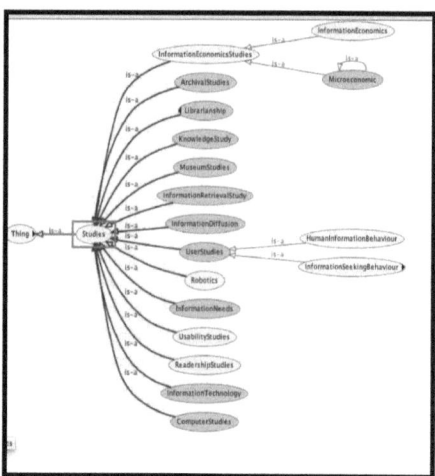

Figure 4-21 Information Economics studies class

4.2.6 Mediator

This entity is a mediator between users and the actor who is provider of information services like libraries, information centres, archives, websites and museums. The Mediator class has 7 subclasses, as follows:

Archives

Libraries

Centres media

Documentation centres

Information Centres

Museums

Websites

An archive is a place where a large number of historical documents are stored. It divided into 3 sub-classes, which are; digital, general and specialised archive. The Film archive came from specialised archive class, see Figure 4-22.

Libraries are places that contain collections of materials organised for usage. The libraries class has 15 subclasses based on its types, for instance academic, archival, art, audiovisual, bibliotheca, government, map, national, picture, school, special, virtual and library media centre.

 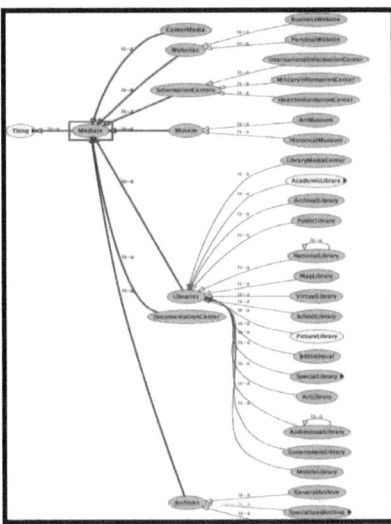

Figure 4-22 Mediator class

4.2.7 Methods

Method is a class about the methods to follow to do something systematically. It can be Quantitative or Qualitative. The Quantitative method was developed in natural science to study natural phenomena. The Quantitative class is divided mainly into five subclasses, namely; Analytic, Archival Methodology, Bibliometrics, statistical Bibliography and Webmetrics, see Figure 4-23.

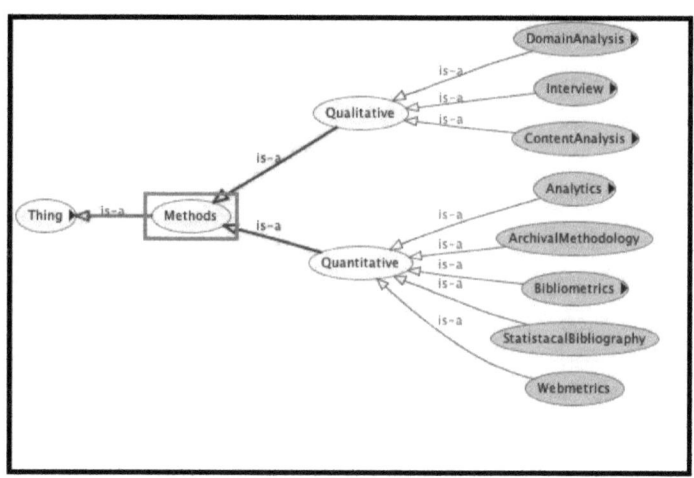

Figure 4-23 Methods class

4.2.8 Resources

Any field has its own information sources related to the field. The Recourses class consists of certain types of information sources which is divided into two main classes, as shown in Figure 4-24; *Documented, Non-documented.* The documented type is structured information that is recorded on specific container, such as; audio, visual, audiovisual and readable resources, while the 'non-documented' resources collect all kind of resources that differ from documented, like stories, informal information, genres, speeches, tacit knowledge and indigenous knowledge.

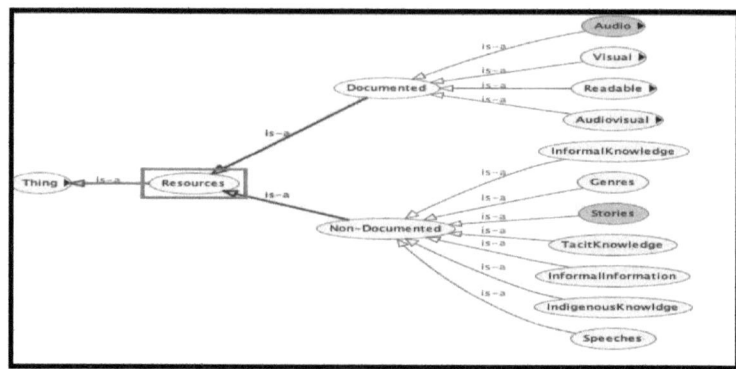

Figure 4-24 Resources class

4.2.9 Tools

Information science uses certain tools that allow the circulation of information and help with the performance of work for each of the users and staff in the field. These tools are used: computers, systems, index, catalogue, communication, presentation tools and abstracts. The abstract is a very important tool for instance for the librarian and information scientist who work in libraries and information centres, as well as the users. It represents the contents of a document. The class abstract consists of; abstract journal, indicative abstract, evaluative abstract and descriptor.

4.2.10 Philosophy and theories

The class Philosophy and Theories structures information about the main theories and philosophies in the domain. It consists of two main sub-classes; philosophy and theories as illustrated in Figure 4-25.

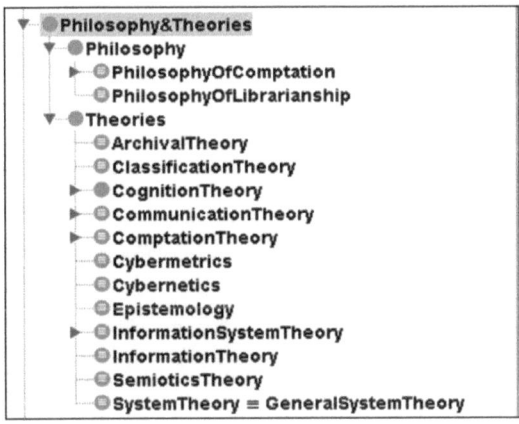

Figure 4-25 philosophy and theories class

4.2.11 Legislation

The class Legislation is related to the law. It consists of all the domain issues that require more control, such as accessibility, archival jurisdiction and standards, copyright, ComputerCrime or InternetCrime. InformationPolicy, and InformationEthics, The concept Accessibility is a hierarchy of related concepts like; AccessCharge, AccessCode, AccessControal, AsseccCopy, AccessPolicy. The sub-class AccessCode has a synonym which is IdentificationCode.

4.2.12 Societal

This structures the knowledge that is related to the social issues of the field, like Informatics communities, education, history, and industry. The information under the CommunityInformatic concept is defined as group of people who have the same interest in the information field. It is structured as follows;

- InformationSociety, which is a society that relies on information by creating, sharing, using, distributing and integrating it.
- InternetSociety – this concept is defined as group of people developing and looking after the internet. That relates to the internet and it is a kind of organisation
- LibraryCommunity – this concept can be defined as group of people who have has interest in the Library field and are related only to it.

4.2.13 Time

The temporal dimension is important in recognising the temporal entities, particularly those that are related to historical periods, and to indicate dates of particular studies or researches. Ontology needs employees in the model to identify the present time and time length. The model represents temporal concepts and temporal properties which are required for Semantic Web applications. It needs to be defined at the present time in its current role by assuming some axioms for interval time. Time is a measurement rather than a representation. Instances of the time can be associated with an instance of an event rather than being made independently. In this study the OIS ontology does not present a temporal aspect, because it is a generic model and as such, it does not include any temporal contents.

4.2.14 Space

The geospatial dimension applies the ontology for applications. Space indicates the entities of places. It could be a word, more than word, city, or street for example; Paris, London. It is still a big challenge in the Ontology community to represent spatial concepts because they can be known by different names. This model does not represent geographic dimension as it provides basic knowledge.

A result, through the OIS ontology creating and modifying subclasses is possible to represent variations of axioms. Therefore, ontologies create links among data to be accessed, manipulated, reused, and readily accessible on the internet.

The OIS ontology is visualised by using OWLViz that integrates with the Protégé –OWL plug-in to enables class hierarchies in OIS ontology to be viewed. It also enables comparison between asserted and inferred models using the same colour schema for both primitive classes and defined classes. Besides this, it saves and loads graphs and settings in xml format, and provides the ability to hide and show individual slots as shown in Figure 4-26.

Figure 4-26 visualizing OIS by OWLViz

4.2.15 OIS Components

The main components of OIS ontology are:

4.2.15.1 Classes

Classes in OIS ontology (also called concepts) are a type of object in the real world, e.g. the class "Tools" models the class of all tools that are used in the domain to facilitate doing and providing services. Classes in OIS ontology are defined to be unique by their definitions. Classes have too many relationships to each other. The relation type indicates that a class has a relationship with other subclasses by specific relations like is-a and part of. If the class "Library" has is-a relationship to class "PublicLibrary", that means the class "PublicLibrary" is a subclass of the class "Library". Also, that means all instances of the class Libraries will be instance of the class "PublicLibrary".

Classes can be subsumed in Protégé as each class is defined as an owl class that can be used to arrange many subclasses. e.g.

> OIS: Library owl: class
>
> OIS: Acquisition owl: class

In Additional, Abstracting is a subclass of Practices as shown in the OWL below in list 3.

        List (3) OWL subclasses

```
<owl:Class rdf:about="#Abstracting">

    <rdfs: subClassOf rdf:practices="#NonConventional"/>

    <rdfs: commen >Processing of creating extract as much information from the document and expression. This process is complementary to the indexing.</rdfs:comment>

</owl:Class>
```

All members of the subclass can be inferred to be members of its superclass.

Thing is a superclass of all classes. Things in Protégé as superclass subsume all other classes. e.g.

(Actors class)is subsumption of (person).

(Actors) is superclass of (person)

(Person) is subclass of (Actors)

Then, all members of (person) are also members of Actors.

Defining classes of OIS in owl

Owl uses many methods to define classes, as shown in diagram 4-27. Classes can be defined by using:

    a. Restrictions.
    b. Equivalent class.
    c. Enumerating class
    d. Disjoint classes

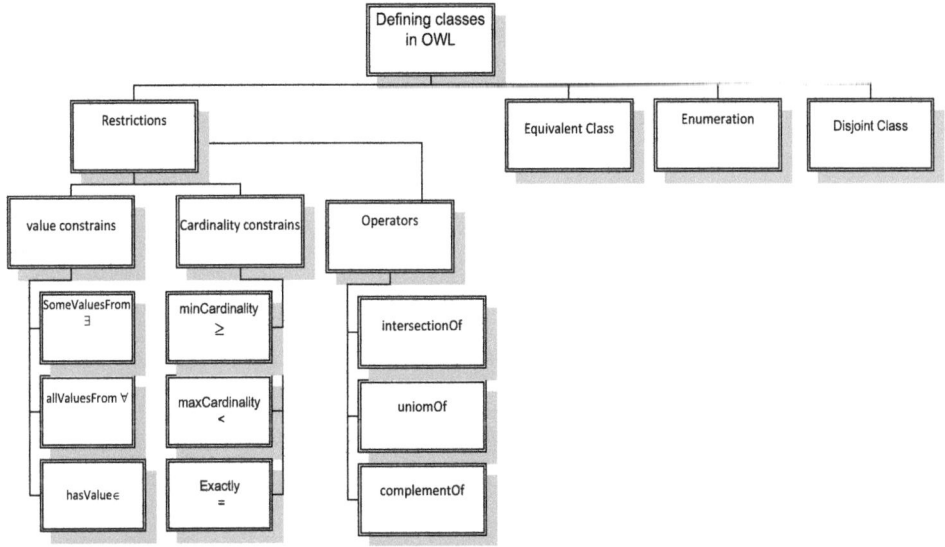

Figure 4-27 methods of defining class in OWL

a. Owl Restrictions

The restrictions in owl are used to describe anonymous classes and define them by adding restriction on some properties. The restriction has two parts, namely:

- It is applied to the restructuration on a specific property such as *owl:onProperty* property.
- It is about what the constraint is in owl, such as **cardinality constraints,** to put constraints on the number of value properties, and **value constraints,** to put constrains on the range of property. Adding these constraints on a property means defining a class that satisfies a specific need (Yu, 2011).

1. Value constraints
- *owl:someValuesFrom constriction*

This restriction is used to ensure that *MobileLibrary* provides service to users using Van. We can make the restriction less by adding that it can be used by residential for example. The class called *MobileLibrary* is defined as a sub-class of *Libraries*, and it has a property called provideServiceTo. Furthermore, at least one value of provideServiceTO property is an instance of students. For expressing the idea, see List 4.

List 4 use owl:someValuesFrom to define Mobile library class.

```
<!--
http://www.semanticweb.org/ontologies/2011/1/Ontology1298894565306.owl#MobileLibrary -->
    <owl:Class rdf:about="#MobileLibrary">
        <owl:Class>
            <owl:intersectionOf rdf:parseType="Collection">
                <rdf:Description rdf:about="#Libraries"/>
                <owl:Class>
                    <owl:intersectionOf rdf:parseType="Collection">
                        <owl:Restriction>
                            <owl:onProperty rdf:resource="#provideServiceTo"/>
                            <owl:someValuesFrom rdf:resource="#Students"/>
                        </owl:Restriction>
                        <owl:Restriction>
            </owl:Class>
```

- ***owl:allValuesFrom constriction***

This restriction is used to ensure that Mobile Library provides services only to students using only Van.. To express this idea, see the List 5 fragment from OIS ontology.

List 5 use owl:allValuesFrom to define Mobile library class.

```
<!--
http://www.semanticweb.org/ontologies/2011/1/Ontology1298894565306.owl#MobileLibrary -->
  <owl:Class rdf:about="#MobileLibrary">
    <owl:Class>
      <owl:intersectionOf rdf:parseType="Collection">
        <rdf:Description rdf:about="#Libraries"/>
        <owl:Class>
          <owl:intersectionOf rdf:parseType="Collection">
            <owl:Restriction>
              <owl: onProperty rdf: resource="#provideServiceTo"/>
              <owl:allValuesFrom rdf:resource="#Students"/>
            </owl:Restriction>
          </owl:Class>
```

2. Cardinality Constraints

Adding Cardinality constraints to anonymous class makes it defined for specific usage and makes the ontology more accurate. These cardinality constraints are; Max, Min, Exactly.

3. *Operator Restrictions (Boolean)*

One of the enhancing powers of owl is using operator restrictions to define classes.

- owl:intersectionOf (and): if c1 is intersectionOf class C2,C3,C4,.... then C1 is subclass of each class C2,C3,C4.

- owl:unionOf (or) : if C1 is UnionOf list of classes such as C2,C3,C4 then each class is subclass of C1
- owl:ComplementOf (not) : if C1 is ComplementOf C2 then all the subclasses of C1 is disjoint with C2, see list 6.

List 6 Definition of class Government Publication using owl:complementOf

```
<!--
http://www.semanticweb.org/ontologies/2011/1/Ontology1298894565306.owl#GovernmentPublication -->

    <owl:Class rdf:about="#GovernmentPublication">
        <owl:Restriction>
            <owl:onProperty rdf:resource="#hasA"/>
            <owl:someValuesFrom rdf:resource="#GovernmentPublication"/>
        </owl:Restriction>
        <rdfs:subClassOf rdf:resource="#Documents"/>
        <rdfs:subClassOf>
            <owl:Class>
                <owl:complementOf rdf:resource="#Libraries"/>
            </owl:Class>
        </rdfs:subClassOf>
        <rdfs:comment
            >Publications issued by the government such as statistical reports, survey and press releases.</rdfs:comment>
```

b. Enumerating class

</owl:Class> Classes can also be defined by enumerating their instances, identifying the equivalent classes and disjoint classes (Yu, 2011). The defining classes in Owl are shown diagrammatically in Figure 4-26; the class *AcademicLibrary* has been defined as the Type of libraries that support all research needs and provide services to some employees and users.

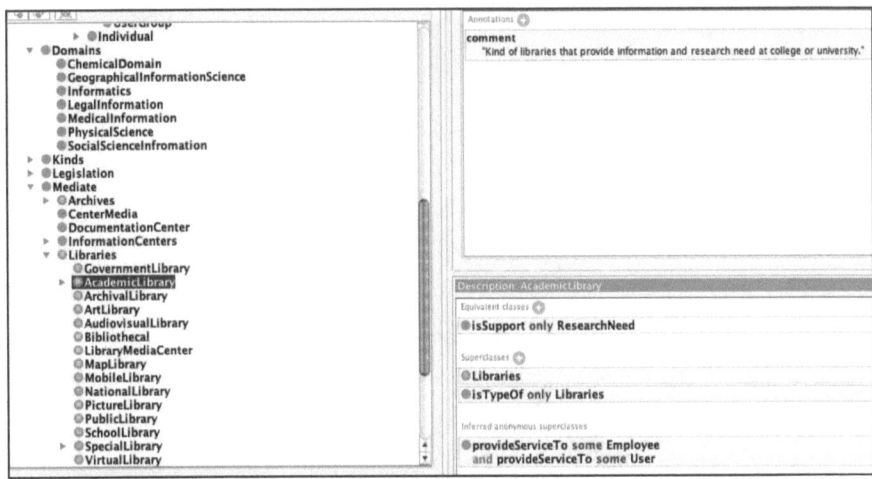

Figure 4-28 defined class in owl

c. **Disjoint classes**

Classes are designed using properties to make restrictions. For example, from a simple taxonomy of OIS ontology, the hierarchy means that

"All computer expert is employee", that

"All employee is person" or

"All computer expert is person"

Does this mean that "employee" and "computer expert" are different? We can assume that both "employee" and "computer expert" are different, unless they have a common child. However, classes in OWL cannot overlap if the disjoint axioms are entered.

The main classes are primitive to describe the primitive domain, so they cannot be defined in the same way as actors, users, methods, practice. We assume that classes overlap. If we state that classes are not disjoint that means an individual cannot be in two classes at the same time. For instance

: *Women owl: DisjointWith: man*

: *Fruit owl : DisjointWith: meat*

From OIS ontology the classes of Practice disjoint with Class Actor as they have different individuals, as illustrated in Figure 4-29.

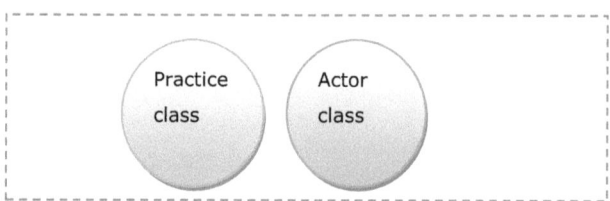

Figure 4-29 an example of disjoint class

Together individuals cannot be joining, whereas, an individual could be in Actors and Domains at the same time.

Also, this kind of definition for concepts and relations provides powered ontology software that enables expression to interpret it correctly. In the meantime, OIS ontology is designed to be relatively small due to the fact that these concepts and assertions should be easy to apply and understand.

4.2.15.2 Axioms

Ontology has axioms which are basic statements; these axioms represent a basic knowledge, e.g. <owl:Class rdf:about="#Film">

    <rdfs:subClassOf rdf:resource="#Audiovisual"/> film class is a subclass of the Audiovisual class - it is an axiom.

4.2.15.3 Properties

In the OIS ontology relationships are called properties in OWL and some other description logic languages. The attributes are created in object properties - Owl: Object property - and data property view - Owl:Data Type property. The object property is the relationship between instances, whilst data property describes the relationships between instances and data values, which link an instance to RDF or to XML schema. The data property is similar to the object property unless it can be just functional in characteristic, not inverse in description. The relations in object properties are shown in list 7 and the graph 4-40.

List 7 defining - hasA property from OIS ontology.

```
<!--
http://www.semanticweb.org/ontologies/2011/1/Ontology1298894565306.owl#hasA -->

  <owl:ObjectProperty rdf:about="#hasA">

    <rdf:type rdf:resource="&owl;InverseFunctionalProperty"/>

    <rdfs:domain rdf:resource="#Actors"/>

    <rdfs:range rdf:resource="#Associations"/>

  </owl:ObjectProperty>
```

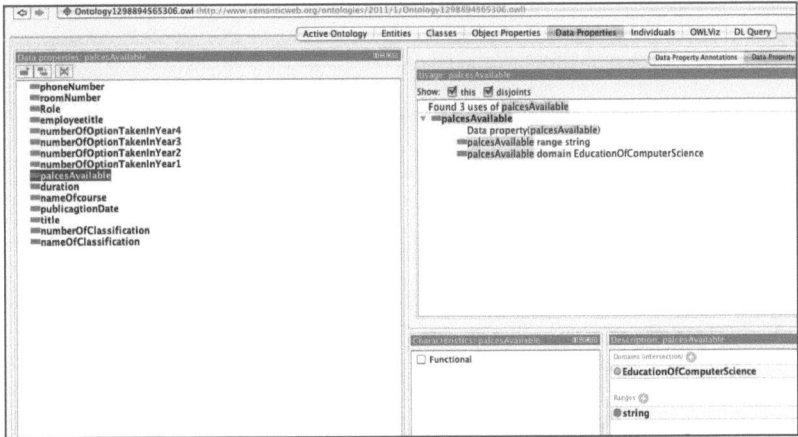

Figure 4-30 object properties

There are two main groups of relations type in OIS ontology, which are:

-Relations between classes to describe type of relation links among two classes.
-Relations between individuals and general concepts in the ontology to describe type of relation links between classes and individuals.

The OIS ontology defines the relations types such as <Is-A> <is Part Of> <has A> between superclass and subclass. Is-A relation is represented in the class hierarchy that is called Generalisation, while *Part of* relations are called Aggregate. If A is a subclass of B, then every instance of A is also an instance of B.

For example, *CopyRightLaw* is a subclass of *Legislation* class. Other taxonomic relations are <*is Part Of*> <*has A*> <*kind Of*>. Table 4-10 illustrates types of relations between classes.

Table 4-10 Types of relations between terms

Term	Relations	Term
Information	Is a part of	Knowledge
Data	Is a piece of	Information
Organization	Is a part Of	Institution
Professional association	Works In	Institution
Canadian Library association	Is kind of	library associations

The properties have many features such as;

    a. Inverse.
    b. Symmetric.
    c. Transitive.
    d. Functional.
    e. Inverse functional.

a. Inverse Property

In OWL this relation is relating between two properties explicitly in case these properties are the same. That means each object property has a corresponding inverse property as shown in both list 8, and diagram 4-31.

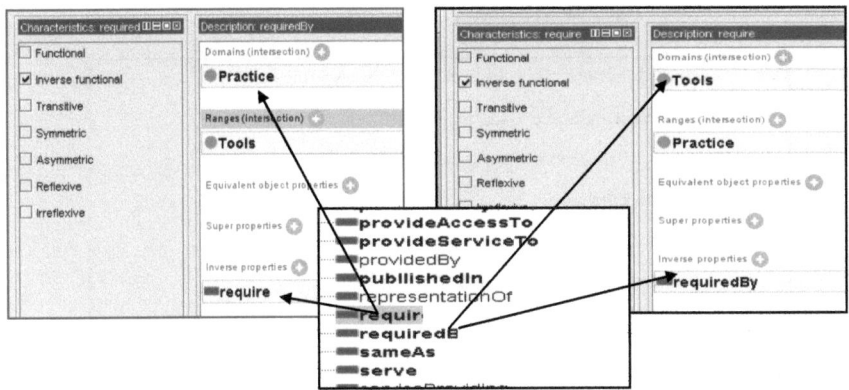

Figure 4-31 InversOf relation

List 8 InversOf relation in OWL

owl: inversOf
<owl:ObjectPr operty rdf:ID="hasAuthor">
<owl: inverseOf rdf:resource="#hasBook"/>
</owl:ObjectProperty>

b. **Symmetric Property**

It is just one facet of a single property to express memberships of a class. This relation could be: studiedIn; owl:inversOf; studiedBy. The symmetric property expresses the relationship between many classes, such as: If C1 connects to C2 by isfriendOf then C3 isfriendOf C1. For the example from OIS ontology see list 9.

145

List 9: symmetric property

```
<owl: Symmetric Property rdf:ID="EmpolyeeIn">
  <rdfs:domain rdf:resource="#Organization"/>
  <rdfs: range  rdf:resource="#Organization"/>
</owl: SymmetricProperty>
         <owl:SymmetricProperty
   <owl:Class rdf:about="# isFriendOf">
  <rdfs:domain rdf:resource="#Editor"/>
  <rdfs:range rdf:resource="#Editor"/>
         </owl:SymmetricProperty>
```

c. Transitive property

This property is representing certain part-whole relations between classes. If Ca is connected to Cb by property A, and Cb is connected to Cd by the same property then Ca is also connected to Cd by property A.

List 10: transitive property

```
<!--
http://www.semanticweb.org/ontologies/2011/1/Ontology1298894565306.owl#hasPolicy -->
  <owl:ObjectProperty rdf:about="#hasPolicy">
    <rdf:type rdf:resource="&owl;TransitiveProperty"/>
  </owl:ObjectProperty>
```

d. Functional Property

In owl, Functional Property is for property that has a single unambiguous value, i.e. for just one value that cannot be repeated. In mathematics, functional property provides one value to one or particular input. For example,

If y2 is a function, so there is one value for y, this means there is one value for y2.

Another way if y= x then y2 = x 2.

List 11: Functional property

```
!--
http://www.semanticweb.org/ontologies/2011/1/Ontology1298894565306.owl#isDescribeA -->

  <owl:ObjectProperty rdf:about="#isDescribeA">

    <rdf:type rdf:resource="&owl;FunctionalProperty"/>

  </owl:ObjectProperty>
```

e. Inverse functional property

This property describes relations between classes, e.g. if class C1 is connected to C2 by property a, then the inverse property a will connect C1 to C2.

List 12: Example of inverse property

```
<!--
http://www.semanticweb.org/ontologies/2011/1/Ontology1298894565306.owl#isPolicyOf -->

  <owl:ObjectProperty rdf:about="#isPolicyOf">

    <rdf:type rdf:resource="&owl;TransitiveProperty"/>

    <owl:inverseOf rdf:resource="#hasPolicy"/>

  </owl:ObjectProperty>
```

f. Annotation property

In Protégé OWL allows classes, individual (instance) and properties to be annotated. Annotations in OWL are to add a piece of information such as references or resources for example. OWL has many pre-defined annotation properties as restrictions to annotate class, individual and property; these annotation properties are namely, Owl: versionInof: which provides information about the ontology version, and Owl:priorVersion, which provides information about the prior ontology version.

Rdfs: comment: This is to add a comment on the class

Rdfs:lable, to offer alternative names of class or property

Rdfs:seeAlso, uses for references as URL (Horridge, 2011)

4.2.15.4 Individuals

Ontology Instances in Protégé are called individuals of classes that are created in the individuals view. Each instance can be described in the description tab as the Type and name of the same individual. The instance Institute of Electronical and Electronical engineering, is described under types as a computing standard and the same name is IEEE. This is shown in Figure 4-32.

Attribute is allocated in data property assertion, and the relations under the object property assertion. It can be seen from diagram 4-34. The class description appears on the description tap above Type; Library Science Courses, and the property assertions shows object property assertions and data property assertions. In this research the individual is not our concern. The research focuses on the classes and object properties only, providing this example to show how the OIS will work in further research, and how it will be useful in the Information science education process.

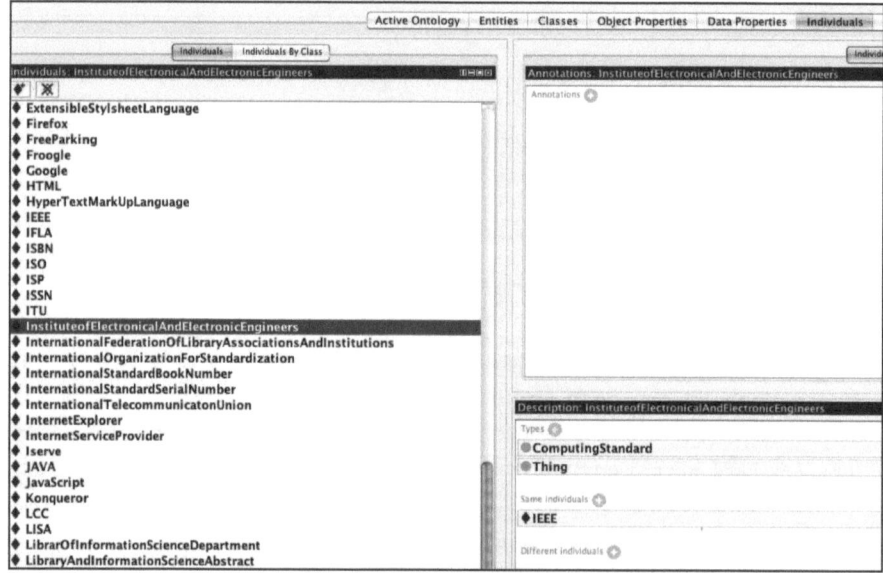

Figure 4-32 Individuals of OIS ontology

Figure 4-33 properties assertions of OIS ontology

4.2.16 Usage Class Tab

Protégé provides a great feature for checking the uses of classes and individuals in the ontology, for example the class *Website* has been used in the ontology eleven times, and to see how many relationships and axioms it has, see Figure 4-43. One of the usages in Analytics is equivalent class to measuring websites which recognise it as methods. The second one is Business website and Personal website, which are subclasses of Website.

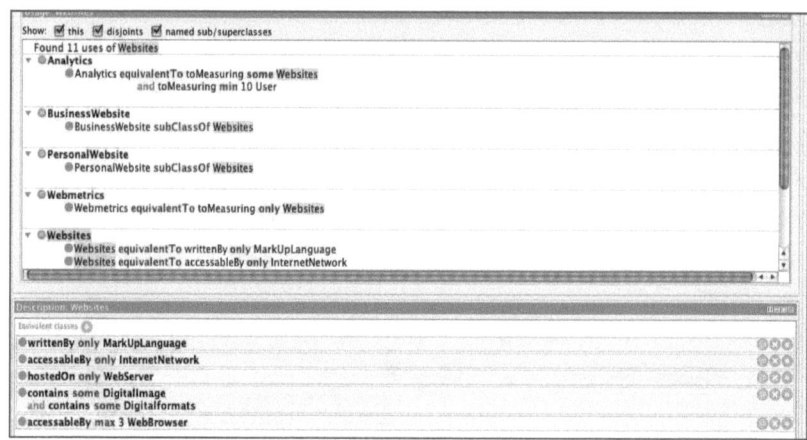

Figure 4-34 usage class tap in protégé

4.3 Ontocop - a system of visualisation of IS knowledge

The Ontocop system is designed by the author of thesis to support group interaction; it allows communication through the community of Information Science IS to enable members to communicate and interact across diverse destinations. Ontocop is a tool to support the OIS ontology.

4.3.1 System Requirements

The system must be usable and sociable. Usability features include consistency between pages and words used in the website, such as title of pages and headings. There should be no difficulty for members in navigating easily and following links easily. The navigation bar is consistent throughout the website, and the main page has a common browser. If users have problems using other browsers, they can use Firefox or Internet Explorer.

To maintain the website's integrity, a registration policy for new members keeps information in the database and other sites under control. This has been introduced because this community exists purely for research purposes and is for information science domain experts only.

4.3.2 System Architecture

This section presents the architecture of Ontocop system in Figure 4-35. The architecture is organised into 5 layers, the first layer is the homepage, which contains the navigation icon to search on Google or on the website itself. The News layer provides recent news about the developing ontology. Tool layer consists of:

- Events: to display Events on the website, to organise the discussion topics to be realised for participation.
- Forum: for debate and discussion about Information Science topics, as well as Chat and E-conferencing online.

The Information layer explains and clarifies some information about the Ontocop and the reasons for supporting the ontology model, and shows frequently asked questions (FAQ), feedback, members' profiles, and contact details.

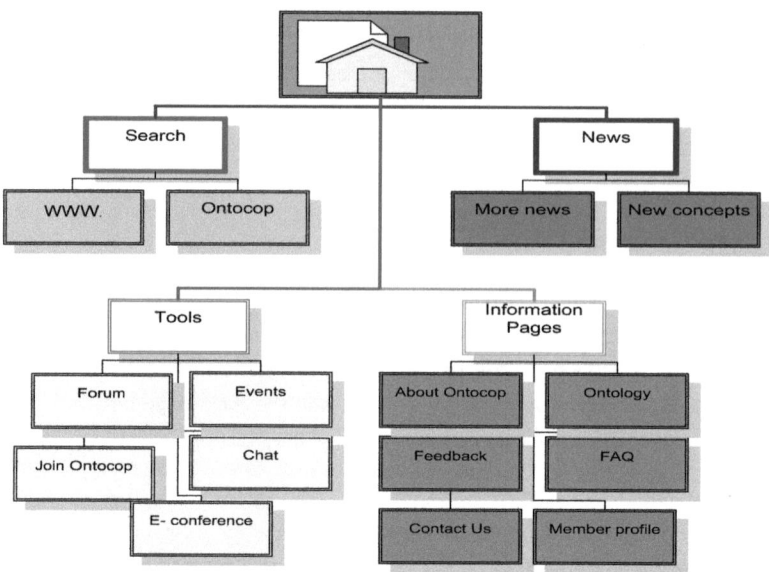

Figure 4-35 website layout

4.3.3 System implementing

Ontocop was launched in November 2009, by inviting people to get involved. The online community was created, designed and moderated by a research student to support her research project. The website designer has chosen to use the chat room features provided free by the phpfree Chat Company and forum features provided free by phpBB3. The site also uses e-conference features. (Koch, 2000).

4.3.3.1 Technical features

Ontocop is hosted by a server in Huddersfield which has proven suitable for this project and which has been developed in this research; the site has been tested on Microsoft Internet Explorer and Mozilla Firefox.

Most of the pages in Ontocop's original WebPages use the following mark-up languages: Hyper Text Mark-up Language (HTML) tag standards and Extensible Hypertext Mark up Language (XHTML). Cascading Style Sheets (CSS) have been used to maintain consistency of style, maintaining the website theme in the background, text, font, image and so on to provide an easy user interface. Also, PHP, JavaScript, and MySQL have also been used. The software has been successfully tested in the following hardware:

Microsoft Windows XP Professional version 2002, Service pack3.Computer intel (R) core (™) Duo CPU ,E 7500@2.93 GHz ,2.96 GHz RAM Physical address.

- Microsoft Windows XP Professional version 2002,Service pack3.Computer intel (R) core (™) Duot CPU ,E 7500@2.93 GHz ,2.96 GHz RAM
- Physical address. Toshiba personal Rating: 1.0 Windows Experience 2 Dou CPU. E 7400@2.80 GHz 2.80 GHz. Memory (RAM) 4.00 GB system type 32-bit operating system, Windows Vista Home Premium , 2007.

4.3.3.2 Aesthetic Features

Ontocop's format has been designed to be helpful for users.

A white background with some bright colours like blue and yellow makes for easy user experience and more proper for human interactions. Multiple colours and fonts have not been used. Yellow is used to draw the visitor's attention to the main menu and left menu, whilst magenta has been used for visited navigational links.

The main fonts used are the verdana, Arial, helvetica, and sans-serif family for the main body and headings. The graphics continue the website theme. Modifications of the main page work with the other pages such as ontology, contact us, FAQ pages, as well as the forum and chat features (Sawsaa and Lu, 2010).

4.3.4 System developments

The core function of VCop is to generate ideas and elaborate tacit knowledge through problem solving and suggesting topics to be discussed. This knowledge could be stored in a multimedia database where it is easier to extract knowledge. Tacit knowledge is shared in VCops through technology using several tools. VCops requires resources to operate its functions, such as space for members' meetings, a database to store discussions, information ideas, ways to share tacit knowledge and also record activities. The designer decided to make the following resources available:

Members' meeting space: members of a community require a place to meet face to face or virtually; this space needs to be easy to access to enable members to interact and communicate asynchronously by leaving comments and ideas. The virtual space is provided online via software such as forums, online chat, virtual meeting rooms and e-conferencing. Figure 4-36 shows the Forum, which is an essential part of the website infrastructure. A professional community should be restricted by rules to follow such as having to register and sending ID and password for users. The access is just for the community members themselves Ontocop is accessible by these criteria.

By inviting people after activation of their account, pseudonyms are not permitted.

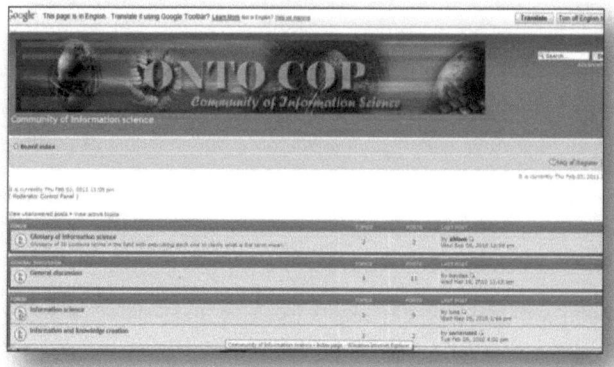

Figure 4-36 Ontocop Forum

Obviously in a physical space members communicate face to face, but in the virtual community members can do this through technology, using e-conferencing and chat. Figure 4-37 shows a Chat page, which provides a communication space for online users to debate specific subject matter.

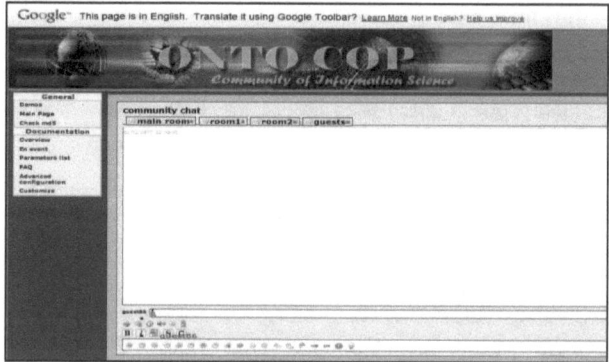

Figure 4-37 Ontocop chatting page

Figure 4-38 shows the Event Management calendar which is the record of the community's activities. The Community needs software to keep concepts to generate ideas for ongoing discussions. These general concepts help to suggest topics and future activity. As a calendar of events or activity it can be in electronic format to be updated frequently, and also as record of past events.

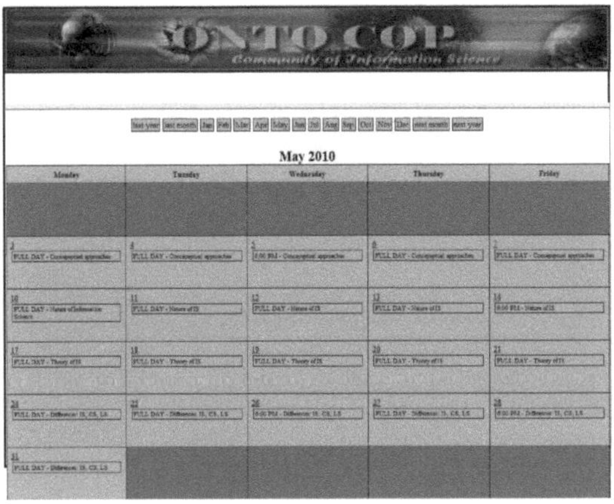

Figure 4-38 : Ontocop chatting page

Figure 4-39 List of members of Ontocop: a community needs to identify its members. Physically members are identified by creating a list of members to clarify who the members of the community are. Members in ontocop have profiles kept verifiable via a record kept in the database. A member profile helps to create a social network by linking members with the same interest.

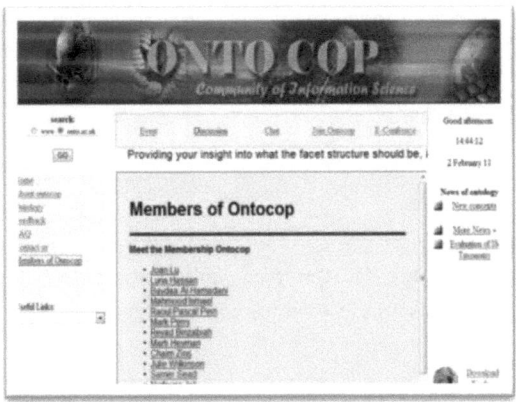

Figure 4-39 Ontocop Members list

Members of the community can stay up-to-date with developments in building the ontology – see Figure 4-40.

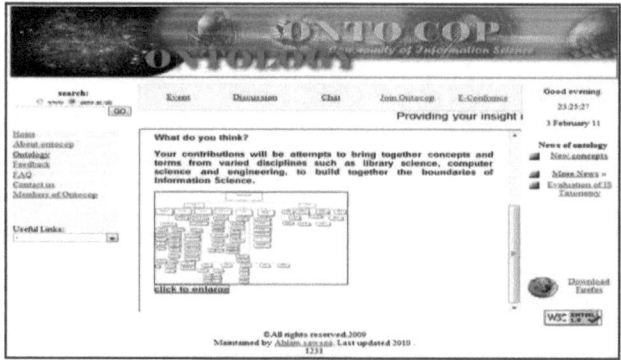

Figure 4-40 Ontology Page

Users can help to improve Ontocop by providing Feedback – see Figure 4-41.

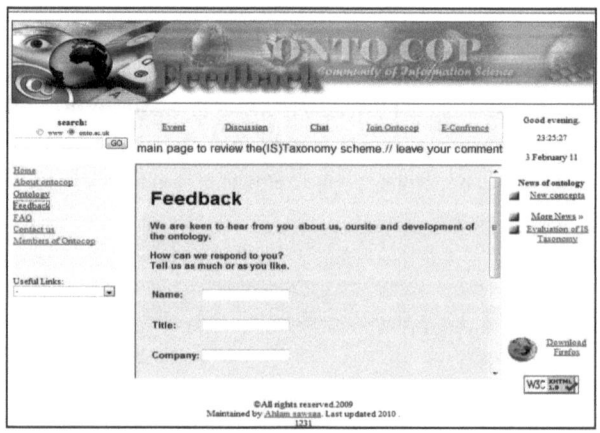

Figure 4-41 Feedback Page

Figure 4-42 shows the space for Questions and Answers and FAQ, which provide clarification about ambiguous areas within the community.

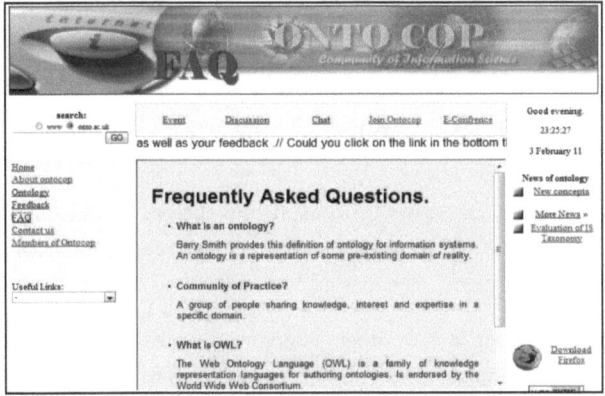

Figure 4-42 FQA Page

Figure 4-43 shows the Contact us page, which allows users to email the moderator to clarify issues or make contact. With regard to links to members of Ontocop, trust is as vital in the online community as in offline communities. The Ontocop can be accessible by using this link: http://ontocop.hud.ac.uk/

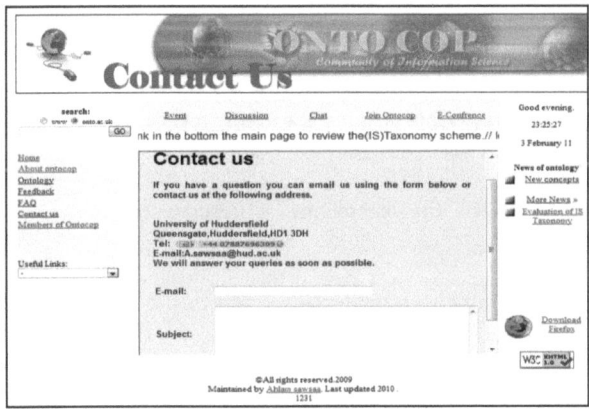

Figure 4-43 Contact Page

4.3.5 Description and potentials of Ontocop components

The process of invitation started by sending emails after collecting information from different universities around the world. Then we repeated the process several times of inviting people to participate. Appendix D comprises the invitation letters and Appendix E summarises the process of cultivating Ontocop.

The members at Ontocop have already collaborated for some time. Thirty 30 participants responded and they are active participants. The core group review events and topics to be discussed from the calendar. The list as indicated in Appendix F.

Here we outline some critical points to measure the success of Ontocop at this stage based on specific criteria. As is widely known, creating a social network is a big challenge.

Trust: Members need to know each other. Interview the potential members of Ontocop by arranging virtual meeting using chat tools, to allow them to introduce themselves and to get know existing members. Furthermore, create members' profile pages to display their information. Also, people need to know the reason for creating an online community and what the specific goal or target is.

Education: Providing some information about the website to educate people first, due to the fact that people will not be involved till they do know how to contribute. Creating a section in the Home page to cover simple guidelines; for these criteria e.g. "Getting Started" to explain the method of registration, see Appendix G.

Guide & Template: there is an assumption about people that they panic on an empty page. Examples have been prepared in the forum to make members participate effectively by writing down some definitions and argument issues and letting them follow the templates.

Refreshing: to encourage the community in keeping the content up to date and interesting for everybody.

Easy access: Ontocop is not a commercial website that is easy to find, but it could be accessed by searching in search engines.

Authentic and personal: present the developer of ontocop in the "About" page to help people to know the person behind Ontocop.

The great challenge in this community is to know how it will develop over time. I will outline a potential future and some intentions for Ontocop:

Potential:

- At the beginning it is essential to find out who will participate in the community and be a member of it, to share common background and experience. This helps to make a new challenge easier.
- The initial stage started with inviting people to be the core group in Ontocop, which began as follows:
    a. Gathering information about people working in IS field and add it to the database, to find out if potential members of Ontocop are interested in joining the project, and ensuring the database is ready at the moment of invitation. The total number of people is 1633 from 58 universities around the world. A part of collected data is indicated in Appendix H.

    b. Collecting data is requested: first name, last name, full address, email address, picture and their Webpages and interests. Thereafter, we send the invitation letter including the URL of the website. This stage helps to determine whether or not they are willing to share the community, by sending an email to set at ease starting. See Appendix I.

4.3.6 Summary

Our consideration is that OIS ontology purpose is to use for a particular knowledge base, its important making a clear distinguishes between knowledge base and application ontology. OIS ontology is describes facts, assertions, and axioms to provide formal and reusable model. The core ontology has constraints between concepts to hold between the concepts. Also, to avoid unambiguous terms, these concepts and constraints were presented in the ontology model. The OIS ontology takes advantages of a formal semantic in OWL language to balance the domain requirements. The conceptualization in a specific domain could be represented, analysed and interpreted in different ways, that dependents on in which contexts and circumstances that created under it. Also, it is formalized based on whom doing it. Therefore, OIS ontology is made to utility the conceptualization to be reusable and sharable on specific context of ontological commitments that were made obviously. The development of OIS ontology that followed Methontology was presented. It starts by introducing OIS designing activities and the main result was introduced.

Furthermore, the modelling design of OIS ontology consisted of fourteen entities that abstract the main components of domain knowledge. The OIS ontology model identifies the terms and definitions in the IS domain. Finally, designing the ontocop system and how it can be a useful platform for supporting and assessing the OIS ontology to be in a comprehensive and consistent manner.

Part 4: Results & Discussion

5 Chapter 5: Results and Discussion

5.1 Results

Ontology development is meaningful and useful for both users and IR, therefore it needs to be evaluated. In this chapter we are going to test and evaluate the results produced in the research, which is the development of the OIS ontology life cycle. It describes the testing and validation which was applied to the whole model from the initial implementation to ensure consistency of modelled knowledge. The evaluation objective was to collect feedback on OIS ontology by using our evaluation system. The Ontocop system is a platform that has been implemented to get feedback from the IS community. The feedback is assessing and eliciting further details that support the ontology development. The evaluation and discussion will be at two levels based on Gòmez-Pérez's view Section 2.1.10.

5.1.1 Evaluation OIS ontology

5.1.1.1 Ontology validation

The validation of the OIS ontology is conducted from two points to measure in which way the ontology has been written, and that the ontology syntax does not contain any errors and anomalies. Thus, we make certain of richness and complexity of syntactic issues of the ontology, not just correctness.

On the one hand, testing the modelled knowledge coherence by the FaCT++ reasoner which is an owl-DI, as mentioned in Section 2.1.12.3 - in OWL semantic languages - the OWL statements are constructed on formal logic to provide high expressive and automated reasoning. The reasoning aims to check the consistency of the ontology entities, relationships, and restrictions.

Significantly, the reasoner checks whether or not the statements and class definitions are consistent. Furthermore, FaCT++ was applied during the developing process of the ontology. With respect to consistency checking of the OIS, the reasoner was used. It achieved this by using the FaCT++ plug-in that combines with Protégé 4.0.2.

This tool infers classification and class hierarchy in the ontology, which helps to correct any errors and inconsistence classes in ontology classification. In fact checking the consistency is necessary to find out if there are any contradictions; to ensure the modelling constructs are being used correctly, and avoid reaching any incorrect inferences.

In Protégé there are two structures of taxonomy; the computed method is called inferred hierarchy and the manual way is called asserted hierarchy. The main evidence of automatic computation of the ontology checking is revealed through appearance of the root of hierarchy (nothing) in red colour in the pane of the inferred hierarchy.

The FaCT++ reasoner shows errors in the classes that had been classified in a red colour. The changing of the OIS ontology model was driven by the discovery of errors during the implementation stage. The process of improving it considered its inadequate performance and improvement of the domain knowledge. The early tests around the reasoner highlighted many errors, some of which arose from adding more information to the model without revising the existing axioms. These errors have been eliminated. However, in practice the first round revealed some errors as shown in Table 5-1

Table 5-1 inconsistence classes

First round of running Fact++ reasoner		Second round		
class	Inconsistence class		class	Inconsistence class
Actors	Analytics	*Legislation*		DataPrivcy, InformationPrivicy
	ArchitectureLibrary			
	Dissemination			
Domain	ElectronicDocumetDelivery			CopyRight, IntellectualProperty
	GovernmentLibrary			
	InformationDiffusion			
Practice	ReallSimpleSyndication			ComputerCriem,InternetCrime.
Resource	SelectiveDisseminationOfInformation			FreeSpeech, FreedomExpression
Space	SpecialLibrary			IdenticationCod,AccessCode

The table reveals that these classes were classified under different meta-classes, such as that *Analytics* is a sub-class of Actors while it should be a subclass of Quantitative class under Methods. Also, the classes ArchitecturLibrary, GovernmentLibrary and SpecialLibrary are classified under the different meta-classes Actors, Domain, and Space whereas they should classified under Libraries Class.

Figure 5-1 illustrates that some classes have circularity in the OIS after running the reasoner second time. These classes are: DataPrivacy, InformationPrivicy, CopyRight, IntellectualProperty, ComputerCrime, InternetCrime, FreeSpeech, FreedomExpression, IdenticationCode, AccessCode.

Figure 5-1 circular classes

Figure 5-2 illustrates that the asserted and inferred hierarchies after running the FaCT++ reasoner are decreased. It can be seen that there is inconsistency in the class *GovernmentLibrary which* appears in red colour under *Domains* class; this means it should be under *Mediator* as sub-class of *Libraries*. Otherwise, after that the reasoner was run many times to ensure there is no difference between the inferred and asserted taxonomies and nothing appeared that indicates tasks to be completed and semantically validated.

Figure 5-2 inferred class hierarchy

This is also to ensure there are no confounding and contradictory concepts. Also, ensuring terms have consistency of meaning with clarity. Ontology should provide mapping according to the meaning of its contents. However, the consistency and the syntax of the generated OWL file can be verified by using an OWL ontology validator. The OIS ontology was verified by using OWL validation as well, for more testing and validation. Once the ontology was uploaded to the validator, the abstract syntax –Full OWL - form says Yes: Why, this means the ontology has succeeded and the results are good. Figure 5-3 shows a segment of the verification results.

```
OWL Species Validation Report

Conclusion

Full: YES Why?

Abstract Syntax Form

Namespace(rdf   = <http://www.w3.org/1999/02/22-rdf-syntax-ns#>)
Namespace(owl   = <http://www.w3.org/2002/07/owl#>)
Namespace(xsd   = <http://www.w3.org/2001/XMLSchema#>)
Namespace(rdfs  = <http://www.w3.org/2000/01/rdf-schema#>)
Namespace(a     = <http://www.semanticweb.org/ontologies/2011/1/Ontology1298894565306.owl#>)

Ontology( <http://www.semanticweb.org/ontologies/2011/1/Ontology1298894565306.owl>

   Annotation(rdfs:comment "Information Science ontololgy that descrips the domain of IS.")
   Annotation(<http://purl.org/dc/elements/1.1/creator> "Ahlam Sawsaa 2011."@en)

   ObjectProperty(a:accessableBy)
   ObjectProperty(a:cannotAccess)
   ObjectProperty(a:collect InverseFunctional)
   ObjectProperty(a:concernedWith Functional)
   ObjectProperty(a:conjectionBetween Functional)
   ObjectProperty(a:contains Functional)
   ObjectProperty(a:continuingTo Functional)
   ObjectProperty(a:conversationAmong Functional)
   ObjectProperty(a:doing)
   ObjectProperty(a:employeeIn InverseFunctional)
   ObjectProperty(a:exploreImpactOf Functional)
   ObjectProperty(a:focusOn Functional)
   ObjectProperty(a:hasA InverseFunctional
     domain(a:Actors)
     range(a:Associations))
   ObjectProperty(a:hasBook Functional)
   ObjectProperty(a:hasDocuments Functional)
   ObjectProperty(a:hasJob Transitive)
   ObjectProperty(a:hasPartA InverseFunctional
     inverseOf(a:isPartOf))
   ObjectProperty(a:hasPolicy Transitive)
```

Figure 5-3 part of OIS ontology verification results

However, after testing and validating the OIS ontology it was introduced to the domain experts to be evaluated.

5.1.1.2 *Ontology verification*

The ontology was evaluated by IS experts. They identified some classes needing to extended and divided further, and added or deleted some layers from the ontology. The next section, the user case scenario, describes the whole process of ontology verification;

5.1.1.3 *Use case scenario of evaluation*

Using the user case scenario provides the main components of ontology evaluation.

1- The developer creates the first version of the OIS ontology in Protégé. During the development the ontology is assisted from ontocop members at the conceptualisation stage to ensure the conceptual model is built correctly.
2- The developer displays the taxonomy of OIS on ontocop to be accessible and viewed. The members have been notified to provide their insights in order to configure the classification of the IS domain and change some parts of the ontology taxonomy. See Figure 5-4 and Appendix K.

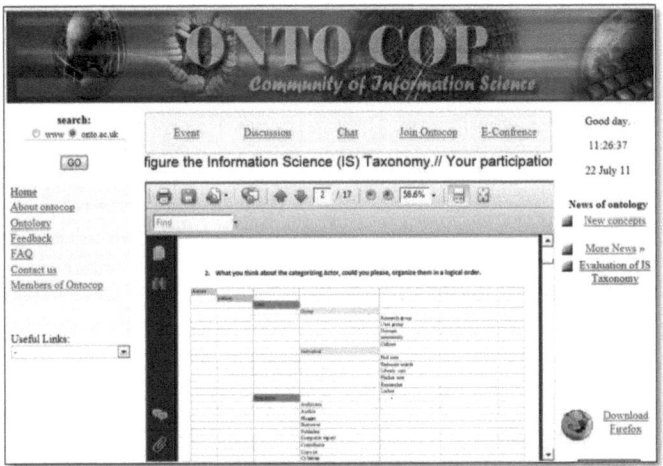

Figure 5-4 Evaluation of IS taxonomy

3- The developer publishes the ontology version on WebProtégé; at the same time another copy is displayed on ontocop in OWL formats. The developer keeps the original copy of the current work to continue working to make edits when the others access the ontology. The OIS ontology is displayed on WebProtégé that can be accessible through Ontology page in Ontocop, as shown in Figure 5-5.

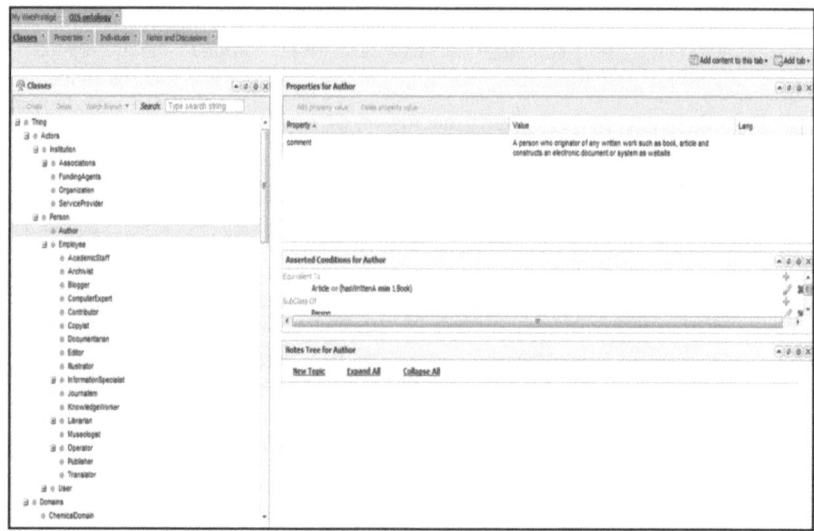

Figure 5-5 snapshot of OIS ontology on WebProtégé

4- Before asking the members to answer the questions on the OIS ontology and sending feedback, some details are displayed on ontocop to give them an overview. It provides how they can search on it, as shown in Figure 5-6.

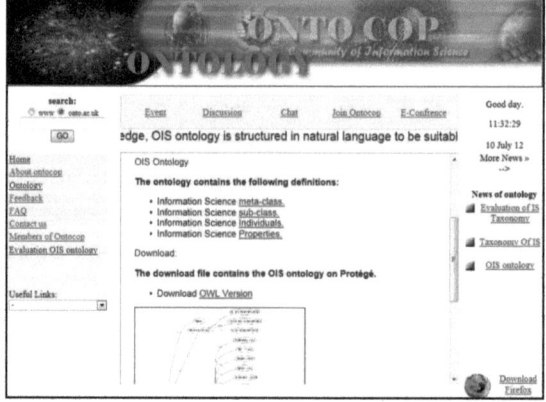

Figure 5-6 OIS documentation

5- The evaluators were asked to complete a web-based survey to evaluate the OIS with indications as to the level of satisfaction, based on the criteria in Section2.1.9. Also, they were asked to answer the following questions as shown in Table 5-1, to obtain information about their impressions of developing the OIS ontology.

Table 5-2 The questions in OIS ontology survey

Q1.	What do you like about the ontology?
Q2.	What do you think needs to be improved?
Q3.	What would you like to add or change at any part of the domain knowledge?
Q4.	Do you think it is a completed ontology?
Q5.	Do you think the ontology has a clean taxonomical structure?
Q6.	Do you think the ontology is mappable to some specific upper ontology?

6- The members' access the ontology by using a direct link in WebProtégé to navigate around the taxonomy tree and look at metadata and properties that are provided. They provide some notes to OIS and make comments on some classes and add suggestions to add new concepts.

7- The developer is notified through an email and the ontocop database. The editing on ontology takes place based on their comments.

8- The developer publishes the new version of the ontology in WebProtégé, and members are notified when the new version is published.

Participants

The members 30 of Information specialists were involved in the evaluation. We asked 30 Information Specialists: 12 Assistant professors, 2 senior Lecturers, 5 professors, 2 knowledge management consultants, 3 adjunct faculty professors, 1 professor Emeritus, and 5 PhD Informatics students.

5.1.1.4 Results of Evaluation

The OIS ontology evaluation was obtained over two months. The survey answers were received through following the link on Ontocop. We asked 30 participants, and 25 of them responded. The gathered data analysed after a fair period of the publishing the ontology on WebProtégé to understand the comments participants made. Discussion results were used to obtain research findings that aided us in addressing research questions. In the survey it was very important to capture the participants' satisfaction about the ontology based on predefined criteria.

The first part of the survey asked about the experts' level of satisfaction, based on predefined criteria. The first criterion was ontology consistency. 64% of respondents indicated level 3 of satisfaction, and others expressed levels 2 and 4 by 20%, 12% respectively, see Figure 5 -7.

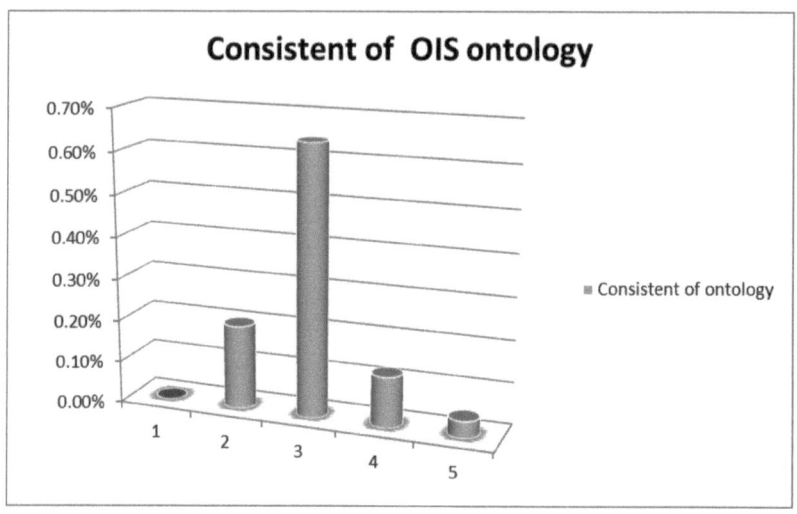

Figure 5-7 ontology consistency

The second criterion was consistency of is-a and part-of –relationships. 14 of the participants indicated their satisfaction with the consistency of ontology relations at Level 3 ,56% while 6 of them 24% pointed to level 2. Figure 5-8 illustrates this.

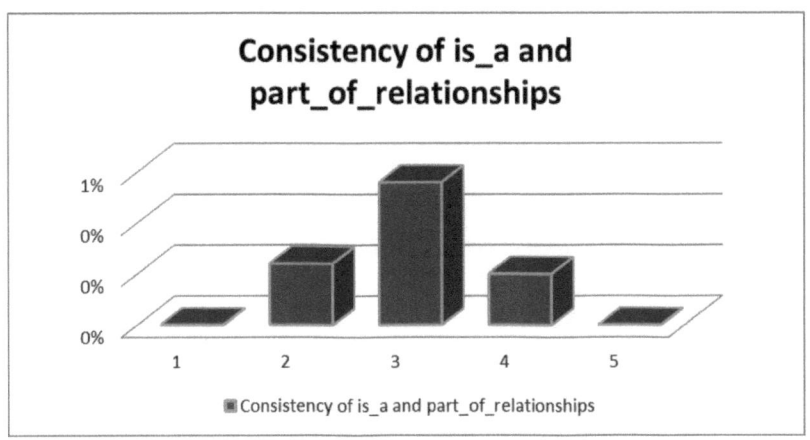

Figure 5-8 Consistency of is-a and part-of –relationships

For the third criterion the majority of participants identified level 3 to indicate their level of satisfaction to assess completeness of OIS ontology which is 48%, in comparison with level 1 and 5. Diagram 5-9 shows the percentage of completeness of the ontology.

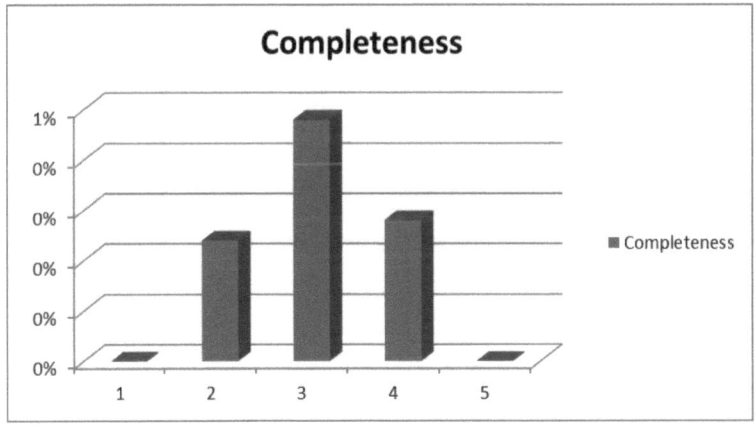

Figure 5-9 completeness of ontology

The fourth criterion was clarity of OIS ontology. The vast majority of participants found that the OIS ontology is clear. Due to the fact that, they were familiar with the most of the ontology concepts. Only one that criticised "Thing" asked why it was the first class. This was a little confusing because Thing is OWL root. However, participants selected both Level 3 and 4 by 40% to identify the level of clarity, while level 2 was chosen by only 20% from the participants. Diagram 5-10 shows the participants' satisfaction levels.

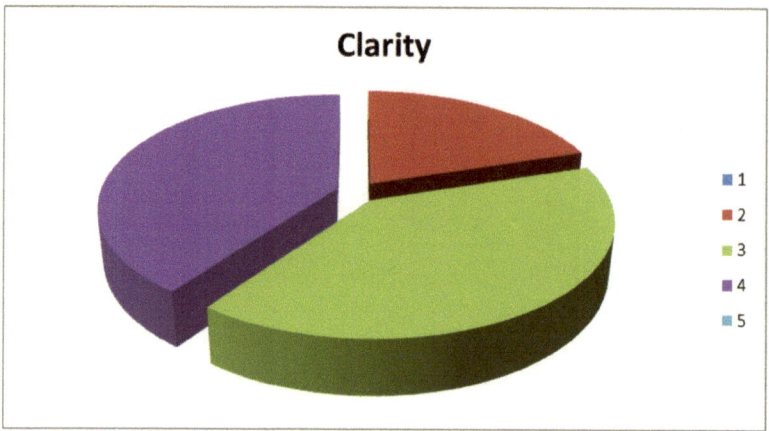

Figure 5-10 Clarity of OIS ontology

The fifth criterion was ontology generality. 88% of participants are satisfied with the Generality criterion of ontology which they indicated by selecting level 3 or 4. Whereas about 12% of participants selected level 2 to point out that they were unsatisfied with the ontology components to cover the whole domain Diagram 5-11 shows the results.

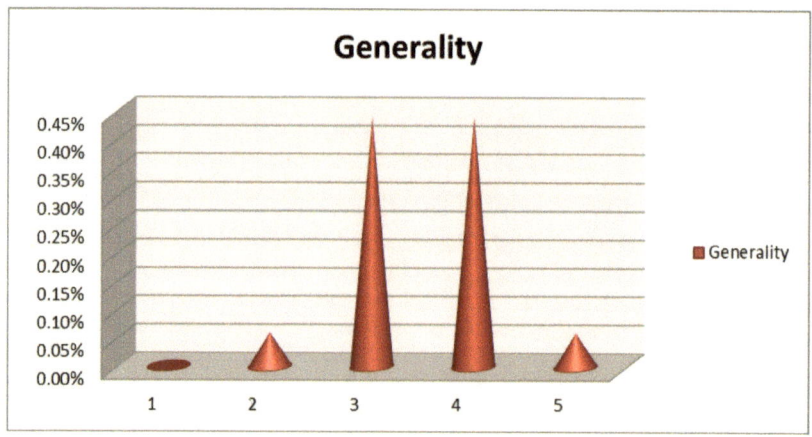

Figure 5-11 ontology generality

The sixth criterion was semantic data richness of the ontology. The results indicated that 12 participants - about 48% - say their satisfaction is at level 3, while 24% identified

172

level 4, but 28% pointed to level 2 because the ontology does not contain instances at this stage. Figure 5-12 illustrates this.

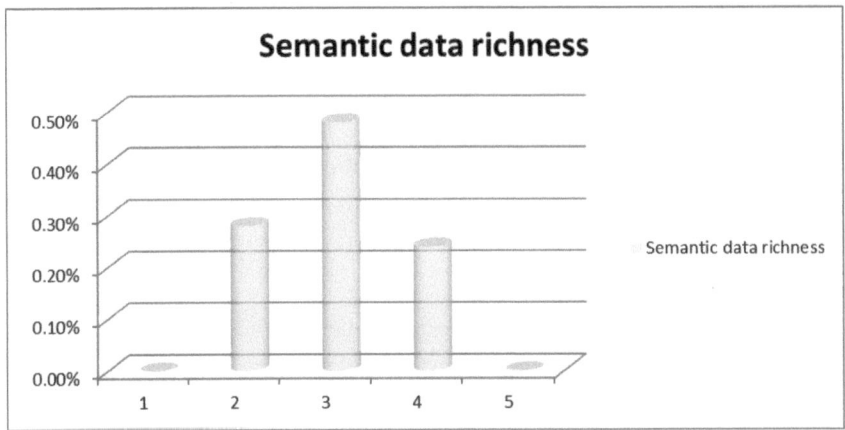

Figure 5-12 semantic data richness of the ontology

The second part of the survey contains six open questions – as stated in Table 5-2 - to ask participants whether the construction approach of the OIS ontology was right and the possibility of improving it, or changing some parts of the domain knowledge.

The first question asked participants what they liked about the ontology. The responses were primarily positive. Most of the responses indicated what they like as whole model and some of them indicated some parts, e.g., one respondent indicated that "she likes [the] inclusion of Standards as a Class".

The second question was asked about whether the ontology needs to be improved. Fifteen out of twenty five responded "yes", it needs some improvements, e.g. one respondent indicated that the subclasses "EvidentialValue" and HistoricalValue" of Standards, and that Value should be in separate classes. Others suggest changing the class "Person" to "People" and "Organization" rather than "Institution" because organization is more general than institution.

The third question asked participants if they would like to add and change any classes in the model. Some responses suggested a number of concepts to be added, e.g., Bibliometrics, scientometrics, and infometrics as subclasses to the Methods class. Also, adding Mathematics, Engineering, Natural science, Chemistry, and Physics to the Domain class. However, one respondent raised an interesting point about the "Author" class; She pointed out that not all "Author" are employee, she said they can be employed or independent, so it needs to be listed directly under "Person". Another suggestion was related to adding facts such as -Mandate, to include accountability, institutional memory, research, and support of human rights, and -Sector to include government, corporate, religious, and academic

The fourth question was asked to point out whether the model covers the domain knowledge. Eighteen out of twenty five answered with a clear "yes" and three of the rest answered I do not know, while six did not answer, i.e., "It seems to cover all the classes I would expect for this domain".

The fifth question asked was about the taxonomy structure of the ontology. Some of the respondents felt that some of the hierarchical relationships could be enhanced or improved, e.g, "Indexer" is not restricted to working at libraries only, he or she could work at publishing companies such as Cengage learning, or resources aggregators for example.

The sixth question was asked about whether the model can be mapped with other specific models or not as a general model according to their theory. Sixteen out of twenty five answered "yes" it could be mappable. Others answered "do not know". Most of the participants indicated to some concepts that could be linked with other ontology for integration of sub-domain ontologies, e.g, People, Methods, Practice, Studies in order of these concepts are general and available in all domains.

The final question was about the general assessment of the model - whether they satisfied or not with the whole model. Twenty of the respondents were positive - "agree" - on the ontology structure. They point this out "Given that no ontology is ever finished" but it is valuable.

In general, the comments of participants were positive on the ontology structure, and overall they agreed with and liked the concepts that were used, see Figure 5-13.

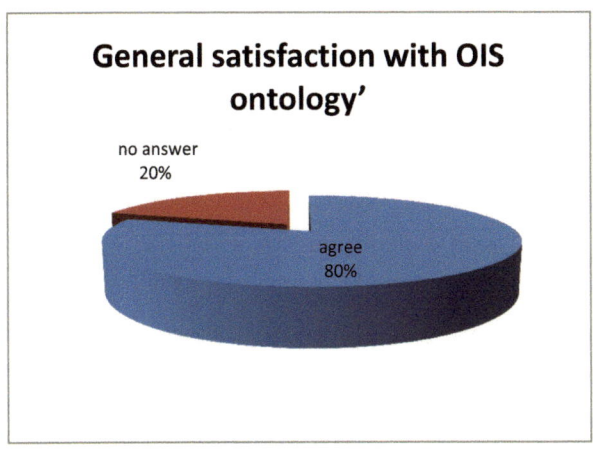

Figure 5-13 The General assessment on OIS ontology

5.1.2 Results of Ontocop System

The core group are professionals who are involved in Library & Information Studies-computer science departments at universities around the world, from different geographic locations, from different universities, and different languages. So the English language is not the native language for many of them, as illustrated in Figure 5-14.

On the other hand, it is important to make members feel that they are participating at a voluntary level and that their participation will keep them up-to-date in their field.

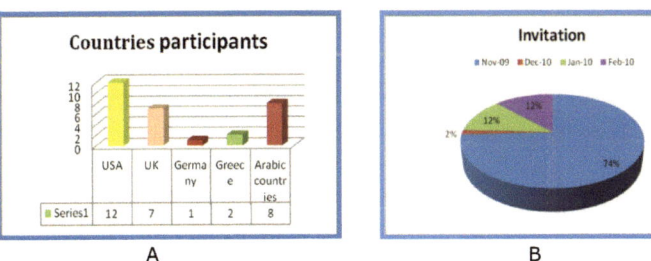

Figure 5-14 participants of Ontocop

To take Ontocop a step forward, the research outlines some actions that have been taken:

Launch the Ontocop with a grand kick-off.

Send 1633 emails in November and December 2009 respectively. At the beginning only 15 people responded offering their support - see some response emails as indicated in Appendix J - while 112 emails had failed through a mistake in the mailing address and the rest did not respond. By January and February 2010 the number had increased to 30 active participants. Overall, most of the emails sent were in November 2009 - about 74% - while approximately 12% were sent in January and February 2010.

The result of potential participations on this project is derived from Piwiki, the website analysis tool. Piwiki provides details on Ontocop website visitors. Using this tool helps to assess how and when users have been visiting the website. Visitors started visiting the community and participating in Jan 2010, and the number increased in Feb, Mar, and April respectively, as illustrated in Figure 5-15.

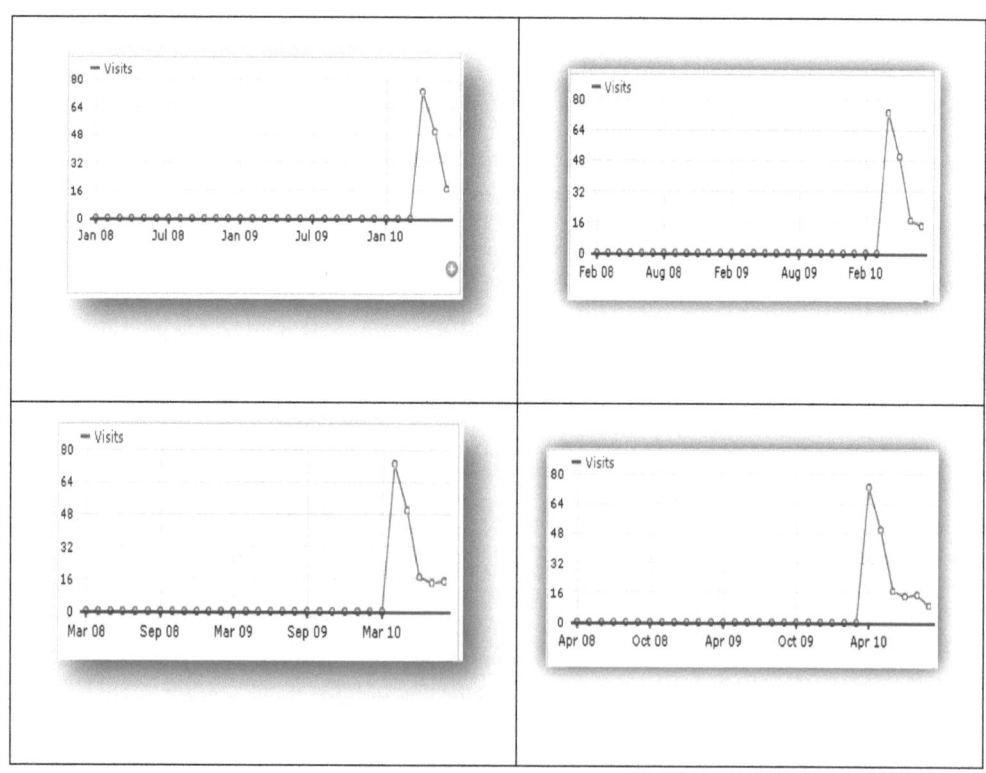

Figure 5-15 visitors of Ontocop

Analysing these results even from this fairly small period, we discovered many interesting points:

1. Users found collaboration in developing the OIS ontology is useful and interesting and involved active discussion.
2. Participants were new to the system and some of them had difficulties with basic usability issues. We have addressed this by providing explanations to help them.
3. Participants at the beginning did not understand aspects of the tool functionality.
4. Language barriers affected their communication.

5.2 Discussion and Analysis

Returning to the research questions that we introduced in Section 1.3, the results of our evaluation attempt to answer these questions to address research objectives; these objectives were fulfilled by assessment of the ontology by domain experts.

Regarding the first question was answered by revealing that the OIS ontology was developed to visualise the domain knowledge. It described the process of developing in a practical way. The workflows of the developing process differ from ontology to ontology. The answer to this question is positive through the results of evaluation, where the participants considered it to be clear and comprehensive. The completeness is verified by checking the OIS ontology has fulfilled the objectives, which have been defined as;

- Domain interest: the OIS was modelled for the IS domain knowledge

- Ontology purpose: creating this ontology for providing a domain model to be used as knowledge base. OIS ontology is providing a formal representation of the domain concepts and describing the relationships between them.

For the question of the knowledge that represent by the ontology, the OIS ontology represents the IS domain knowledge - its scope covers the tree branches which are; library science, archival science, and computer science. By describing the domain's content, the ontology's construction considered the users by answering these questions: who are the users of the OIS? What are the problems it attempts to solve? What could we do with the OIS ontology? For instance the users of OIS are domain experts and ordinary users - it helps users to search and studying the relations in the domain's content as mentioned in Section 4.1.1. It can be used for database components to be integrated with other components such as lexical resource and supporting analysis of natural languages.

The third and fourth questions were answered by analysing different ontology methods and determining the ones that are most efficient in constructing ontology. The OIS Ontology expresses the domain conceptualization at formal level. It represents IS concepts by formal language using OWL 2 which gives a clear expressiveness and the semantic syntax, and was coded by using ontology editor Protégé and WebProtégé, as stated in Section 3.3.

The question of the ontology relationships that have been used, in the OIS ontology two types of relationships were implemented, as contained below;

-Relations between classes to describe type of relations links among two classes.

-Relations between individuals and general concepts in the ontology to describe type of relations links between classes and individuals, as stated in Section 4.2.15.

The relations definition between concepts needs to be more flexible for extra modifications in the future and for introducing new domain specifications.

The ontology is structured in the taxonomy tree and visualisation is complete by OWLVis plug-in in protégé.

Regarding the value of using tool such Ontocop system this study indicated that

Examining Winger's communities of practice theory, particularly his constructs of common engagement and sharing community memory, a community of practice consists of the domain, practice and community. Through a process of negotiation of meaning, learning takes place within identity formation. Because of the importance and value of tacit knowledge, many developers of knowledge-based systems are spending significant time in obtaining information from experts, which is considered as a tacit knowledge, and making it accessible and machine-readable. On the basis of Winger's theory some specific requirements for the visualisation approach were conducted.

Collaboration with experts helps to overcome inconsistencies in the building process. Although there is a difference in views about classifying the knowledge according to their subject background, but it increases the richness of the ontology. The Ontocop community supports the developing process at different stages to validate the ontology construction. During this study they know about the ontology in its early stages to be familiar with it.

The final answer to these research questions is an implementation of OIS ontology. The OIS ontology was designed based on specific criteria that were mentioned in Section

2.1.19 to meet the requirements. Also, in chapter 2, we have reviewed different evaluation approaches in Section 2.1.10. The produced model was evaluated based on specific criteria.

The OIS was structured as a generic model to visualise the IS domain by unifying the domain knowledge to model the real world. The implementation acts as an example of how the actual research problem can be solved. Overall, the process of creating the OIS ontology was successful and the work proceeded without any significant problems.

In comparing with the related work in the area such as Zins' work (2007). it has clarified the relationships between concepts in the field, but there are many concepts still to be explored; for instance, in researching this study, a range of subdivisions have been uncovered so the study does not reflect the most current knowledge. One of the reactions to Zins' knowledge map is about the validation of its findings, as the participators provide assumptions about the domain as it is now. As we know, the IS field is a fast paced discipline.

Furthermore, Anthony Debons (one of the evaluator in Zin's study) indicates the diversity of IS and its language, which need to be agreed between the information scientists by creating lexicon to rely on during the work. In this study scientists have provided 57 definitions of Data, Information and Knowledge using different terminology; they used same terms that describe different meanings. Consequently, terms can be misleading and need to be clarified to get consensual meaning.

Overall, the nature of IS domain is less structured such as legal or social domains, which posed major challenges to the ontology development. Furthermore, the lack of domain ontology in this area made necessary to develop OIS ontology from scratch, although, there are ontologies that related to this area such as CIDOC-CRM which is focused on cultural heritage documentation, and FRBR to develop relational model of OCLC's catalogue, and ontology of cultural heritage resources is focused on modelling prototypes collection of Tobacco Bag Stringing (TBS) in Section 2.1.8 . They considered specific division of the domain, while OIS ontology is more general focuses to develop knowledge base for the whole domain, is not considered any specific ontology for Library, museum or archive. It is as basic for the IS domain that facilitates creating or developing further domain ontologies for specific applications, such as archival collections, or library collections.

The research finding were encouraging about the potential of OIS ontology to benefit IS studies for instance. The evaluation outcomes provide an approach led to strengthen modelling results and receiving suggestions on how to improve it, as deliberated in previous Section 5.1.1.4.

The produced model of OIS ontology was assessed in this study. The results of the OIS ontology evaluation revealed that the OIS ontology model can offer adequate functionality to meet user's requirements on supplementary information modelling. Furthermore it can help to build semantic capturing with objects designed to support semantic sharing between other disciplines. We have found the results to be satisfactory and the model is valid.

The evaluation results are reflected in the ontology; we made approximately 35 changes to the OIS ontology. Most of the changing was on the class based on the Domains Object class, with 19 classes entered, which were:

-Natural Science

- Astronomy
- Biology
- Chemistry
- Physic
- Earth science
  - Atmospheric Science
  - Oceanography

-Social Science

- Anthropology
- Economics
- Geography
- Political Science
- Psychology
- Art
- Humanities.

-Applied Science

- Engineering
- Medicine and Biology.

The participants were asked to indicate to their level of satisfaction on the ontology in general and the quality of term definitions, as illustrated in Figure 5-16

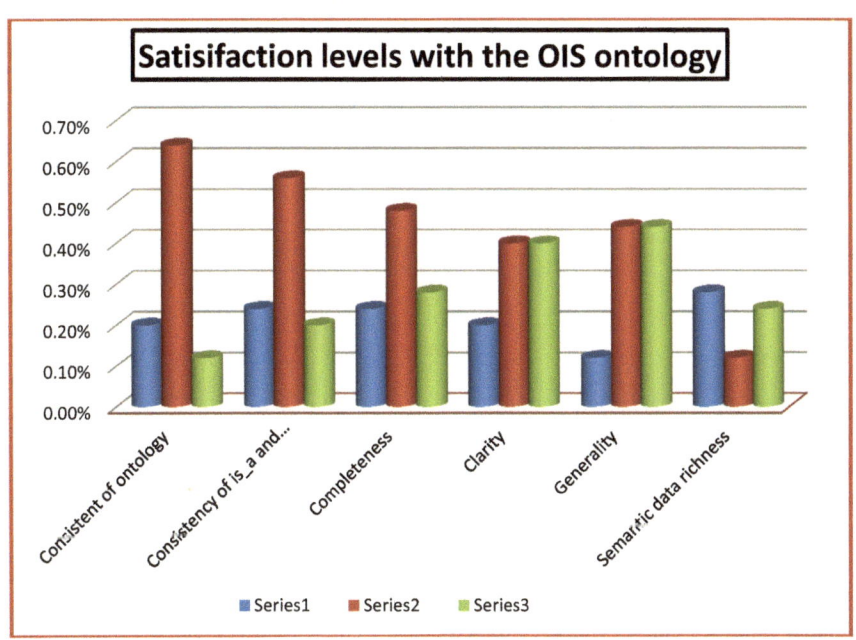

Figure 5-16 satisfaction levels with the OIS ontology

The chart shows the satisfaction levels of the experts with the OIS ontology. The consistency of the ontology and relationships were satisfied. It is notable that the respondents expressed their level of satisfaction by choosing level three which is the middle level of evaluation, while, the same level decreased to 10% on semantic data richness criterion. The consistency of the ontology was remarked upon by 60% in comparison with the generality and clarity which are 44% and 48% respectively, as illustrated in Figure 5-17 and Table 5-3.

Table 5-3 level 3 of satisfaction on ontology based on specific criteria

Criteria	Percentage
Consistent of ontology	0.64%
Consistency of is_a and part_of_relationships	0.56%
Completeness	0. 48%
Clarity	0.40%
Generality	0.44 %
Semantic data richness	0.48%

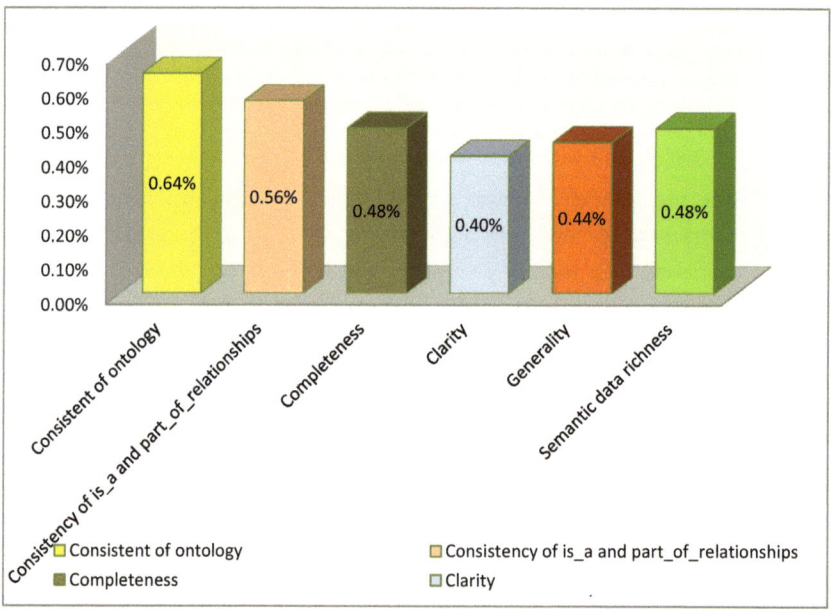

Figure 5-17 evaluation criteria at level 3

It is notable that the OIS ontology was evaluated at levels 2, 3, and 4. Meanwhile, participants did not indicate level 1 and 5 which means the ontology is neither negative nor completely sufficient. The choosing of middle levels revealed evidence that the ontology met the designing criteria and it is an appropriate model. The findings of the evaluation stage provided a rich source of data that has been considered in refining the current model.

The Analysis of the results points to many interesting issues: firstly;

- The evaluation of ontology model is not a communal practice in knowledge engineering, also it is uncommon when conducted from VCops. Furthermore, the main challenge in this part of the study was related to designing issue such designing and evaluation criteria. It is usual to evaluate ontology using systems performance or testing formal quality of ontology.
- Collaboration on such a virtual community of practice is interesting; some of the participants found the idea of using VCop valuable, it can be used to develop any universal software collaboratively.
- Respondents were new to using the ontology in WebProtégé software. So some of them had difficulties in accessing the ontology. Some of these difficulties were caused by using different internet browsers.
- The WebProtégé tool made the access to OIS ontology easier to browse and navigate through the ontology components, with concerns arising in online discussions about how to navigate and browse at the same time in quick and easy ways. Through WebProtégé, users can search on concepts and their relationships with other classes and where they were used. For example, the result of searching on the concept Information provides 64 result that indicate uses of this concept through the ontology such as:
  - Information Broker
  - HealthInformationCenterInfromationTransfer
  - InformationSearch
  - InformationCentres
  - GeneralInformation
  - LibraryOfInformationDepartment
  - InformationManagementSystem
  - InformationSeekingBehaviour
  - InformationRetrievalSystem

The graph 5-18 shows some of these results.

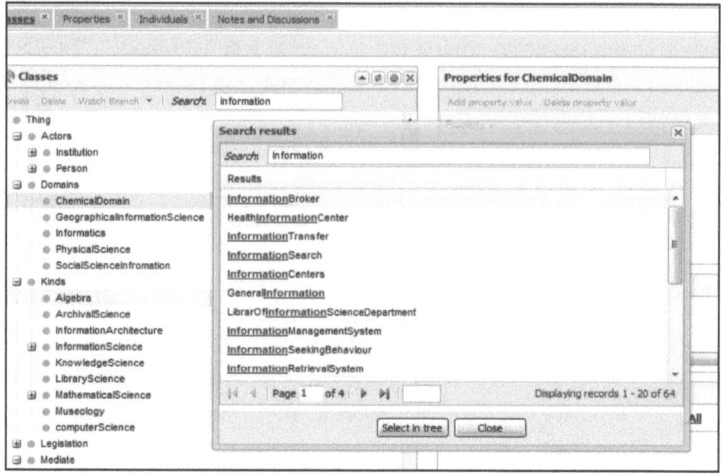

Figure 5-18 Searching on WebProtégé

Overall, the aim of this study was visualise the IS domain by providing the framework to share a common understanding of Information science, and the ultimate aim was creating ontology model of IS.

5.3 Revised OIS model

The OIS was changed after some comments had been gathered. The comments were made on the classification to enrich the ontology such as:

- Domains need to include arts, humanities
- Divide the science in the Domains into natural science, applied science and social science to add more subclasses under each one.
- Add Mandate as it has subclasses such as; accountability, institutional memory, research and support of human rights.

The final version of the OIS ontology has 706 classes, 70 object properties, 99) individuals. We can see this from the ontology matrices and ontology diagram 5-19.

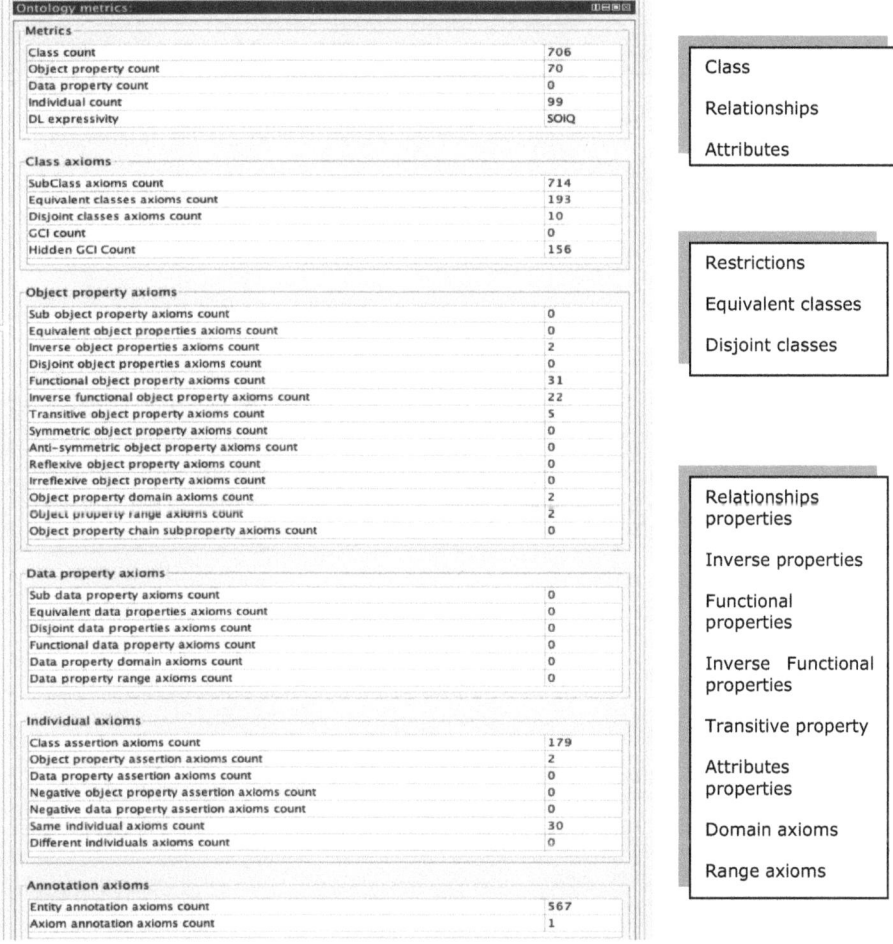

Figure 5-19 ontology matrices

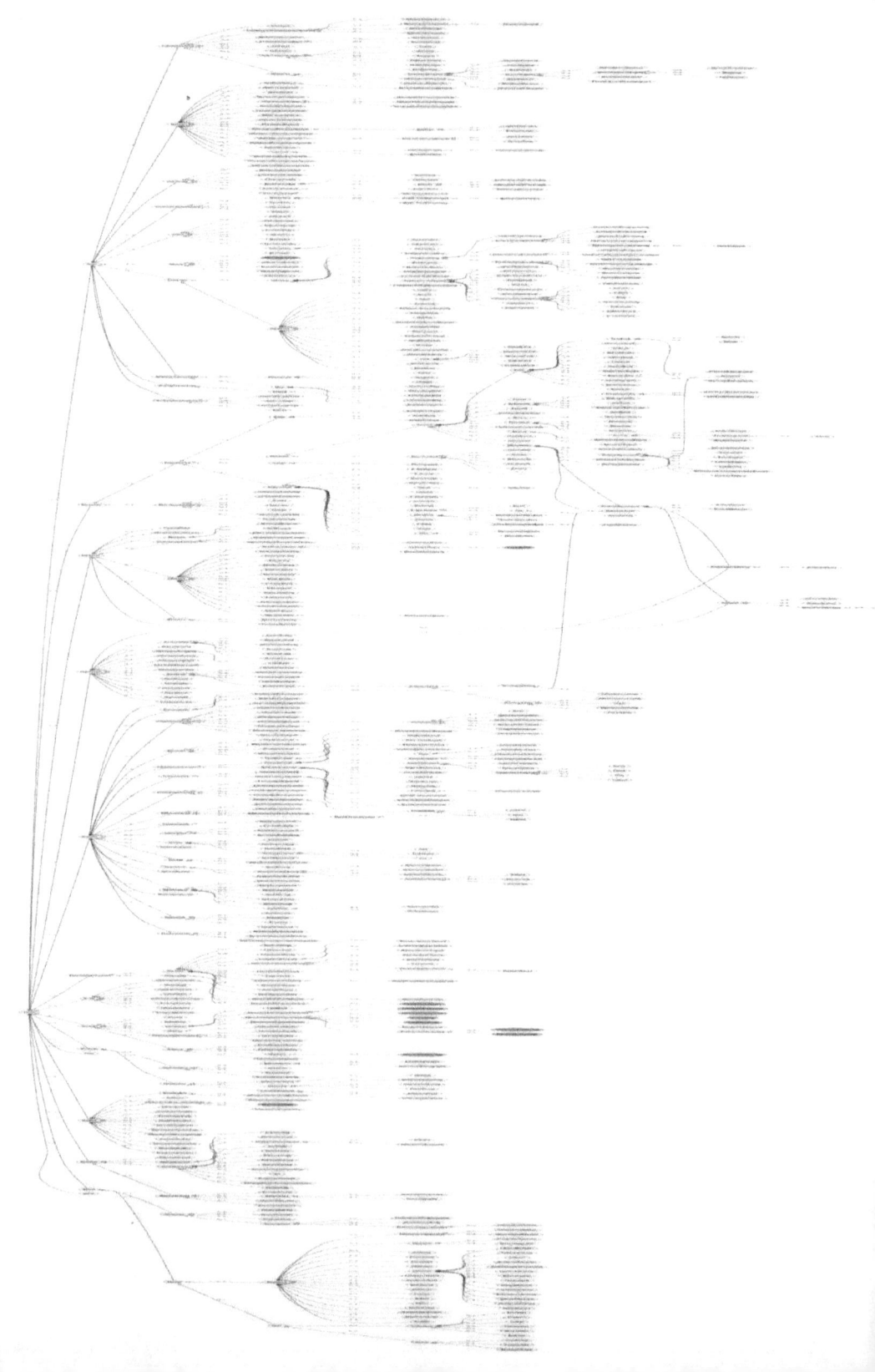

Part 4: Conclusion & Future Work

6 Chapter 6: Conclusion & Future Work

This study is concluded in this chapter. The research problem and questions derived from it are answered. In addition, the achievements and the limitations of this study are discussed. The research started with identifying the problem. To achieve these objectives, the OIS was designed and developed. Feedback and evaluation from the domain's experts has led to constant improvement in the ontology's development. The current version of the OIS ontology is presented in this thesis. At the end of this chapter, possible research leads for the future are suggested.

The study aimed at the creation of OIS ontology of Information Science domain to visualise its knowledge, in order to be integrated with other ontologies to be applied for a specific application. The resulting ontology covers three main areas of domain knowledge: library science, archival science and computing science. The vocabularies of these branches are formalised in class hierarchy with relations which are interconnecting concepts from all these areas, in order to define a sufficient model of the Information Science domain.

6.1 Contributions

The main contributions in this study are presented in Figure 6.1, which are:

1. Designing ontology of Information Science (OIS): is presented to design OIS domain ontology to visualize a specific area. The OIS contains 706 concepts. These concepts identified to provide a clear definitions for classes that would be interest to the domain users and developers. Also, identify the associated attributes and characteristics of the objects with their relations. Each entity has attributes and type of relations for operating between these entities. The study intent to provide conceptual model serve as base to related specific relations and attributes. Furthermore, the research is focusing on analysis IS data to be defined in a systematic way in which way that how the information can be used.
2. A new strategy of conceptual representation of the domain knowledge that supported by both human and machine.
3. Developing IS taxonomy which is a novel methods to classify the domain knowledge. It describes the main concepts in a hierarchy tree. Our approach is overlapping on shortcomings of the classification systems that are widely acknowledged amongst the scientific community based on (FAS) and reinitialized previous classification schemas.

4 Designing Ontocop system a novel method presented to support the developing process as specific virtual community of IS.

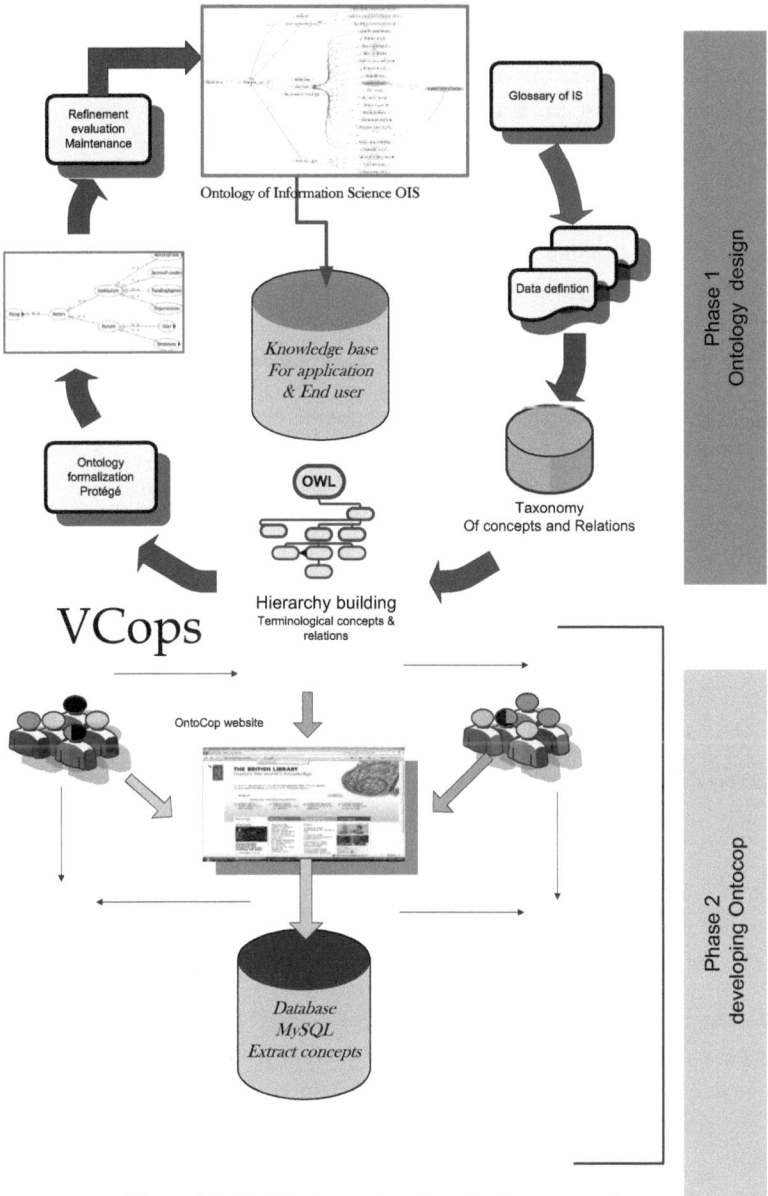

Figure 6-1 Architecture of system design approach

6.2 Achievements

The main achievement of this study is the creating a new model of OIS ontology. The OIS ontology was implemented in the process of the life cycle of ontology development, which was strongly influenced by Methontology. The creation process divided mainly into four processes: specification, conceptualisation, formalisation, and evaluation. The evaluation was essential to gather results on the produced model. The information resources were acquired manually and semi-automatically from domain's publications, books and dictionaries, where the text analysis and annotation techniques have been used. Conceptualisation essentially relied on the identification of concepts and groups of concepts and in building specific classification trees. The knowledge model was then formalised using Protégé, and WebProtégé to use the OIS ontology; it was also used to generate the ontology code automatically. Another relevant issue was using a standard evaluation methodology to check if the ontology satisfied needs.

The OIS is a data model representing set of concepts and sets of relations that connect the concepts; each instance is restricted by some axioms.

This model aimed to provide a shared terminology among agents and specialists in the domain and to define the meaning of all concepts in an accurate manner.

Identifying a research problem and justifying its need for a solution, required devoting an artefact as a solution. The research problem of the study was defined in Section 1.2.

The research problem was solved by answering the research as mentioned in Section 5.2.

The problems that were considered were:

- The IS domain was too broad for the specific time of the study.

- Since the beginning of the 1990s ontologies have been developed without clear guidance for developers. Nevertheless, some design criteria, principles, methods and methodologies must be followed.

-Despite some problems we have faced, the OIS ontology has reached a usable state. The concepts of the domain were structured and documented. The ontology is currently published in WebProtégé, since that work will be used for an application of IS domain to be used in specific purposes. At the end of this study, the implemented approach was evaluated.

6.3 Future work

For reusing, sharing, and maintenance of the OIS ontology, there are future issues that relate to our ontology that need to be considered. In the OIS module there is always space for improvement. Ontologies are changing over time, due to changes in the domain and conceptualisation, so its structure should be extensible and flexible;

-It has the potential to be a collective knowledge base for the information science domain.

- Improve it by adding new or missing concepts and adding new classifications based on different criteria and perspectives.

- Most Information Science concepts were considered. Another, more interesting, possibility would be to link this general model with other science that is related to the domain.

- The OIS ontology is a key piece in the future development of Informatics applications such as Geographical information system, Management Information systems, and decision support systems.

- Translate ontology into another language, Spanish and Arabic for example. Once the ontology has been conceptualized, all the terms can be translated into another language using Multilanguage thesaurus and electronic dictionary.

- The main purpose of the OIS ontology is supporting knowledge sharing and exchange of data among databases as a generic model e.g. Actors, Domains, Kinds, Practice and so on. This ontology can be extended to create instances to general classes such as Author name.

- The subclass author can be defined as follows: author: (author, name) the author is a subclass of person that indicates to any author must be a person (person, author) and each author has associated name and has some document, at least one book or article.

This ontology can be used by knowledge engineers or domain analysts. It requires search modules to provide a basic mechanism for searching. The OIS ontology uses natural language or keywords. Also, it provides advance research to retrieve specific knowledge that users are seeking for, see Figure 6-2

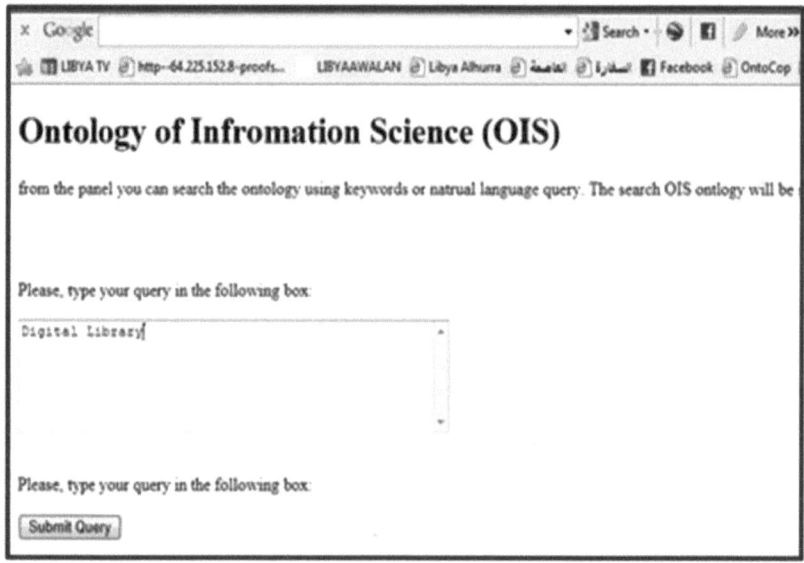

Figure 6-2 Interface of OIS ontology searching

The search module is to facilitate:

- Reuse of the ontology components by equipping the application to deal with certain ontologies.
- Sharing knowledge that is contained in the repository.
- Helps users to retrieve any subsection of the OIS ontology for use in applications.

OIS can be used in many applications that range from knowledge base systems to information systems, for instance in information retrieval.

The OIS ontology is a domain ontology that will be used as a foundation for task ontologies, which provides a defined vocabulary to data ontology and database. The task ontology provides vocabulary for applications, whereas application ontology is designed for solving specific problems, which are accessed by the application, by implementing the semantics in sets of axioms to enable OIS ontology to deduce the answers of questions about the IS domain automatically. The relationship between these ontologies is shown diagrammatically in Figure 6-3.

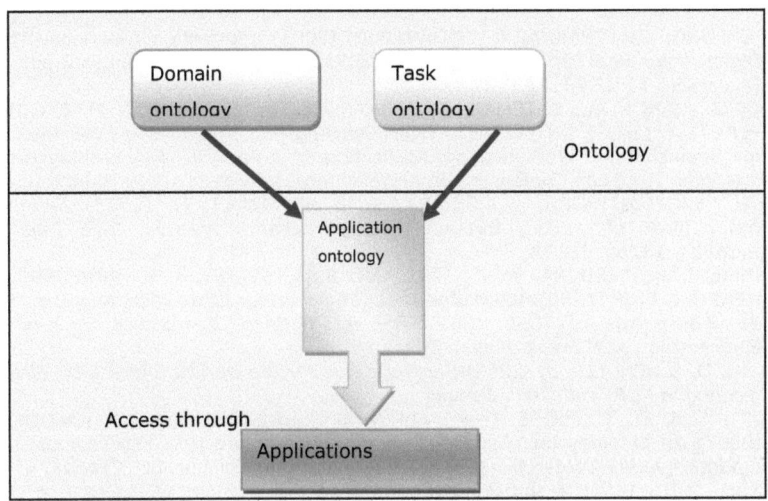

Figure 6-3 **Relationships between ontologies**

The model of OIS is possible using application ontology. The appropriate use of OIS ontology is in Information science education; it helps teachers and students to obtain more details about their courses. It can provide outlines and summaries of topics that are covered in the courses. Also, it can answer questions such as:

What are the courses in the domain?

How many courses are in the domain?

How many places are available to each course?

How many students are studying each year?

Bibliography

AFTAB, CHEUNG, KIM, THAKKAR & YEDDANAPUDI (2001) Information Theory and The Digital Age. Final Paper. http://mit.edu/6.933/www/Fall2001/Shannon2.pdf [Accessed: 11.12.2012].

AGUADO, G., BANON, A., BATEMAN, J., BERNARDOS, S., FERNANDEZ, M. & GÒMEZ-PÉREZ, A. (1998) ONTOGENERATION: Reusing domain and linguistic ontologies for Spanish text. Workshop on Application of ontologies and problem-solving methods. *European Conference on Artificial Intelligence (ECAI'89).* Brighton, UK.

ALANI, H., DASMAHAPATRA, S., O'HARA, K. & SHADBOLT, N. (2003) Identifying communities of practice through ontology network analysis. *IEEE Intelligent Systems,* 18, pp. 18–25.

ALEXANDER, J. H., FREILING, M. J., SHULMAN, S. J., STALEY, J. L., REHFUSS, S. & MESSICK, S. L. (1986) Knowledge Level Engineering: Ontological Analysis. *AAAI-86 Proceedings of ICSE 1991: The international Conference on Software Engineering.* ACM Press. Austin, Texas.

ALLEMANG, D. & HENDLER, J. (2008) *Semantic web for the working ontologist: effective modling in RDFs and OWL*, Elsevier.

AMIRA, T., ADIL EL, G., ROSE, D.-K., ALAIN, G., CHRISTINA, C., G & RALDINE, V. (2007) An ontology for supporting communities of practice. *Proceedings of the 4th international conference on Knowledge capture.* Whistler, BC, Canada, ACM.

ANDERSON, J. R. (1983) A spreading activation theory of memory. *Journal of Verbal Learning and Verbal Behavior,* , 22, pp. 261-295.

ANDREW, N., TOLSON, D. & FERGUSON, D. (2008) Building on Wenger: communities of practice in nursing. *Nurse Education Today,* 246-252.

ANTONIOU, G. & HARMELEN, F. V. (2004) *Semantic web primer*, Massachusetts Institute of Technology.

ANUPRIYAN, A. SYCARA, K. HERBSLEB, J. KRAUT, R. & WELTY, C. (2006) Supporting online problem-solving communities with the semantic web. Proceedings of the 15th international conference on World Wide Web. Edinburgh, Scotland, ACM.

ARAUJO, L. (1998) Knowing and learning as networking *management Learning* 29, pp.317-336.

ARDICHVILI, A., PAGE, V. & WENTLING, T. (2003) Motivation and barriers to participation in virtual knowledge -sharing communities of practice. *Knowledge management* 7, pp.64-77.

ARPIREZ, J. C., GOMEZ-PEREZ, A., LOZANO, A. & PINTO, H. (1998) Reference ontology and ONTO Agent: the ontology yellow pages. Workshop on Application of ontologies and problem-solving methods. *European conference on artificial Intelligence (ECAI'89).* Brighton, UK.

AWODEY, S. (2006) Category Theory. Oxford Science publication, http://www.google.co.uk/#hl=en&q=on%20catego [Accessed: 18.05.2010].

BAADER, F. & NUTT, W. (2003) *The description logic handbook: theory, implementation, and application*, Cambridge University Press.

BARRY, S. (1996) Mereotopology: A Theory of parts and boundaries. *Data and knowledge Engineering,* 20, pp:287- 303.

BATISTA, F., PARDAL, J. P., MAMEDE, N. J., VAZ, P. & RIBEIRO, R. D. (2006) Ontology construction: cooking domain http://www.inesc-id.pt/pt/indicadores/Ficheiros/3615.pdf [Accessed :30.11.2010].

BAWDEN, D. (2011) Brookes equation: The basis for a qualitative characterization of information behaviours. *Journal of Information Science,* 37, pp. 101-108.

BECHHOFER, S., HORROCKS, I., GOBLE, C. & STEVENS, R. (2001) OilEd: a Reasonable Ontology Editor for the Semantic Web. *In Joint German/Austrian conference on Artificial Intelligence.* Berlin,2001, Springer.

BELLO, A. (2010) Ontology and Phenomenology. IN POLI, R. & SEIBT, J. (Eds.) *Theory and Applications of Ontology: Philosophical Perspectives.* London New York, Springer.

BERNERS-LEE, HENDLER, J. & LASSILA, O. (2001) The Semantic Web. *Scientific American,,* 284, pp. 34-43.

BERNERS-LEE, T. (2000) Semantic Web on XML. Keynote presentation for XML 2000. http://www.w3.org/2000/Talks/1206-xml2k-tbl/slide1-0.html. [Accessed :02.10.2009].

BERNER-LEE, T. (2001) The Semantic Web Made Easy. http://www.w3.org/RDF/Metalog/docs/sw-easy [Accessed: 11.02.2009].

BHATT, M., RAHAYU, W., SONI, S. P. & WOUTERS, C. (2009) Ontology driven semantic profiling and retrieval in medical information systems. *Web Semantics: Science, Services and Agents on the World Wide Web,* 7, pp.317-331.

BLÁZQUEZ, J. FERNANDEZ, M. GARCÍA-PINAR, J. & GÓMEZ-PÉREZ, A. (1998) Building ontologies at the knowledge level using the ontology design environment. Knowledge Acquisition of knowledge- Based System Workshop(KAW).

BLUM, B. I. (1996) *Beyond programming* Oxford Unversity Press, New York.

BOURNE, C. P. (1980) On-line systems: History, technology and economics. *Journal of the American Society for Information Science,* 31, pp.155-160.

BREWSTER, C. ALANI, H. DASMAHAPATRA, S. & WILKS, Y. (2004) Data Driven Ontology Evaluation. *In: International Conference on Language Resources and Evaluation,24-30 May.* Lisbon, Portugal.

BROUGHTON, V. (1999) Notational expressivity, the case for and against the representation of internal subject structure in notational coding. *Knowledge Organization,* 26, pp.140-148.

BROUGHTON, V. (2001) Faceted classification as a basis for knowledge organization in a digital environment; the Bliss Bibliographic Classification as a model for vocabulary management and the creation of multidimensional knowledge structures'. *New Review of Hypermedia and Multimedia,* 7, pp.67-102.

BRUSA, G., CALIUSCO, M. L. & CHIOTTI, O. (2006) A Process for Building a Domain Ontology: an Experience in Developing a Government Budgetary Ontology. *Conferences in Research and Practice in Information Technology,.* Hobart, Australia.

BUBENKO, J. A. & ORCI, I. P. (1989) Knowledge base management system *Foundation of knowledge base management system.* New York, Springer,Verlag.

BUCKLAND, M. K. & LIU, Z. (1995) History of information science. . *Annual Review of Information Science and Technology,* pp. 385–416.

BURTONJONES, et. al (2005) A semiotic metrics suite for assessing the quality of ontologies. *Data & Knowledge Engineering* 55, p.p 84-102.

CALERO, C., RUIZ, F. & PIATTINI, M. (2006) *Ontologies for software engineering and software technology,* Springer.

CATHERINE, C. M., FRANK M. SHIPMAN, III & RAYMOND, J. M. (2000) Making large-scale information resources serve communities of practice. *Journal Manage Information System,* 11, pp.65-86.

CHAN, K. W. & LI, S. Y. (2010) Understanding consumer- to consumer interactions in virtual communities: The salience of reciprocity. *Journal of Businees Research,* pp.1033-1040.

CHAUDHRI, V., FARQUHAR, A., FIKES, R., KARP, P. & RICE, J. (1998) OKBC: A programmatic foundation for knowledge base interoperability. *In Proceedings 15 th National conference on artificial Intelligence AAAI-98.*

CHI, Y.-L., HSU, T.-Y. & YANG, W.-P. (2006) Ontological techniques for reuse and sharing knowledge in digital museums. *Electronic Library,* Vol. 24, pp.147 - 159.

CLEVERDON, C. (1087) Historical note: Perspectives. Journal of the American. *Society for Information Science,* 38, pp. 152–155.

COAKES, E. & CLARKE, S. (2008) Boundaries in Communities. *Encyclopedia of Communities of Practice in Information and Knowledge Management.*

CORCHO, O., et. al (2002) Building legal ontologies with METHONTOLOGY and WebODE. http://academic.research.microsoft.com/Paper/1856108.aspx [Accessed: 23.10.2011].

COX, A. (2005) What are communities of practice? A comparative review of four seminal works *Journal of Information Science,* 31, pp.527-540

CRISTANI, M. & CUEL, R. A. (2005) Survey on Ontology Creation Methodologies. *International Journal of Semantic Web and Information Systems (IJSWIS),* 1, pp: 49-69.

CUNNINGHAM, H., MAYNARD D. & TABLAN, V. (2000) JAPE: a Java Annotation Patterns Engine (Second Edition). *Research Memorandum CS-00-10,* . Department of Computer Science, , University of Sheffield, November 2000.

CURTIS, J., MATTHEWS, G. & BAXTER, D. (2005) On the Effective Use of Cyc in a Question Answering System. *In: Papers from the IJCAI Workshop on Knowledge and Reasoning for Answering Questions.* Edinburgh, Scotland: 2005., pp61-70.

DACONTA, M., OBRST, L. J. & SMITH, K. (2003) The semantic web: a guide to the *future of xml web services, and knowledge management.,* Indianapolis, Ind. : Wiley Pub,2003 .

DALKIR, K. (2005) *KM in theory and practice,* Oxford., Elsevier Butterworth-Heinemann,.

DAVENPORT, T. H. (1998) Some Principles of knowledge management http://www.strategy-business.com/article/8776?gko=f91a7 [accessed :10.03.2010].

DAVENPORT, T. & PRUSAK, L. (2000) working knowledge: how organisations mange *what they know* Boston, Mass. , Harvard Business School.

DAVIS, R., SHROBE, H. & SZOLOVITS, P. (1993) What is a knowledge Representation? *AI Magazine,* 14, 17-33.

DELIISKA, B. (2007) Thesaurus and Domain ontology of Gioinformatics. *Journal Compilation,* vol,11, pp. 637-651.

DMTERIE, J. & VERBEEK, F. J. (2008) Information visualisation from ontology. *Formal ontology in information systems Fifth international conference FOIS2008.*

DOMINGUE, J. (1998) Tadzebao and Webonto: Discussing, Browsing and Editing ontologies on the web . *11th knowledge Acquisition workshop (KAW98),* . Banff.1998.

DOMINGUE, J., ENRICO, M., BUCKINGHAM, S. S., MARIA, V.-V., YANNIS, K. & NICK, F. (2001) Supporting ontology driven document enrichment within communities of practice. *Proceedings of the 1st international conference on Knowledge capture.* Victoria, British Columbia, Canada, ACM.

DU, T. C., LI, F. & KING, I. (2009) Managing knowledge on the Web - Extracting ontology from HTML Web. *Decision Support Systems,* 47, 319-331.

DUBE, L., BOURHIS, A. & JACOB, R. (2006) Towards a Typology of virtual communities of practice. *Interdisciplinary Journal of Information, knowldge and Management,* 1, 71-93.

ELENA, T. (2006) Creating an Historical Archive Ontology: Guidelines and Evaluation. *Digital Information Management, 2006 1st International Conference on 6-6 Dec. 2006.*

F ERNANDEZ-LOPEZ , M. & GOMEZ - P EREZ, A. (2002) Overview and analysis of methodologies for building ontologies. *The Knowledge Engineering Review* Vol. 17:2,, pp. 129–156.

FACEBOOK (2011) Facebook statistics. https://www.facebook.com/press/info.php?statistics [Accessed :20.03.2012].

FANG, Y.-H. & CHIU, C.-M. (2010) In justice we trust: Exploring knowledge- shaing continuance intentions in virtual communities of practice. *Computers in Human Behavior,* 235-246.

FARKAS-CONN, I. (1990) *From documentation to information science: The beginning and early development of the American Documentation Institute American Society for Information Science,* New York, Greenwood.
FARQUHAR, A., FIKES, R. & RICE, J. (1996) The Ontolingua Server: a Tool for Collaborative Ontology Construction. *10th knowledge Acqisition for knowledge - based systems workshop (KAW96).* Banff,1996.
FEATHER, J. & STURGES, P. (2003) International Encyclopedia of Information and Library Science (2nd edition). IN STURGES, J. F. A. P. (Ed. London and New York, NY, Routledge International Encyclopedia of Information and Library Science (2nd edition) [accessed: 04.05.2010].
FERNADEZ-LOPEZ, M., et. al (1999) Building a chemical ontology using methontology and the ontology design environment *IEEE Intelligent System & Their applications,* 4, pp.37-46.
FERNADEZ-LOPEZ , M. & GOMEZ - PEREZ, A. (2002) Overview and analysis of methodologies for building ontologies. *The Knowledge Engineering Review* Vol. 17:2,, pp. 129–156.
FERNÁNDEZ-LÓPEZ, M. (1999) Overview of methodologies for building ontologies. *In: Workshop Ontologies and Problem-Solving Methods : Lessons Learned and Future Trends de la conferencia International Joint Conference for Artificial Intelligence (IJCAI'99),* August 1999. Stockholm, Sweden.
FERNÁNDEZ-LÓPEZ, M., GÓMEZ-PÉREZ A & JURISTO, N. (1997) Methontology : from ontological art towards ontological engineering. *Proceedings of the AAAI97 Spring Symposium Series on Ontological Engineering.*
FLUIT, C., SABOU, M. & HARMELEN, F. V. (2002) Ontology-based Information Visualisation. *In visualisation the semantic web.* Springer, Verlag.
FOX, M. S. (1992) The Tove project: towards a common-sense model of the enterprise. *Industrial and Engineering Applications of Artificial Intelligence and Expert systems .* pp. 25-34.
GAOYUN, J., JIANLIANG, W. & SHAOHUA, Y. (2010) A method for consistent ocean ontology construction *Industrial and Information Systems (IIS).*
GARTNER, N. R. (2006) Emerging Technologies Hype Cycle Highlights Key Technology Themes.
GASCUEÑA, J. M., FERNÁNDEZ-CABALLERO, A. & GONZÁLEZ, P. (2006) Domain Ontology for Personalized E-Learning in Educational Systems *vanced Learning Technologies, 2006. Sixth International Conference on* 5-7 July 2006.
GASEVIC, D., DEVEDZIC, V. & DJURIC, D. (2006) *Model driven architecture and ontology development* Berlin, Springer.
GENEONTOLOGY (2009) Welcome to the Gene Ontology website! , http://www.geneontology.org/ [Accessed: 20.04.2011].
GERVASSIS, N. J. (2004) In Search of the Value of Online Electronic Personae: Commercial MMORPGs and the Terms of Participation in Virtual CommunitiesAbstract. *Journal of Information, Law and Technology.*
GOLBECK, J., FRAGOSO, G., HARTEL, F., HENDLER, J., OBERTHALER, J. & PARSIA, B. (2008) The National Cancer Institute's Thesaurus and Ontology. http://www.mindswap.org/papers/WebSemantics-NCI.pdf [Accessed : 01.09.2009].
GÓMEZ-PÉREZ, JURISTO, N. & PAZOS, J. (1995) *Evaluation and Assesment of knowledge sharing Technology. Towards very large knowledge base,* Amsterdam, IOS.
GÓMEZ-PÉREZ, A., CORCHO, O. & FERNÁNDEZ-LÓPEZ, M. (2003) Methodologies, tools and languages for building ontologies. Where is their meeting point? *Data & Knowledge Engineering,* 46, 41-64.
GÒMEZ-PÉREZ, A., FERNANDEZ-LOPEZ, M. & CORCHO, O. (2004) *Ontological Engineering :with examples from the areas of knowledge management,e-commerce and the semantic web,* Springer.

GÒMEZ-PÉREZ, A. & ROJAS, M. D. (1999) Ontological Reengineering and reuse. *European knowledge Acquisition workshop (EKAW).*
GOMEZ, R. (1998) The nostalgia of virtual community: a study of computer- mediated communications use in Colombian non- governmental organisation. *Information Technology & People,* 11, pp. 217-234

GOURLAY, S. (2001) knowledge management and HRD. *Human Resource Development International* 4, 27-46.
GOURLAY, S. (2002) Tacit knowledge or behaving? . *European Conference on Organizational Knowledge.* Athens, Gourlay.
GROUP, D. S. W. (2008) The CIDOC Conceptual Reference Model
GRUBER, T. R. (1993) Toward principles for the design of ontologies used for knowledge sharing. IN GUARINO, N. & POLI, R. (Eds.) *formal ontology* kluwer Academicpuplishers.
GUARINO, N. (1997) Understanding, building and using ontologies. *International Journal of Human-Computer Studies,* vol. 46, pp. 293-310.
GUARINO, N. (1998) Formal Ontology and Information Systems. *Proceedings of FOIS'98.* Trento, Italy, 6-8 June 1998. Amsterdam, , IOS Press.
GUARINO, N. & GIARETTA, P. (1995) Ontologies and Knowledge Bases :Towards a Terminological Clarification. Amsterdam.
GURUNINGER, M. & FOX, M. S. (1995) Methodology for the design and evaluation of ontologies. *In: Workshop on Basic ontological issues in knowledge sharing* Montreal, 1995.
NORIKO, H. & KHE, F. (2007) knowledge-sharing in online community of health-care professional. *Information Technology & People* 20, pp.235-261.
HANSON, C. W. (1968) The first ten years. *The Information Scientist,,* 2, pp1-2.
HARTMANN, N. (1952) *The new ways of ontlogy,* Chicago.
HERRE, H. (2010) The Ontology of Mereological Systems: A Logical Approach. IN POLI, R. & SEIBT, J. (Eds.) *Theory and Applications of Ontology: Philosophical Perspectives.* London ,New York, Springer.
HERRING, S. C. (2008) Virtual community IN GIVEN(ED), L. M. (Ed. *Encyclopedia of Qualitative Research Methods.*
HILDRETH, P., KIMBLE, C., WRIGHT, P. & LUMINY, D. D. (1998) Computer mediated communication and Cops *Ethicomp'98.* Erasmus university.
HONG-YAN, Y., JIAN-LIANG, X., MO-JI, W. & JING, X. (2009) Development of domain ontology for e-learning course. *IEEE International Symposium on* vol.1, pp.501-506.
HORRIDGE, M. (2011) A Practical Guide To Building OWL Ontologies Using Protege 4 and CO-ODE Tools. Edition 1.3 ed., The University Of Manchester.
HORRIDGE, M. & PATEL-SCHNEIDER, P. F. (2009) OWL 2 Web Ontology Language Manchester Syntax. IN NOTE, W. C. W. G. (Ed.
HORROCKS, I., PATEL-SCHNEIDER, P. & VAN HARMELEN, F. (2003) From SHIQ and RDF to OWL: The making of web ontology language. *Web Semantics* pp: 7-26.
HU, L. & WENG, J. (2010) Geo-ontology integration Based on Category Theory *International conference on computer Design And applications (ICCDA2010).*
HUBER, G. P. & DAFT, R. L. (1987) *The Information Environments of Organizations,* Newbury Park, Ca.: Sage Publications.
HUSSERL, E. (1970) *Logical Investigations,* London, Routledge and Kegan Paul.
INGWERSEN, P. (1992) Information and Information Science in context. *Libri,* 42, pp. 99-153.
JANSEN, W. & STEENBAKKERS, H.(2002) knowledge management and virtual communities IN WHITE, D. (Ed.) knowledge mapping and management. IRM press.
JEPSEN, T. C. (2009) Just what is an ontology. *IEEE computer society,* 11, pp.11-23.

JOHNSON, M. & DAMPNEY, C. N. G. (2001) On category theory as a (meta) ontology for information systems research. *Proceedings of the international conference on Formal Ontology in Information Systems - Volume 2001* Ogunquit, Maine, USA.

KABILAN, V. (2007) Ontology for Information Systems (O4IS) Design Methodology: Conceptualizing, Designing and Representing Domain Ontologies. *School of Information and Communication Technology, Department of Computer and Systems Sciences.* The Royal Institute of Technology.

KOCH, M. (2000) Learning from civilization. Line Zine. http://linezine.com/3.1/features/mklic.htm [accessed :15.04.2009].

KRIVOV, S., VILLA, F., WILLIAMS, R. & WU, X. (2007a) On visualization of OWL ontologies. *Semantic Web* Springer.

KRIVOV, S., WILLIAMS, R. & VILLA, F. (2007b) GrOWL: A tool for visualization and editing of OWL ontologies. *Web Semantics: Science, Services and Agents on the World Wide Web,* 5, pp.54-57.

KRÖTZSCH, M. HITZLER, P. EHRIG, M. & SURE, Y. (2005) Category theory in ontology research: Concrete gain from an abstract approach. Karlsruhe, Germany, Institut AIFB, Universität Karlsruhe,

LABORATORY, E. I. (2011) TOVE Ontology Project. University of Toronto. Toronto, http://www.eil.utoronto.ca/enterprise-modelling/tove/ [Accessed : 30.06.2011].

LAWVERE, W. (1969) Adjointness in foundations. *Dialectica,* 23, pp: 281-296.

LEIMEISTER, J., SCHWEIZER, K. & LEIMEISTER, S. (2008) Do virtual communities matter for the social support of patients? Antecedents and effects of virtual relationships in online communities. *Information Technology And people,* 21, pp.350-374.

LENAT, D. & GUHA, R. (1990) Building Large Knowledge-Based Systems: *Representation and Inference in the Cyc Project*, .Addison-Wesley.

LIN, F.-R., LIN, S.-C. & HUANG, T.-P. (2008) Knowledge sharing and creation in a teachers' professional virtual community. *Computers & Education,* 50, pp.742-756.

LLLUM, S. F., IVANOV, S. H. & LIANG, Y. (2010) Using virtual communities in tourism research. *Tourism Management,* 31, pp.335-340.

LOMBARDI, V. (2003) Noise between stations meta data glossary. http://www.noisebetweenstations.com/personal/essays/metadata glossary/meta data glossary.html [Accessed : 19-9-2011].

LOZANO-TELLO, A. & GOMEZ-PEREZ, A. (2004) ONTOMETRIC: A Method to Choose the Appropriate Ontology. *Journal of Database Management (JDM),* 15, pp.1-18.

LU, Y. & YANG, D. (2011) Information exchange in virtual communities under extreme disaster conditions. *Decision Support Systems,* pp.529-538.

MACHLUP, F. & MANSFIELD, U. (1983) *The Study of Information,* New York, Wiley.

MAEDCHE, A. (2003) *Ontology learning for the semantic Web* Kluwer Academic publishers.

MAEDCHE, A. & STAAB, S. (2002a) Measuring Similarity between Ontologies. *EKAW '02 Proceedings of the 13th International Conference on Knowledge Engineering and Knowledge Management. Ontologies and the Semantic Web* Springer-Verlag London, UK.

MAEDCHE, A. D. (2002) *ontology learning for the semantic web*, Kluwer Acadmic

MAEDCHE, E. & STAAB, S. (2002b) Measuring Similarity between Ontologies *in Proceedings of the European Conference on Knowledge Acquisition and Management (EKAW).*

MALHOTRA, Y. (2002) Enabling knowledge exchanges for e-business communities. *Information Strategy.* http://www.brint.org/EnablingKnowledgeExchanges.htm [Accessed:15.06.2010].

MARKMAN, A. B. (1999) *Knowledge Representation* London, Lawrence erlbaum Associates.

MCCARTHY, J. (1980) Circumscription- A form of Non-Monotonic Reasoning. *Artificial Intelligence,* 5, pp.27-39.
MCDERMOTT, R. (1999) Nurturing three dimensional cops: How to get the most out of human networks. http://home.att.net/~discon/KM/Dimensions.pdf [Accessed:14.11.2009].
MCIIWAINE, I. & BROUGHTON, V. (2000) The classification Research Group: then and now. *Knowledge Organization,* 27, pp.195-199.
MCILWAINE, I. C. (1997) The Universal Decimal Classification: Some Factors Concerning Its Origins, Development, and Influence. *Journal of the American Society for Information Science.,* 48, pp.331-339.
MERRILL, G. H. (2011) Ontology, ontologies, and science. *Humanities, Social Sciences and Law* Volume 30, pp. 71-83.
MIKSA, F. L. (1998) *The DCC, the universe of knowledge, and the post- modern library,* Albany, Network, Forst Press.
MILLS, H. & HEVNER, A. R. (1995) Box-structured requirements determination methods. Decision Support Systems, Volume 13, p.p 223-239.
MIZOGUCHI, R. (2003) Tutorial on ontological engineering. *New Generation Computing* 21, pp. 363-384.
MOENS, M.-F. (2006) *Information Extraction: algorithms and prospects in a retrieval context,* Springer.
MOHAMED, A. H., LEE, S. P. & SALIM, S. S. (2006) Managing Evolution in Software-Engineering Knowledge Management Systems *Digital Information Management,* 3, pp.19 - 24
MOMMERS, L. (2010) Ontologies in the Legal Domain. IN ·, R. P. & SEIBT, J. (Eds.) *Theory and Applications of Ontology: Philosophical Perspectives.* London New York, Springer.
MORBACH, J., WIESNER, A. & MARQUARDT, W. (2009) OntoCAPEis a large–scale ontology for chemical process engineering. Engineering Applications of Artificial Intelligence. *Computers & Chemical Engineering,* 20, pp.147-161.
MSEB (2010) Mathematical Science Education Board http://www7.nationalacademies.org/mseb/ [Accessed :27.11.2010].
MURILLO-OTHON. (2006) Searching for Virtual Communities of Practice in the discussion network. Bradford, Bradford.
NICOLAE, D. (1961) Information Science Syllabus and Teaching Practice within the Higher Education. *Georgia Institute of Technology.* (USA).
NIRENBERG, J. (1995) From team building to community building. *National Productivity Review,* pp.51 - 62.
NIRENBURG, S. & RASKIN, V. (2001) Ontological semantics, formal ontology and ambiguity. *proceedings of FOIS.*
NIRENBURG, S. & RASKIN, V. (2004) *Ontological semantics,* MIT Press, Cambridge.
NOLAN, T., BRIZLAND, R. & MACAULAY (2007) Individual trust and development of online business communities. *Information Technology and People,* 20, pp.53-71.
NONAKA, I. & KONNO, N. (1998) The concept of Ba: Building a Foundation for Knowledge Creation California Management Review.
NONAKA I., T., H. (1995) *The knowledge creating company: how Japanese companies create the dynamics of innovation.,* New York, oxford University press.
NOY, N. F. (2004) Semantic Integration: A Survey Of Ontology-Based Approaches. *SIGMOD Record* Vol. 33, pp 65 -70.
NOY, N. F. & MCGUINNESS, D. L. (2001) Ontology Development 101: A Guide to Creating Your First Ontology. http://liris.cnrs.fr/alain.mille/enseignements/Ecole_Centrale/What%20is%20an%20ontology%20and%20why%20we%20need%20it.htm [Accessed:15.11.2010].
NOY, N. F. & MUSEN, M. A. (2000) PROMPT: Algorithems and tools for automated ontology merging and alignment *17th National conference on Artificial Intelligence (AAAI'00).* Austin-Texas.

O'HARA, K., ALANI, H. & SHADBOLT, N. (2002) ONTOCOPI: Methods and Tools for Identifying Communities of Practice. *In: IFIP 17th World Computer Congress - TC12 Stream on Intelligent Information Processing, August 25-30,* . Montreal, Quebec, Canada., http://eprints.ecs.soton.ac.uk/6521/[Accessed: 04.07.2011].

OCLC (2010) Dewey Decimal Classification (DDC) system., http://www.oclc.org/dewey/versions/ddc22print/intro.pdf [Accessed: 20.4.2011].

OGDEN, C. K., RICHARDS, I. A., MALINOWSKI, BRONISLAW & COROOKSHANK, F. G. (1949) *The meaning of meaning : a study of the influence of language upon thought and of the science of symbolism,* London, Routledge & Kegan Paul.

PANTELI, N. & DUNCAN, E. (2004) Trust and Temporary Virtual Teams: alternative explanations dramaturgical relationships. *Information Technology and people,* 17, pp.423-441.

PATTUELLI, M. C. (2011) Modeling a domain ontology for cultural heritage resources: A user-centered approach. *Journal of the American Society for Information Science and Technology,* 62, pp.314-342.

PEREZ-SOLTERO, A., SANCHEZ-SCHMITZ, G., BARCELO-VALENZUELA, M., PALMA-MENDEZ, J. T. & MARTIN-RUBIO, F. (2006) Ontologies as Strategy to Represent Knowledge Audit Outcomes. *INTERNATIONAL JOURNAL OF TECHNOLOGY, KNOWLEDGE AND SOCIETY,* 2, pp 43-53.

PETERSEN, T. (1994) Art & architecture thesaurus. New York: Oxford University Press. ,http://www.getty.edu/research/tools/vocabularies/index.html [Accessed : 26.11.2010].

PINTO, H. & MARTINS, J. (2001) A methodology for ontology inegration. *International Conference on Knowledge CaptureK-CAP'01* Victoria, British Canada.

POLANYI, M. (1974) *Personal knowledge: toward a past-critical philosophy,* Chicago, The University of Chicago Press.

POLI, R. (2002) Ontological methodology. International Journal of Human-Computer Studies, 56, pp.639-664.

POLI, R. (2003) Descriptive, formal and formalized ontologies, university of Trento' Husserl's Logical Investigations Reconsidered- Dordrect, pp.183-210.

POLI, R. (2010) Ontology: The Categorial Stance. IN POLI, R. & SEIBT, J. (Eds.) Theory and Applications of Ontology: Philosophical Perspectives. London ,New York, Springer.PORRA, J. & PARKS, M. M. (2006) Sustainable virtual communities : suggestions from the colonial model. Springer-verlag 4, pp.309- 341.

PORZEL, R. & MALAKA, R. (2004) A Task-based Approach for Ontology Evaluation. *In: Proc. of ECAI 2004 Workshop on Ontology Learning and Population* Valencia, Spain: August 2004 . .

POWER, D. J. (2000) The decision support system glossary. *DSS Resources.com.* http://dssresources.com/glossary/[Accessed:07.04.2011].

PRIETO-DIAZ, R. (2003) A faceted approach to building ontologies *Information Reuse and Integration IRI 2003.* IEEE International Conference . .

PROTÉGÉ (2011a) Welcome to Protégé http://protege.stanford.edu/doc/faq.html [Accessed :20.10.2011].

PROTÉGÉ (2011b) What is protégé? , http://protege.stanford.edu/overview/ [Accessed: 02.05.2009].

RANGANATHAN, S. R. (1962) *Elements of library classification* New York: Asia Publishing House.

ROBERTS, J. (2000) From know-how to show-how? Questioning the role of information and communications technologies in knowledge transfer. *Technology Analysis & Strategic Management,* 12, pp. 429-443.

ROBERTS, J. (2006) Limits to Communities of Practice. *Journal of Management studies* 43, pp. 624-639.

ROBERTS & AMIN, A (2008) Knowing in action: Beyond communities of practice. *Research policy,* 37, pp. 353-369.

SABOU, M., WORE, C., GOBLE, C. & MISHNE, G. (2005) Learning domain ontologies for web service descriptions; an experiment in bioinformatics. *www2005*. China, Japan.

SAWSAA, A. & LU, J. (2010) Ontocop: A virtual community of practice to create ontology of Information sciecne. *International Conference on Internet Computing (ICOMP'10)*. Las Vagas.

SAWSAA, A & LU, J (2011) Extracting Information Science concepts based on Jape Regular Expression. *In: WORLDCOMP'11The 2011 World Congress in Computer Science, Computer Engineering, and Applied Computing, 18-21 July 2011, .* Las Vegas, Nevada, USA

SCHWEN, T. M. & HARA, N. (2003) Community of Practice: A metaphor for online design. *The Information Society*, 27, pp.1-23.

SCIE (2010) Social care online subject taxonomy. http://www.scie.org.uk/publications/misc/taxonomy.asp [Accessed: 13.10.2010].

SENGE, P. (2003) Creating desired futures in a global economy. *Reflections*, 5, pp. 1-12.

SHADBOLT, N. & MILTON, N. (1999) From knowledge Engineering to knowledge management *British Journal of Management*, 10, pp.309-322.

SHARRATT, M. & USORO, A. (2003) Understanding knowledge –sharing in online communities of practice. *Electronic Journal of Knowledge Management* 1.

SHERA, J. H. (1983) Librarianship and information science. IN MANSFIELD, E. B. F. M. A. U. (Ed.) *In: The Study of Information.* New York, Wiley.

SHERA, J. H. & CLEVELAND, D. (1977) The history and foundation of information science. . *Annual Review of Information Science and Technology*, pp.250–275.

SMITH, B. (2003) Ontology and Information Systems. Oxford Blackwell http://ontology.buffalo.edu/ontology(PIC).pdf [Accessed:03.03.2011].

SOWA, J. (2005) Distinction, combination, and constraints,. *Proceeding of IJCAI-95 workshop on basic ontological issue in knowledge sharing.*

SOWA, J. F. (1984) *Conceptual Structures: Information Processing in Mind and Machine.*, Addison-Wesley.

SOWA, J. F. (2000) Knowledge Representation: Logical, Philosophical, and Computational Foundations. Brooks Cole Publishing Co. Pacific Grove, CA, http://www.jfsowa.com/krbook/ [Accessed: 11.08.2011].

SOWA, J. F. (2012) Ontologies Website. http://www.jfsowa.com/ontology/index.htm[Accessed: 01.04.2011].

NISO Standards- 2006 (2006) ANSI/NISO Z39.19 Guidelines for the Construction, Format, and Management of Monolingual Controlled Vocabularies.

IEEE 1074-1995, (1996) IEEE Standard for developing software life cycle process, IEEE Computer Society, New York (USA), 1996, ISBN: 0-7381-0414-0

IEEE 1074-2006, (2006) IEEE Standard for Developing a Software Project Life Cycle Process, IEEE Computer Society, New York (USA), 2006, ISBN: 0-73814957X

STEWART, T. (1997) The invisible key to success. *Fortune*, pp.173-176.

STONIER, T. (1990) *Information and the internal structure of the universe: An exploration into information physics.*, Springer.

SURE, Y., ERDMANN, M., ANGELE, J., STAAB, S., STUDER, R. & WENKE, D. (2002) OntoEdite: collaborative ontology engineering for the semanticweb. *First International Semantic Web Conference (ISWC'02)*. Sardinia ,Italy, pp.221-235.

SURE, Y., STAAB, S. & SUDER, R. (2008) *Ontology Engineering Methodology*, Springer.

SWARTOUT , B. E. A. (1997) Toward distributed use of large -scale ontologies. *AAAI Symposium on Ontology Engineering* Stanford, 1997.

TAPPEDIN (2010) Community of educational domain. http://tappedin.org/tappedin/ [Accessed: 20.10.2010].

TENNANT, N. (2007) Parts,Classes and Parts of Classes : An Anti-Realist Reading of Lewisian Mereology *The SAC conference on David Lewis's contributions to formal philosophy September 2007.* Copenhagen.

THRYSOE, L., HOUNSGAARD, L., DOHN, N. B. & WENGER, L. (2010) Participating in a community of practice as a prerequisite for becoming a nurse- Trajectories as final year nursing students. *Nurse Education in Practice*, pp.361-366.

TIFOUS, A , ADIL, E. & ROSE, D. (2007) Ontology for supporting communities of practice. Proceedings of the 4th international conference on Knowledge capture *K-CAP '07* http://dl.acm.org/citation.cfm?id=1298415 [Accessed:13.09.2010].

TILLETT, B. (2004) FRBR: A Conceptual Model for the Bibliographic Universe. Library of Congress Cataloging Distribution Service.

TROMBERT-PAVIOT, B., RODRIGUES, J., ROGERS, J. & BAUD, R. (2002) GALEN: A Third Generation Terminology Tool to support multipurpose National Coding System for surgical procedures. *International Journal of Medical Informatics*, 58, pp. 71- 85.

TSUI, E., WANG, W. M., CHEUNG, C. F. & LAU, A. S. M. (2009) A concept-relationship acquisition and inference approach for hierarchical taxonomy construction from tags. *Information Processing & Management*, 46, pp.44-57.

TUDORACHE, T., & et.al (2010) Ontology Development for the Masses: Creating ICD-11 in WebProtégé. 17th International Conference, EKAW 2010, Lisbon, Portugal.

TUDORACHE, T., & et.al (2011) WebProtégé: A Collaborative Ontology Editor and Knowledge Acquisition Tool for the Web. *Semantic Web* 11, pp.154-165.

TUOMI, I. (2000) Data is more than knowledge: Implications of the reversed knowledge hierarchy for knowledge management and organizational memory. *Journal of Management Information Systems* 16, pp103-117.

TURNER, J. G. & MACCLUSKY, T. L. (1994) The construction of formal specifications An introduction to the model- based and Algebraic Approaches, McGRAW-HILL England.

USCHOLD, M. & GRÜNINGER M. (1996) ONTOLOGIES: Principles, Methods and Applications *Knowledge Engineering Review* 11, pp. 93-155.

VARZI, A. (1996) Parts, wholes, and part-whole relations: The prospects of Mereotopology. *Data and knowledge Engineering* 20, pp.259–286.

VASCONCELOS, J., KIMBLE, C. & GOUVEIA, F. R. (2000) A design for a Group Memory system using Ontologies. . *Proceedings of 5th UKAIS Conference,*. University of Wales Institute,, Cardiff, McGraw Hill.

VOGRINCIC, S. & BOSNIC, Z. (2011) Ontology- based multi-label classification of economic articles. *ComSIS*, Vol8, pp.101-119.

VRANDECIC, D. (2010) Ontology Evaluation.

WALSH, M. & CRUMBIE, A. (2011) Initial evaluation of Stilwell:A multimedia virtual community. *Nurse Education in Practice*, pp.136-140.

WANG, Y.-H. & JHUO, P.-S. (2009) A Semantic Faceted Search with Rule-based Inference. *Proceedings of the International MultiConference of Engineers and Computer Scientists IMECS 2009, March 18 - 20, 2009,* . Hong Kong.

WEBSTER'S (2010) Definition of ontology. *Webster's third new international dictionary.* http://www.merriam-webster.com/dictionary/ontology [Accessed: 10.11.2010].

WEBSTER (2011) Defintion of Knowledge., http://www.merriam-webster.com/dictionary/knowledge?show=0&t=1316553888 [Accessed:05.09.2011].

WELTY, C., LEHMANN, F., GRUNINGER, G. & USCHOLD, M. (1999) Ontologies: Expert Systems all over again? IN AAAI-99, I. P. A. (Ed. *The National Conference on Artificial Intelligence.* Austin.

WENGER, E. (1998) *Communities of practice: Learning, Meaning, Identity*, Cambridge, Cambridge University Press.

WENGER, N., WHITE, J. & SMITH, K. (2005) Technology for communities. http://technologyforcommunities.com/ [Accessed: 30.10.2009].

WENGER , R. M., W SNYDER (2002) *Cultivating Communities of practice: A guide to managing knowledge*, Harvard Business School Press.

WIEDERHOLD, G. (1986) *Knowledge Base Management System.*, New York, Springer.

WIELINGA, B. J. & SCHREIBER, A. T. (1993) Reusable and searchable knowledge bases: a European perspective. *First international conference on building and sharing of very large-scaled knowlegde base.* Japan -Tokyo.

YAO, H., ORME, A. M. & ETZKORN, L. (2005) Cohesion Metrics for Ontology Design and Application. *Journal of Computer Science* 1, pp.107-113.

YU, L. (2011) *A Developer's Guide to the Semantic Web* Springer.

YUEXIAO, Z. (1988) Definitions and Sciences of Information. *Information Processing and Management,* 24, pp.479-491.

ZHANG, W. & WATTS, S. (2008) Online communities as communities of practice: a case study. *Journal of Knowledge Management,* 12, pp. 55-71.

ZINS, C. (2007a) Conceptions of, Information Science. *Journal of the American society for information science and technology,* 58, pp.335-350.

ZINS, C. (2007b) Conceptual Approaches for defining data, information, and knowledge. *Journal of the American society for information science and technology,* 58, pp.479-493.

ZINS, C. (2007c) Knowledge Map of Information Science. *Journal of the American society for information science and technology,* 58, pp.526-535.

ZINS, C. (2007d) Knowledge mapping: of information science. *Journal of the American society for information science and technology,* 58, pp.526-535.

Appendices

A. Evaluation Report
B. Taxonomy of IS
C. Glossary
D. Invitation Letter Ontocop
E. Information about participation process
F. List of Ontocop's participants
G. Initiation of participation process
H. Examples of collected Data
I. Letter sent to participants
J. Response emails from participants
K. Evaluation of the Taxonomy
L. Part of OIS ontology in OWL format
M. Lessons learned

Appendix A: Evaluation Report

Ontology of Information Science (OIS).

This report has been designed to evaluate Ontology of Information Science (OIS) from domain expert's' point of views. It aims to ensure the quality of terms and definitions in ontology and taxonomy of OIS.

Could you please indicate your level of satisfaction of each the following criteria.

On a scale of 1-5 within being 5 very satisfied or 1 dissatisfied, tick the appropriate number that indicate how satisfied you are.

Criteria	Description	satisfaction				
		5	4	3	2	1
consistent of ontology	referring to the absence of contradictory information in the ontology					
consistency of *is_a* and *part_of* relationships	Relations between concepts					
Completeness, *if there any:* • *Imprecisely defined;* • *Missing concepts;* • *Partially defined* • *Disjointnes properties* • *Redundancy of class, instance or relations*	referring to how well the ontology covers the whole domain of Information Science					
Clarity	referring to how effectively the intended meaning is commutated					
Generality	referring to the possibility of using the ontology for various					

	purpose inside the fixed domain				
Semantic data richness:	determine richness of ontology's conceptualization				

What do you like about this ontology? Please, write below

What do you think if it needs to be improved? Please, write below

What do you like to add or change any part of the domain knowledge?
Please, write below

Do you think it is a completed ontology? Please, write below

Do you think it is a Clear taxonomical structure of ontology? Please, write below

Do you think the ontology mappable to some specific upper ontologies?
Please, write below

Over all, I am satisfied with the ontology?

Strongly disagree	
disagree	
agree	
Strongly agree	

Appendix B: Taxonomy of IS

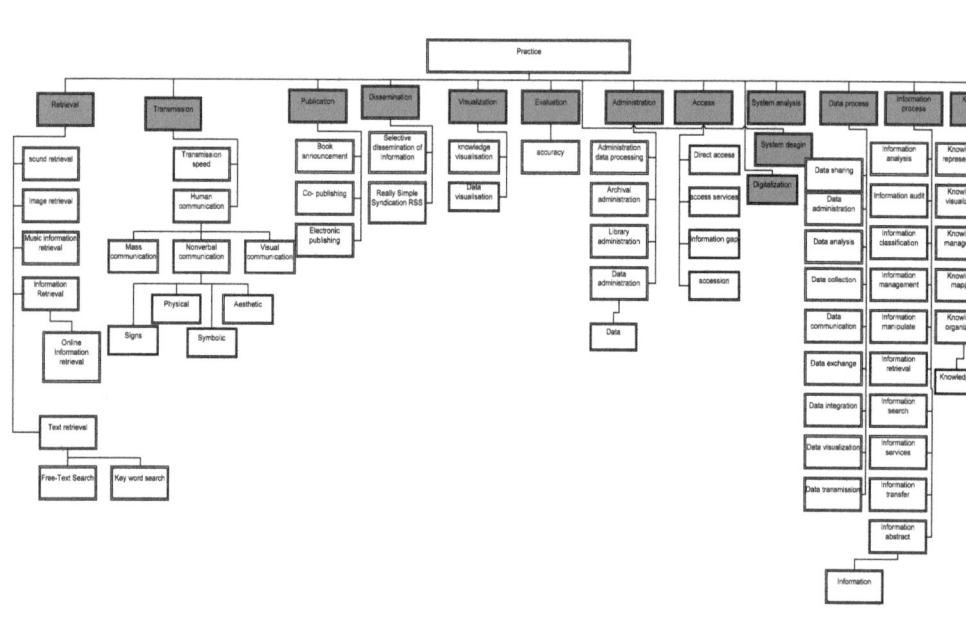

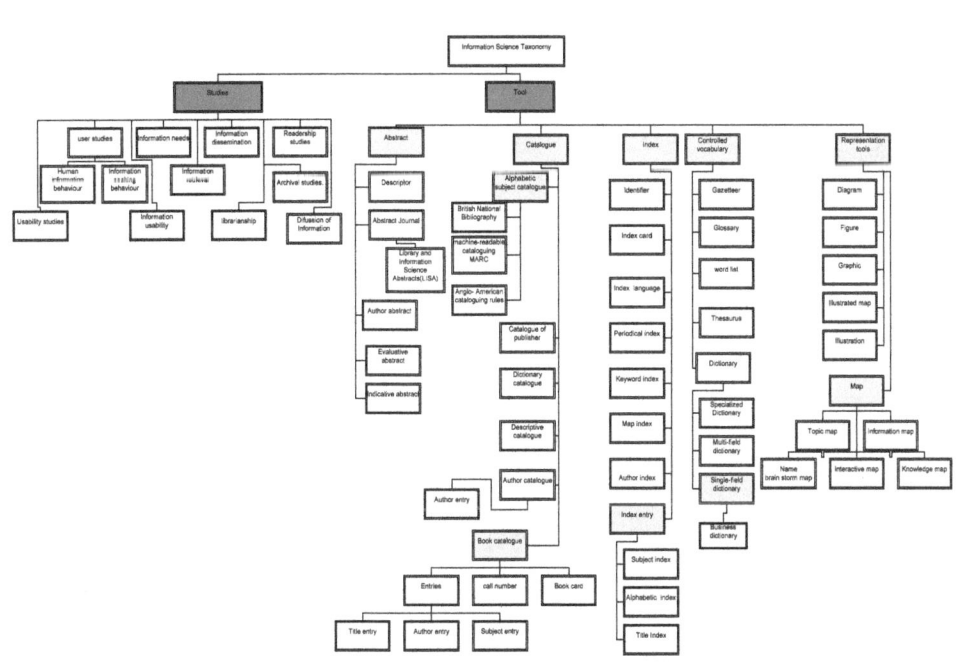

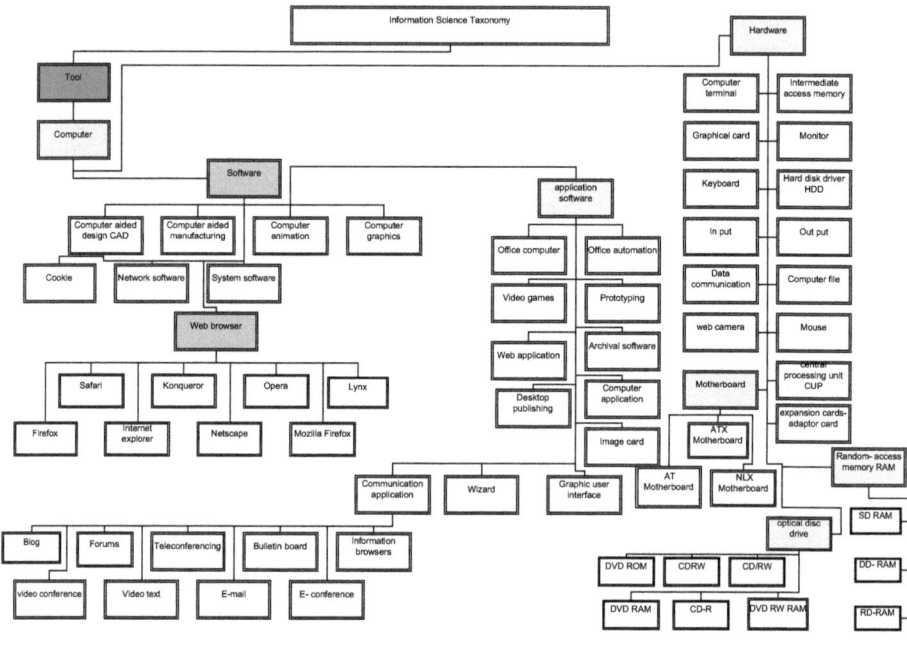

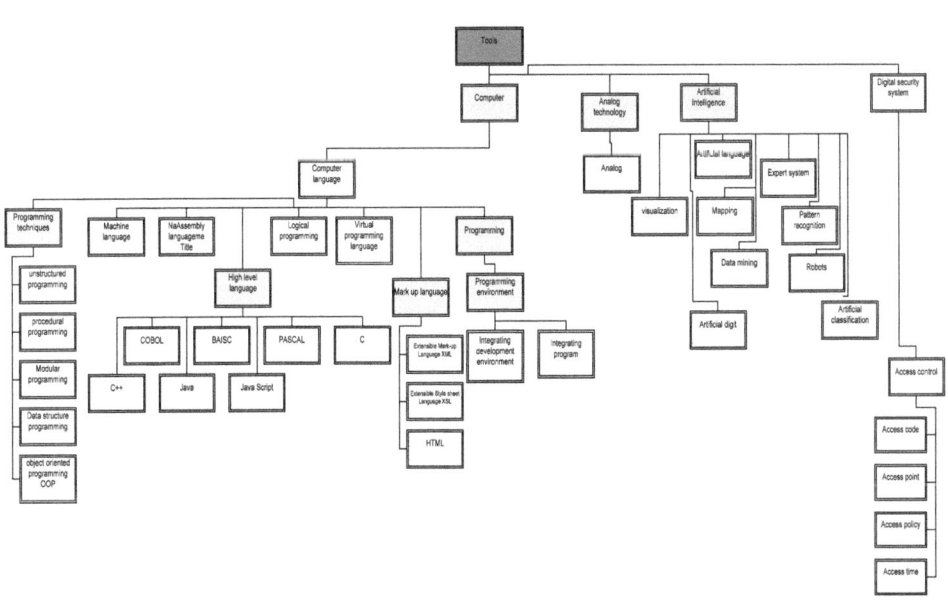

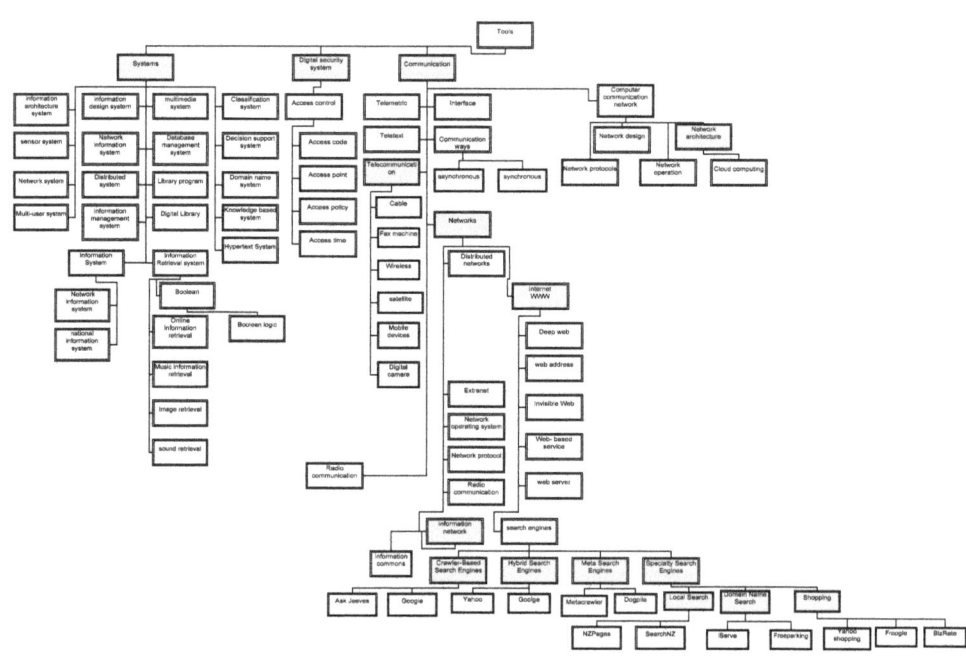

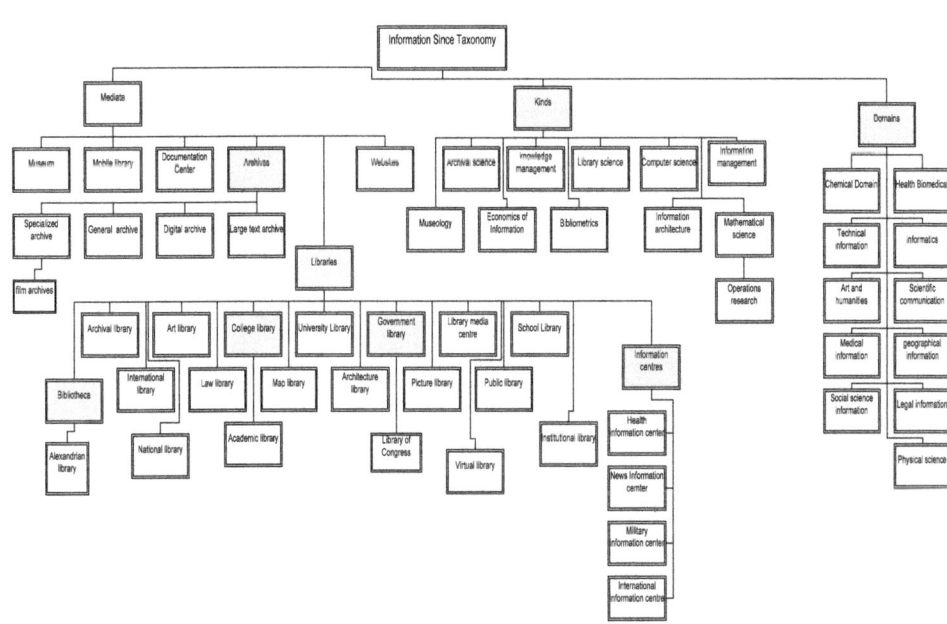

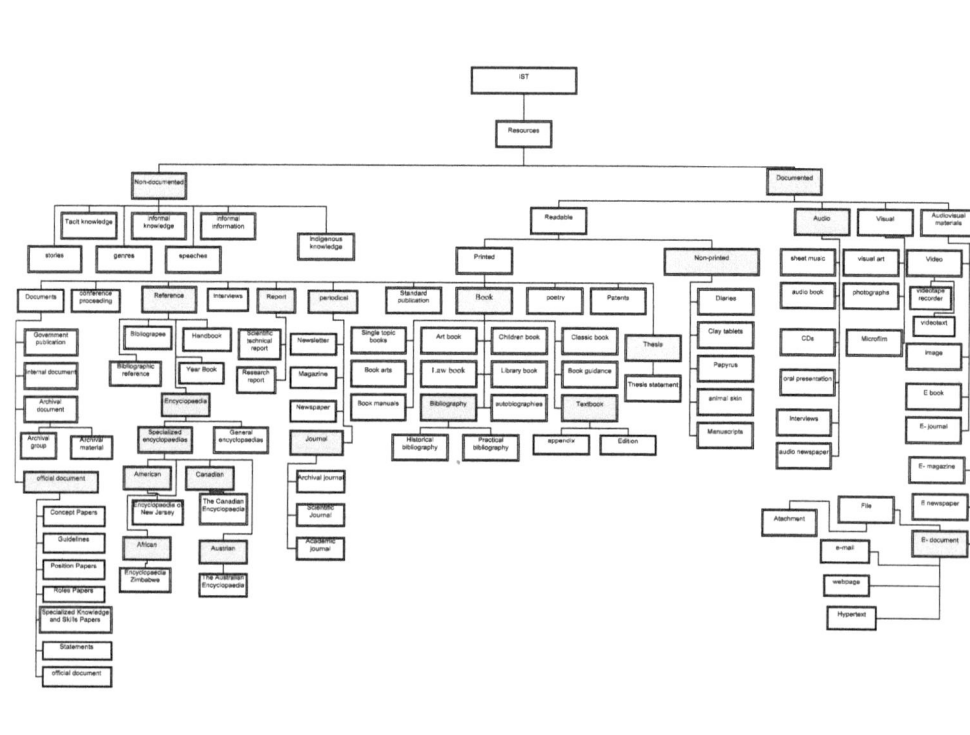

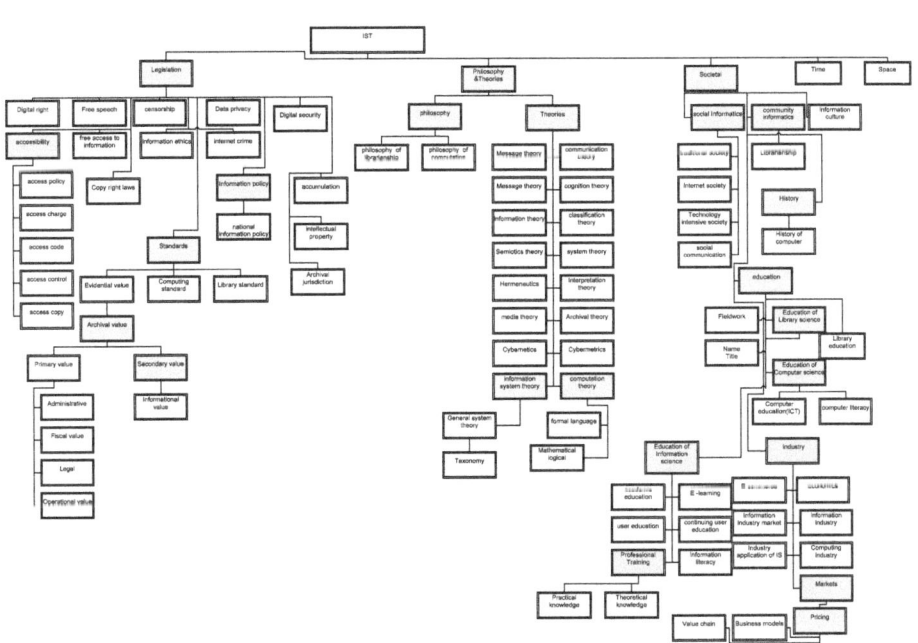

Appendix C: Glossary

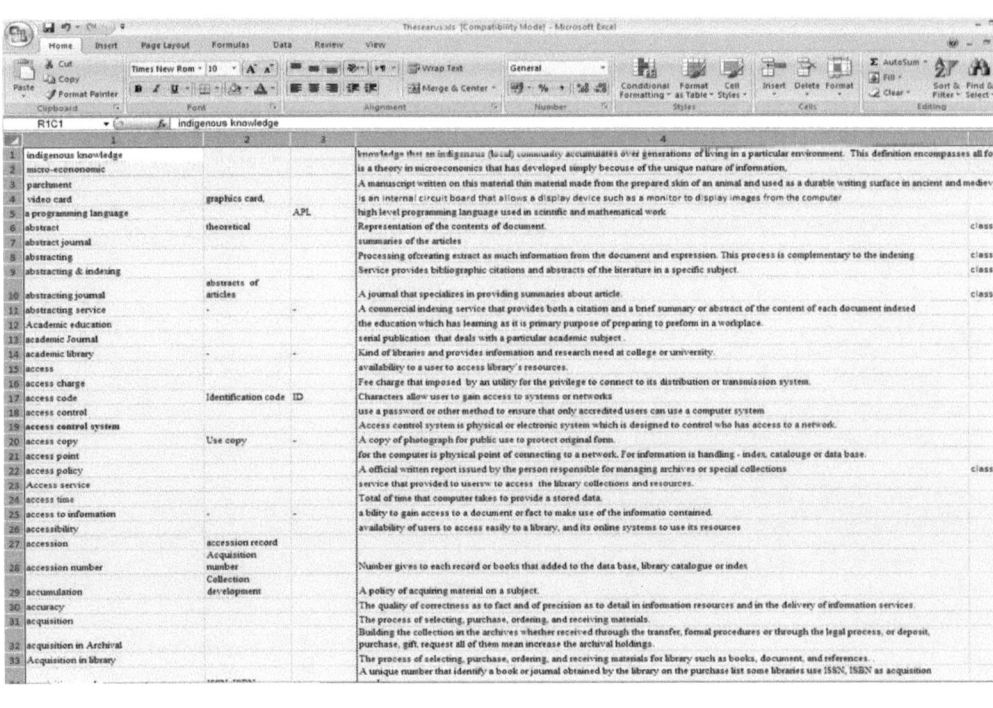

Appendix D: Invitation Letter Ontocop

Dear Sir/Madam,

I would like to invite you to join the virtual communities of practice of Information science (OntoCop), this website is a part of a PhD project. The purpose of this project is to build an ontology in the domain of Information Science (IS), which is machine readable. The essential goal is to clarify the ambiguous nature of concepts and terms in the domain. Furthermore, to develop the process of information retrieval.

The Link for the website is http://ontocop.hud.ac.uk. It contains several tools.

Currently:

Chat: enabling communication between participants to interact synchronously, and discuss topics by typing text.

Forum: enabling participants to communicate asynchronously by leaving messages and texts to be responded later by others.

Coming soon:

E-conference: will be added to assist synchronous communication by both text and visual interaction.

Voice chatting: will enable members to communicate efficiently verbally.

In the meantime, the researcher would like to let you know that the website is a result of her efforts (own project), and it is only at the primary stage. More updated versions will appear in the near future, adding more capabilities and tools as indicated above. You will be informed what extent the ontology has developed. Feedback from you would be welcome in order to rectify and clarify where needed.

As you know, this website is essentially has been designed for scientific research purposes, based on concepts of Communities of Practice (CoPs). Due to the importance of the mutual trust needed between the members, which will have a significant influence on the project progress and the community's success, we hope to gain your permission to create a profile for each member. Each member will have a specific page to provide information about them to be thus creating a directory for all members. This will allow participants to learn more about their colleagues in the field. If you agree to be included in this, please let me know.

Note that the website just deals with experts, scientists, scholars and researchers in the information science domain to ensure the validity of the ontology. Others from outside the domain will not be permitted.

Due to the fact that the website is still in the primary stages, if you find delay on downloading as (chatting software, e.g.) you could use the Firefox browser. According to our research Firefox is faster than other browsers to active the web site.

Finally, here is some guidance to explain how to start interaction through the website:

- Register as a member in the member profile page.
- Review the calendar which contains a regular basis of topics for discussion and the dates (which will be update).
- Register in the forum and wait for activation which will be sent to your e-mail.
- Start participating (If unsure where to start, see the categories in the forum and select which topic is familiar with or suggest new one.

Thank you for your cooperation and I am looking forward to meeting you in the OntoCop

Ahlam Sawsaa
PhD Research Student
School of Computing & Engineering
University of Huddersfield
United Kingdom
a.sawsaa@hud.ac.uk

Appendix E: Information about participation process

Process of inviting to Ontocop

Data	Progress
9.12.2009	Invite people to participate in ontocop1213 emails
15.12.2010	Invite participants to discuss online , but Time zone was the problem
28.01.2010	23 email
01.02.2010	103 emails
02.02.2010	45 emails
03.02.2010	53 emails
07.02.2010	-Prepare some topics to discuss through ontocop- send emails to ensure participants are registered in the forum .(30) participants such as Nature of IS-The main concepts in the domain.-Theory of IS
09.02.2010	Send 30 emails which titled How to getting started
10.02.2010	24 emails
02.03.2010	30 email re-encourage them to register at the form
09.03.2010	Resend emails to inform people about the topic of discussion
10.03.2010	Create member profile page
11.03.2010	Send emails to members to take permission
12.03.2010	Thankful for their interest
06.04.2010	Update the discussion topic by send members question to raise the discussion with a link of diagram uploaded on the ontology page of website
17.05.2010	Calling part of participants by phone
18.05.2010	Calling the reset of them in USA
21.05.2010	Send emails to members for asking them to use their publications.

Appendix F: List of Ontocop's participants

ID	First name	Last name	Company	Job title	Email	Tel	Fax
1.	Reyad	Binzabiah	Huddersfield University	Research student	rkblib@yahoo.com		
2.	Mark	Perry	Brunel Uni.	Senior lecturer	mark.perry@brunel.ac.uk	44 (0)1895 266008	+44 (0)1895 269732
3.	Mahmood S	Ismael	Mosul Un.	Professor	mahmoodismaeel@yahoo.com		
4.	Marti	Heyman	iScool Drexel	Adjunct Faculty	marti@mkheyman.com	-	-
5.	Rupert	Ward	Huddersfield Un.	Head of Department: Informatics	rupert.ward@hud.ac.uk		
6.	Pascal	Pein	Huddersfield Un.	Research student	r.p.pein@hud.ac.uk		
7.	Julie	Wilkinson	Huddersfield Un.		j.wilkinson@hud.ac.uk		
8.	Chaim	Zins			chaimzins@gmail.com		
9.	Anne	Gilliand			gilliland@gseis.ucla.edu		
10.	Mohamed	Salahat	Huddersfield Un.		mohamedsalahat@yahoo.com m.salahat@hud.ac.uk		
11.	Samer	Saed	Tikrit Un.-Iraq	Assistant professor	Samersaed20012002@yahoo.com		
12.	Joan	Lu	Huddersfield Un.	Reader in Informatics	j.lu@hud.ac.uk		

3.	Judy	Jeng	Univ. Of clarion	Assistant professor	judyjeng@comcast.net jjeng@clarion.edu	814-393-2469	
4.	Bhojaraju	Gunjal	Karnataka- India	K.M. consultant	Bhojaraju [dot] G@gmail .com		
5.	Rea	Gaitanou	Athens-Greece	c	rgaitanou@gmail.com		
6.	Mohammed	Allehaibi	Umm Al-Qura Un. Makka	Assistant professor	انتظار رد	0096625501000	
7.	Donald	Kraft	Louisiana State Univ. SLIS	Adjunct Professor	kraft@csc.lsu.edu	225-578-2253	
8.	Christos	Papatheodorou	Dep. Of Archive and Library science Lonian-Greece	Reader	c.papatheodorou@dcu.gr papatheodor@ianio.gr		
19.	Talal	Azzuhairi	Almustansiryah Un.	Assistant professor	talalalzuhairi@yahoo.com		
20.	Mohamed	Aliwi			Mohamedaliwi@yahoo.com		
21.	Ray	Lyons			raylyons@gmail.com		
22.	Michael	Buckland	Berkeley iSchool	Professor Emeritus	buckland@ischool.berkeley.edu	(510) 642 3159 - skpy	(510) 642 5814.
23.	Anthony	Debons			debons@lis.pitt.edu		

#	First	Last	Institution	Title	Email	Phone	Fax
24.	Andrea	Prati			Andrea.prati@unimore.it		
25.	Nancy	Zimmerman	Univ. Of South Carolina- SLIS	Associate Professor	npz@sc.edu	(803) 777-1215	
26.	Feili	Tu	Univ. Of South Carolina- SLIS	Associate Professor	feilitu@sc.edu	803 777-1026 skype	(803) 777-7938
27.	Ellen	Pearlstein	Univ. Of California- SLIS	Associate Professor	epearl@ucla.edu	(310) 794-4940	
28.	Anne	Gilliland	Univ. Of California- SLIS	Chair and Professor	gilliland@gseis.ucla.edu		
29.	Carl	Drott	The iSchool at Drexel	Associate Professor	drott@drexel.edu	+1 (215) 895-2487	+1 (215) 895-2494
30.	Julia	Gelfand	Arizona uni	Adjunct Faculty	jgelfand@uci.edu	949-824-4971 949-824-4971	
31.	Brain	Atkinson			Atkinson@u.arizona.edu		
32.	Rahim	Aboud			Rahim_aboud@yahoo.com		
33.	Blaise	Cronin	Editor of Journal of American society for IS & technology		bcronin@indiana.edu		
34.	Loriene	Roy			loriene@ischool.utexas.edu		

35.	Giannis	Tsakonas	University of Patras, Greece		john@lis.upatras.gr		
36.	Constanti	a Kakali	Panteion University		nkakal@panteion.gr	http://www.ionio.gr/~nkakali/index_en.htm	
37.	Angelos	Mitrelis	Patras, Greece		angelo@lis.upatras.gr		
38.	Abdelhamed	Nada	King Faisal Un.	Assistant Professor	Dr.Abdelhamednada@Yahoo.Com abnida@kfu.edu.sa hamednda@aun.edu.eg	+966509294670 002- 5677320-010-	
39.	Saleh	Mohammed AL-Turki	King Faisal Un.	Assistant Professor	smalturki@kfu.edu.sa	5887082 Ext:138	
40.	ALI	SAAD ALALI	Umm alqura	Assistant Professor	asaali@uqu.edu.sa asaalali@gmail.com	(02) 5501000 تحويله 580	
41.	Mohamed	Menai,	King Saud Un.	Associate Professor	menai@KSU.EDU.SA	4670687	

Appendix G: Initiation of participation process

Dear Sir

We are going to discuss the topic of the nature of Information science through Onto Cop Forum during this week 08-14/02/2010. So, please, could you join us and leave your comments, statements or articles on it.

The nature of Information science

There are multiple perspectives of natural of Information science, e.g.(G. Salton,1969) point out the Information science contains three parts as followed:
1. The study of Information and data.
2. The study of computer organization
3. The study of automatic text processing system purview of statute

While,(C.Zins,2007),called Information Science by this name is problem, which contains three related concepts; information, data and knowledge. And he suggested redefining it by knowledge science rather than information science.

So far, there is no full agreement on nature of information science, perhaps because of the nature of science, which is variable and highly diversity in its meaning.

Also, Ingwersen, Peter (1994). Mentioned that the core of the Information science consists of :
1. Information seeking.
2. Information retrieval
3. Information management
4. Information retrieval systems design
5. Informatics

Please, give your opinion about it.

To participate, I hope that you kindly register in the forum (Onto Cop) to activate your account and to begin participation. For further information on registration read (Getting started) by click on this link http://ontocop.hud.ac.uk/index.php

For registration in the Forum click on this link. .
http://ontocop.hud.ac.uk/phpBB3/ucp.php?mode=register

With best regards
Ahlam Sawsaa

Getting started

Welcome to Onto Cop community. This page gives you the basic knowledge that you need to use the forum effectively. If you encounter any difficulties with the discussion, contact the moderator from contact link from the main menu.

مرحبا بكم في المجتمع الافتراضيOnto Cop. هذه صفحة تتيح لك المعارف الأساسية التي أنت في حاجة الى استخدام المنتدى بشكل فعال. إذا كنت أنت تواجه أي صعوبات مع المنتدي، عليك الاتصال برئيس الجلسة.

Reading Discussions

Anyone with WWW access can read discussion on the forum. TO read discussions, navigate to the debate of interest by single clicking on the link from the list of tools,(Forum). Also you can navigate backwards using the navigation bars at the top of each page.
Otherwise, review our calendar, click on a subject category then read a discussion subject that appears in the Schedule, and log on to the "forum" by using your password.

قراءة النقاش فى المنتدى:
أي شخص لديه الانترنت www يمكنه قراءة المناقشات في المنتدى. من يرغب فى قراءة المناقشات و الإبحار للنقاش عليك النقر على وصلة منتدي (Forum)من قائمة الأدوات فى الصفحة الرئيسية. كما يمكنك الرجوع باستخدام زر الارجاع في أعلى كل صفحة. وايضاً يمكنك مراجعة التقويم(Calendar)واختيار الموضوع category ثم تلا ذلك مناقشة الموضوع الذي ترغب فى المشاركة بعد التسجيل في "المنتدى" باستخدام كلمة السر الخاصة بكم بعد تفعيل الاشتراكز

Contributing to Discussions

To add a topic to an existing discussion, click on "new topic" box at the top in the Forum. After writing your contribution click on "submit". Before submit the topic you need to create a user account (user name and password) follow the instructions on the forum to supply the necessary credentials for posting. Where available, you can click on -New Topic -botten to start a new discussion. This will add a subtopic with the subject you specify and start a conversation with initial message that you specify. After filling in the subject line, post a message.

المشاركة فى النقاش:
لأضافة موضوع إلى الموضوعات الموجودة فى المنتدى أنقر على المربع "new topic" الموجود فى المنتدي، بعد أن كتابة إسهامكم أنقر على "إرسال"(submit). بعد إنشاء (اسم المستخدم كلمة السر) ياتباع التعليمات المتعلقة بذلك فى المنتدى.
إذاسبق وان قمت بالتسجيل , يمكنك النقر علي new topic للبدء من جديد بالنقاش والبدأ في محادثة مع المشتركين برسالة من سيادتكم..

http://ontocop.hud.ac.uk/index.php

Appendix H: Examples of collected Data

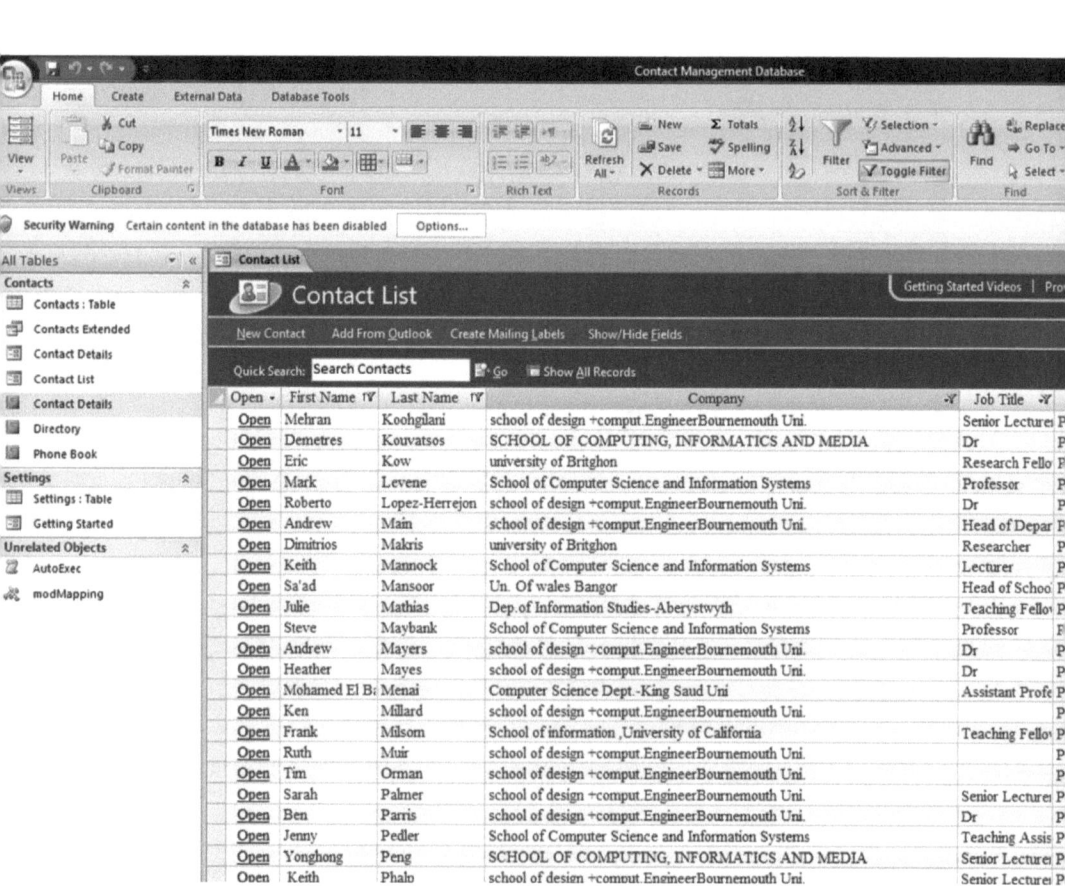

Appendix I: Letter sent to participants

Dear Sir /Madam

I am a PhD researcher in the initial stages of developing an experimental Virtual Community of Practice (VCop) for Information Scientists (IS).

I have established from my initial literature review that some of the key benefits for VCops are typically:

- The ability to meet in a virtual space and communicate via the Internet
- That people are brought together, by means of a technical platform, who might never meet in reality
- That the very existence of the VCop can aid identification of an idea or task Groups can self-select
- That member's interests are usually related to a specific Knowledge Domain.
- Members can establish social relationships or a sense of belonging to the group.

As an information scientist myself with nine years of experience in Information and documentation centres, then as a lecturer and researcher in the Department of Library and Information Science at the University of Garyounis [Libya], I am very aware of how collaborative and co-operative information scientists can be.

Therefore, I am canvassing the support of some four hundred IS experts worldwide to gain their agreement in principle, including yours, to join my experimental VCop.

Please complete the following details.

What would you regard as most beneficial in a VCop for IS?

Perhaps, for starters, some key topics of discussion –e.g. Nature of Information Science (IS) as a domain, (please highlight all that apply):

>Conceptual approaches to define: Data, Information, knowledge, wisdom.
>Boundaries of IS
>Theory of IS
>Resource of IS e.g. Primary & secondary resource
>Knowledge workers
>Technologies of IS
>Users
>Other: Please state:
>...

....

Please re-confirm your contact email addresses below IF you agree in principle to be contacted again by me with a personal invitation to join my VCoP:

....

(All data will be held securely on university servers only and used solely for the purpose of this PhD research and the VCop, as per UK Data Protection Act (1998))

Yours Faithfully

Ahlam Sawsaa
PhD Research Student
School of Computing & Engineering
University of Huddersfield
Queens gate
HUDDERSFIELD
HD1 3DH
United Kingdom
a.sawsaa@hud.ac.uk
Mobile: +44 (0)7887 696309

Appendix J: Response emails from participants

1. ZIMMERMAN, NANCY [NPZ@sc.edu]

Because of the time demands of my position as Associate Dean, I will not
be able to participate in your study. If you wish to include someone
from our university, I recommend Dr. Feili Tu, an associate professor in
LIS. Her area of expertise is medical informatics and reference,
including virtual reference and Second Life. Her email is:
TUF@mailbox.sc.edu should you wish to ask her to participate.
Nancy P. Zimmerman, PhD
Associate Dean for Academic Affairs
The Graduate School
University of South Carolina
901 Sumter Street, 3rd Floor
Columbia, SC 29208
Voice: (803) 777-9086
FAX: (803) 777-8749
Email: npz@sc.edu

---

2. Ellen Pearlstein [epearl@ucla.edu]

Dear Ahlam Sawsaa,

My primary field is in conservation and preservation, so I am not sure
that I am the best person to participate in your VCop. Please let me
know if you wish for me to forward this to the Information Studies
students at UCLA so they may elect to participate.

All best,

Ellen Pearlstein

On Mon, 2 Nov 2009 17:5

My biggest question about your proposal is why? Why do any of these
topics need discussing and what good would it do for the practice of
information science?

Take for example: "Conceptual approaches to define: Data, Information,

knowledge, wisdom." I am quite sure that you and I would not agree on
the definition of these terms, but what is the disadvantage in that?
Would either of us do better Information Science if we somehow had the
"right" definitions?

Or consider "Technologies of IS" There are far too many and they are
far too diverse. For example, just now I am interested in a particular
set of add-ons for a Windows-based Apache server. I am interested
because a colleague wants to try some collaborative software that needs
these tools. In another two weeks I'll be done and on to something
else. If I find out anything worthwhile, I'll put a document on my
website. If someone wants to know they can Google it.

If you want me as a participant, I'll be happy to join, but most of
these topics sound vague and unachievable.

---

3. Carl Drott [drott@drexel.edu]

Ahlam Sawsaa wrote:
> Dear Drott,
>
> I am a PhD researcher in the initial stages of developing an experimental Virtual Community of Practice (VCop) for Information Science (IS).
> I have established from my initial literature review that some of the key benefits for VCops are typically:
> ·   The ability to meet in a virtual space and communicate via the Internet
> ·   That people are brought together, by means of a technical platform, who might never meet in reality
> ·   That the very existence of the VCop can aid identification of an idea or task Groups can self-select
> ·   That member's interests are usually related to a specific Knowledge Domain.
> ·   Members can establish social relationships or a sense of belonging to the group.
>
> As an expert in the field of information science myself with nine years of experience in Information and documentation centres, then as a lecturer and researcher in the Department of Library and Information Science at the University of Garyounis [Libya], I am

> very aware of how collaborative and co-operative information experts can be.
>
> Therefore, I am canvassing the support of some four hundred IS experts (IT, Computer science, Library and Information science, Information systems, Archives and documentation, Information management.....) worldwide to gain their agreement in principle, including yours, to join my experimental VCop.
> Please complete the following details.
>
> What would you regard as most beneficial in a VCop for IS?
> Perhaps, for starters, some key topics of discussion –e.g. Nature of Information Science (IS) as a domain, (please highlight all that apply):
>   Conceptual approaches to define: Data, Information, knowledge, wisdom.
>   Boundaries of IS
>   Theory of IS
>   Resource of IS e.g. Primary & secondary resource
>   Knowledge workers
>   Technologies of IS
>   Users
>   Other: Please state:

---

4. Judy Jeng [jjeng@clarion.edu]

Yes, I am willing to participate in your VCop.

Judy

Ahlam Sawsaa wrote:

5. ALI SAAD ALI ALALI [asaali@uqu.edu.sa]

Dear Ahlam Sawsaa
Wish you the success and I'll be happy to be part of this exciting experimental project.
Regards,
Ali AlAli

---

6. noreply@boxbe.com [noreply@boxbe.com]

Hello Ahlam Sawsaa,

You just sent me an email about "Invitation of participation".

I'll be more likely to see your email and future messages if you are on my priority Guest List.

Click here to be put on my Guest List

Thank you,
nzamanj@gmail.com

About this Notice
This courtesy notice is part of a free service to make email more reliable and useful. Boxbe (www.boxbe.com) uses your existing social network and that of your friends to keep your inbox clean and make sure you receive email from people who matter to you.

Say Goodbye to Email Overload
www.boxbe.com

---

7. Mark Perry [dr.mark.j.perry@googlemail.com]

I am happy to participate.

Mark Perry
(mark.perry@brunel.ac.uk)

---

8. Mohamed Menai, PhD. [menai@KSU.EDU.SA]

Ok, I agree.

Best wishes

Mohamed El Bachir Menai, PhD

http://faculty.ksu.edu.sa/menai

9. Lori Franklin [lfrankli@emporia.edu]

Hello Ahlam,

I am sending this e-mail reply to confirm particiapting in your VCop.

Sincerely,

Lori Franklin, Library Media Specialist
National Board Certified Teacher
Olathe East High School

---

10. Kraft, Donald H CIV USAF USAFA USAFA/DFCS [donald.kraft@usafa.edu]

I am happy to be involved but since I have retired my ability to do too much is limited. Don Kraft

Appendix K: Evaluation of the Taxonomy

Dear Members of Ontocop,

Providing your insight into what the facet structure should be, it helps to configure the Information Science (IS) Taxonomy. Information science is multidiscipline as remarked in the literature; many studies have investigated to identify this science. Information Science (IS) has a fundamental root of its theory which is emerged from other sciences such as: Library science, computer science and archival science.

1. In this part which is the High level of the taxonomy of assessment could you please, let me know to any extent you are agreeing with this division. Also, check the fundamental facets at the general level of Information science ontology, by
    a. *revising or adding further concepts*
    b. *Formulated it in a new schema. which are namely :*

---

1. Actors

2. Method

3. Practice

4. Studies

5. Mediate; (between actors)

6. Kinds, (internal Disciplines)

7. Domains; (external relations)

8. Resources

9. Legislation

10. Philosophy & theories

11. Societal

12. Time

13. Space

2. What you think about the categorizing Actors, could you please, organize them in a logical order, if you are disagreeing.

Actors						
	person					
		User				
			Group			
					Research group	
					User group	
					Domain	
					community	
					Culture	
			Individual			
					End user	
					End-user search	
					Library user	
					Flicker user	
					Researcher	
					Lurker	
		Employee				
			Archivists			
			Author			
			Blogger			
			Borrower			
			Publisher			
			Computer expert			
			Contributor			
			Copyist			
			Cyberian			
			Documentarian			
			Documentray editing			
			Operator			
			Translator			
			Mentoring			
			Career outlook			
			Graphical environment manager			
			Editor			
			Journalism			
			Knowledge worker			
			Illustrator			
			Information specialists			
					Information broker	
					Information manager	
					Information specialist	
			Libarian			
					Library assistant	
					Library cooperation	
					Library director	
					Library staff	
					Indexer	
					bibliographer	
					audiovisual librarian	
					Reference Libaraian	
					school librarian	
					special librarian	
					public librarian	
					academiclibrarian	
					Childern librarian	
	Institution					
		Orgnizations				
		Funding agents				
		service provider				
		Associations				
			Professinal association			
					Library association	
						American library association ALA
						Canadian Library AssociationCLA

Methods						
	Known					
		Quantitative				
			Bibliometrics			
			Informatics			
			Algorithm			
			Archival methodology			
			Information Economic			
			webmetrics			
			Boolean logic			
		Qualitative				
			General system theory			
			Citation search			
			Data structure			
			Domain analysis			
			Subject analysis			
				subject heading		
						Library of congress heading database
				subject heading types		
					Topical	
					Name	
					Title	
	Unknown				Genre	
		new emarging by using new technique				

tice (activities)	activities that actors doing when they praper information						
	Manipulation						
	Information service	Conventional					
			Bibliographic service				
			Loan				
					Inter library loan		
					Internal domestic borrowing		
			Archival reference service				
			classification				
					classification schemes		
						Colon classification	
						Dewey Decimalclassification DDC	
						Universal Decimal classification UDC	
		Non-conventional				Library of Congress classification LCC	
			Abstracting			Bibliographic classification BC	
			Indexing				Bibliographic citation
			Ask librarian				Call number
			Current Awareness				
			Digital reference				
	Acquisition						
		Acquesation sections					
			acquisition in Library				
					Acquisition number		
						International standard Book NumberISBN	
						International standard Serial NumberISSN	
					Acquisition policy	Access list	
						Book selecting	
					Acquisition way		
						Exchange	
						Deposit formal documents	
						Purchase	
			acquisition in Archival				
		Preservation					
			Digital preservation				
			Traditional preservation				
	Storage						
		Data storage representation					
	Retreival						
		Traditional					
			Thesauras				
			Index				
					Author index		
			catalogue				
					Author catalouge		
						Author entry	
					Book catalogue		
						Book card	
						Call number	
					card catalogue		
			Abstract				
					Authoatic abstract		
		Electronical					
			computer				
			Online catalogue				
			Q &A fact retrieval system				
			Image retreaivl				
			soundretreavil				
			Key word search				
	Transmission	Transmission speed					
		Human communication					
			Nonverbal communication				
					Physical		
					Aesthetic		
					Signs		
					Symbolic		
			Viusal communication				
			Mass communication				
		Telecommunication	Cable				
			Wireless				
			Distrubuted networks				
			Electronical				

	Publication			
		Book announcement		
		Co- publishing		
		Electronic publishing		
	Dissemination			
		Current Awareness		
		Selective dissemination of Information DSI		
		RSS		
	Visualization			
		knowledge visualisation		
		Data visualisation		
	Evaluation			
		accuracy		
	Administration			
		Administration data processing		
		Archival administration		
		Library adimnstration		
		Data administration		
			Data	
	Access			
		Direct access		
		access services		
		information gap		
		access code		
		accession		
	System analysis			
	System desgin			
	Data process			
		Data sharing		
		Data administration		
		Data analysis		
		Data collection		
		Data communication		
		Data exchange		
		Data integration		
		Data visualization		
		Data transminssion		
	Information process			
		Information analysis		
		Information audit		
		Information classification		
		Information management		
		Information manipulate		
		Information retrieval		
		Information search		
		Information services		
		Information transfer		
		Information abstract		
	Knowledge process	Knowledge representation		
		Knowledge visualization		
		Knowledge management		
		Knowledge mapping		
		Knowledge organization		
	Digitalization			

Studies			
	user studies		
		Human information behavior	
		Information seeking behavior	
	Information needs		
	Information dissemination		
	Readership studies		
	Difussion of Information		
	Usability studies		
	Information usability		
	Information retrieval		
	librarianship		
	Archival studies.		

Tool	to utilize in doing activity			
	Non-IT Tool			
	Abstract	Descriptor		
		Abstract Journal		
			Library and Information Science Abstracts (LISA)	
	Catalouge			
		Alphabtic subject catalouge		
			Anglo- American ataloguing rules	
			machine-readable cataloguing MARC	
		Catalogue of publisher		
		Dictionary catalouge		
		Descriptive cataloging		
		Author catalouge		
			Author entry	
		Book catalogue		
			Book card	
			call number	
			Entrys	
				Title entry
				Author entry
	Index	Identifier		Subject entry
		Subject index		
		Alphabtic index		
		Index card		
		Index entry		
		Index language		
		Periodical index		
		Keyword index		
		Map index		
	Controlled vocabulary			
		Gazetteer		
		Glossary		
		Dictionary		
		encyclopaedia		
		word list		
	Representation tools			
		Diagram		
		Figure		
		Graphic		
		Illustrated map		
		Illustration		
		Map		
			Information map	
			Topic map	
			Knowledge map	
			Interactive map	
			brain storm map	

IT Tool						
	Computer					
		Software				
			Computer aided design CAD			
			Computer aided manufacturing			
			Computer animation			
			Computer graphics			
			Cookie			
			Network software			
			System software			
			Web browser			
				Safari		
				Konqueror		
				Opera		
				Lynx		
				Firefox		
				Internet explorer		
				Netscape		
				Mozilla Firefox		
			Basic software			
		Hardware				
			Computer terminal			
			Intermediate access memory			
			Graphical card			
			Monitor			
			Motherboard			
				AT Motherboard		
				ATX Motherboard		
				NLX Motherboard		
			central processing unit CUP			
			Random- access memory RAM			
				SD RAM sinigle data rate access memory		
				DD- RAM Dual data rate synchronous dynamic random access		
				RD-RAM Rambus dynamic random access memory		
			expansion cards- adaptor card			
			optical disc drive			
				CD-R compact disk read only memory		
				CD/RW compact disk read writie		
				CDRW compact disk re- writieable		
				DVD ROM digital vedio disk read only		
				DVD RAM digital vedio disk random access memory		
				DVD RW RAM digital viedo disk re- writeable Random access memory		
			Hard disk draiverHDD			
			Keyboard			
			In put			
			Out put			
			Data communication			
			Computer file			
			web camera			
			Mouse			
		Computer language				
			Machine language			
			Assembly language			
			High level language			
				COBOL		
				BAISC		
				PASCAL		
				C		
				C++		
				C #		
				Java		
				Java Script		
			Mark up language			
				Extensible Markup Language XML		
				Extensible Stylesheet Language XSL		
				HTML		
			Programming environment			
				Integrating development environment		
				Integrating program		
			Virtual programming language			
			Artifical language			
			Logical programming			
			Programming techniques			
				unstructured programming		
				procedural programming		
				Modular programming		
				Data structure programming		
				object oriented programming OOP		

			application software	Office automation			
				Office computer			
				Prototyping			
				Video games			
				Archival software			
				Communication application (interface)			
				Computer application			
				Web application			
				Image card			
				Desktop publishing			
				Graphic user interface			
				Wizard			
				Comunication application	E- conference		
					E-mail		
					video conference		
					Video text		
					Information broawsers		
					Bulletin board		
					Teleconferencing		
					Blog		
		Internet			Forums		
			World Wide Web				
			Invisible Web				
			Deep web				
			web adderss				
			web application				
			Web- based service				
			Internet protocol				
			web server				
			Free-text search (keywords)				
			search engins				
				Crawler-Based Search Engines			
					Google		
					Ask Jeeves		
				Hybrid Search Engines			
					Yahoo		
					Google		
				Meta Search Engines			
					Metacrawler		
					Dogpile		
				Specialty Search Engines			
					Shopping		
						Froogle	
						Yahoo Shopping	
						BizRate	
					Local Search		
						NZPages	
						SearchNZ	
					Domain Name Search		
						iServe	
						Freeparking	
				Image search engin			

	Analog technology					
		Analog				
	Systems					
		Information system				
			evaluation of information system			
			national information system			
		information architecture system				
		information design system				
		multimedia system				
		sensor system				
		Classification system				
		Database management system				
		Decision support system				
		Distributed system				
		Domain name system				
		Information management system				
		Library programm				
		Multi-user system				
		Digital archive				
		Digital Library				
		Knowledge based system				
		Information Retrieval system				
		Boolean				
		Network system				
		Network information system				
		Online system				
			Online Information retreival			
		Hypertext system				
Digital securty system						
		Access controal				
			Access code			
			Access point			
			Access policy			
			Access time			
Document mangement System						
		Image retreaival				
		text retreaival				
		sound retreaival				
		Image scan				
	Communication	Interface				
		Telecommunication				
			Cable			
			Wireless			
			satellite			
			Mobile devices			
			Digital camera			
			Fax			
			Fax machine			
		Telematics				
		Teletext				
		Networks	Distrubuted networks			
			Internet			
			Intranet			
			Extranet			
			Network oprating system			
			Network protocol			
			Radiocommunication			
			Computer communication network			
				Network design		
				Network protocals		
				Network operation		
				Network architecture		
			Information network			Colud computing
				Information commons		
		Communication ways				
			asynchronous			
			synchronous			
	Catalouge					
		universal machine-readable cataloguing MARC				
		British National Bibliography				
	Controlled vocabulary					
		e-Gazetteer				
		e- Glossary				
		e-Dictionary				
		e- encyclopaedia				
		e- word list				

Mediate	(Between actors)		
	Libraries		
		Bibliotheca / historical library	
			Alxandrian library
		Archival library	
		Art library	
		College library	Academic library
		University Library	
		Government library	
			Library of Congress
		Library media center	
		Library school	
		Institutional library	
		National library	
		International library	
		Law library	
		Map library	
		Architecture library	
		Picture library	
		Public library	
		Virtual library	
		Mobile library	
	Information centers		
		Health information center	
	Archives		
		public archives	
		film archives	
		Large text archive	
	Museum		
	Websites		

Kinds (Discpline)	Archival science	
	Library science	
	Computer science	
	Museology	
	Economics of Information	
	Libarainship	
	Bibliometrics	
	Information architecture	
	knowledge management	
	Information management	
	Mathematical science	
		Operations research

Domains (External)		
	Chemical Domain	
	Health Biomedical	
	Technical information	
	informatics	
	Art and hummanties	
	Scientific coomunication	
	geographical information	
	Music information retreival	
	Medical information	
	Social science information	
	Leagal information	
	Physical science	
	Culture	

Resources									
	Non-documented								
		Tacit knowledge							
		informal knowledge							
		informal information							
		stories							
		genres							
		speeches							
		indigenous knowledge (native)							
	Doumented								
		Readable							
			Printed						
				Book	Textbook				
							appendix		
							Edition		
					Single topic books				
					Art book				
					Childern book				
					Classic book				
					Book arts				
					Law book				
					Library book				
					Book guidance				
					Book manuals				
					Bibliography				
							Historical bibliography		
							Practical bibliography		
					autobiographies				
				Standdard publication					
				poetry					
				Pantents					
				Data					
					Datum				
					Metadata				
							Descriptive metadata		
					Digit				
					statistics				
					knowledge based				
					Datasheet				
					Attribute				

				Information					
					machine-readable (information)				
				Knowledge					
					formal knowledge				
					meta-knowledge				
					Explicit knowledge				
				periodical					
					specilized periodical				
							Magazine		
							newsletter		
					General periodicals				
							Magazine		
							newspapre		
				Reference					
					Bibliographic reference				
					Thesauri				
					Encyclopedia				
							General encyclopedia		
					bibliographee				
					Gazatteer				
					dictionary	Language dictionary			
						Data dictionary			

			Thesis				
				Thesis statement			
			Interviews				
			Official publication				
			conference proceeding				
			Scintific technical report				
			Research report				
			Journal				
				Journal article			
				Archival journal			
				Academic journal			
			Documents				
				offical doc			
					Concept Papers		
					Guidelines		
					Position Papers		
					Roles Papers		
					Specialized Knowledge and Skills Papers		
					Standards		
					Statements		
					access		
					policy		
				Govirnoment publication	Decision document		
				Internal document			
				Archival document			
			Abstract		Archival material		
				Author abstract	Archival group		
				Evaluative abstract			
				Indicative abstract			
			letters				
			Bulletins				
			Programming documentation				
		Non-printed					
			Diaries				
			Clay tablets				
			Papyrus				
			animal skin				
			Manuscripts				
	Audio						
		sheet music					
		E book					
		E- journal					
		CDs					
		oral presentation					
		Interviews					
		audio book					
		audio newspaper					

		Visual				
			visual art.			
			photographs,			
			Video			
				Video Compact Discs		
				video conferencing		
				Video games		
			Documentary	Video text		
			Documentary drama			
			File			
				Attachment		
			Microfilm			
			Digital image			
			Image			
			Interviews			
			film archives			
			videotape recorder			
		Audiovisual materials (r	videotext			
			CDs			
			Floppy disc			
			Compact Disc-Recorder CD	DVD-RAM		
			Compact Disc-Rewritable C|	DVD- ROMDVD-RW		
			Digital video disc DVD			
			E book	Video		
			E- journal	Video Compact Discs		
			E- file			
			E- magazine			
			E newspaper			
			E- document			
				e-mail		
				webpage		
				Hypertext		
			Database			
				Cross reference database		
					Cross reference	
				Bibliographic database		
				Full text database		
				Image database		
				Numeric database		
				Abstract database		
				Citation database		
				Data warehouse		

egislation	Copy right laws				
	Free speech				
	censorship				
	Data privacy				
	accessibility	access policy			
		access charge			
		access code			
		access controal			
		access copy			
	national information policy				
	intellectual properity				
	Archival jurisdiction				
	Digital right				
	Digital scurity				
	internet crime				
	free ccess to information				
	Standards				
		Evidental value			
			Archival value		
				Primary value	
					Administrative
					Fiscal value
					Legal
					Operational value
				Secondary value	
					Informational value
					Archival value
		Computing standard			
			ITU (International Telecommunication Union)		
			ISO (International Standards Organization)		
			IEEE (Institute of Electronical and Engineers)		
		Libarry standard			
			American National Standards Institute ANSI		
	information ethics				
	Information policy				
	accumulation				

Sociatal				
	social Informatics			
		traditional society		
		Internet society		
		Technology intensive society		
		social communication		
	community informatics			
	Information culture		Librarianship	
	education			
		Fieldwork		
		Education of Information science		
			academic education	
			Professional Training	
				theoratical knowledge
				Practical knoweldge
			E-learning	
			user education	
			continuing user education	
			Information literacy	
		Education of Computer science		
			computer literacy	
			Computer education(ICT)	
		Education of Library science		
			Library education	
	industry			
		Markets		
			Pricint	
		E-commerce		Business models
		Economics		Value chain
		Information industry		
		Information industry market		
		Industry application of IS		
		Computing industry		
	History			
		History of computer		
Time				
Space				

Feedback:

1. Gilliland, Anne [gilliland@gseis.ucla.edu]

Dear Mr. Sawsaa,

Thank you for your interesting message. In response to your questions, while topics would likely evolve fairly quickly, those that would seem to be of most interest to someone like me right now would be the following:

Nature of Information Science (IS) as a domain - this whole area is very much the current preoccupation of the iSchool movement in North America.

Conceptual approaches to define: Data, Information, knowledge, wisdom - to this I would add Records and Metadata, and, more generically, Information Objects.

Boundaries of IS - especially interdisciplinarity and transdisciplinarity

Theory of IS - yes, need more theory-building, especially in some areas

Resource of IS e.g. Primary & secondary - understanding the nature of primary sources and their relationships to derivative objects is becoming increasingly important across all information environments.

Sincerely,

Anne Gilliland.

Appendix L: Part of OIS ontology in OWL format

```xml
<?xml version="1.0"?>
<!DOCTYPE rdf:RDF [
    <!ENTITY owl "http://www.w3.org/2002/07/owl#" >
    <!ENTITY dc "http://purl.org/dc/elements/1.1/" >
    <!ENTITY xsd "http://www.w3.org/2001/XMLSchema#" >
    <!ENTITY owl2xml "http://www.w3.org/2006/12/owl2-xml#" >
    <!ENTITY rdfs "http://www.w3.org/2000/01/rdf-schema#" >
    <!ENTITY rdf "http://www.w3.org/1999/02/22-rdf-syntax-ns#" >
    <!ENTITY Ontology1298894565306 "http://www.semanticweb.org/ontologies/2011/1/Ontology1298894565306.owl#" >
    <!ENTITY CD "http://www.semanticweb.org/ontologies/2011/1/Ontology1298894565306.owl#CD/" >
    <!ENTITY Philosophy "http://www.semanticweb.org/ontologies/2011/1/Ontology1298894565306.owl#Philosophy&amp;" >
]><rdf:RDF xmlns="http://www.semanticweb.org/ontologies/2011/1/Ontology1298894565306.owl#"
    xml:base="http://www.semanticweb.org/ontologies/2011/1/Ontology1298894565306.owl"
    xmlns:dc="http://purl.org/dc/elements/1.1/"
    xmlns:rdfs="http://www.w3.org/2000/01/rdf-schema#"
    xmlns:owl2xml="http://www.w3.org/2006/12/owl2-xml#"
    xmlns:CD="&Ontology1298894565306;CD/"
    xmlns:owl="http://www.w3.org/2002/07/owl#"
    xmlns:xsd="http://www.w3.org/2001/XMLSchema#"
    xmlns:rdf="http://www.w3.org/1999/02/22-rdf-syntax-ns#"
    xmlns:Philosophy="&Ontology1298894565306;Philosophy&amp;"
    xmlns:Ontology1298894565306="http://www.semanticweb.org/ontologies/2011/1/Ontology1298894565306.owl#">
```

```xml
<owl:Ontology rdf:about="">
    <rdfs:comment
        >Information Science ontololgy that descrips the domain of IS.</rdfs:comment>
    <dc:creator xml:lang="en"
        >Ahlam Sawsaa 2011.</dc:creator>
</owl:Ontology>
    // Annotation properties
    <owl:AnnotationProperty rdf:about="&dc;title"/>
    <owl:AnnotationProperty rdf:about="&dc;creator"/>
    //
// Object Properties
<!-- http://www.semanticweb.org/ontologies/2011/1/Ontology1298894565306.owl#accessableBy -->
    <owl:ObjectProperty rdf:about="#accessableBy"/>
        <!-- http://www.semanticweb.org/ontologies/2011/1/Ontology1298894565306.owl#collect -->
    <owl:ObjectProperty rdf:about="#collect">
        <rdf:type rdf:resource="&owl;InverseFunctionalProperty"/>
    </owl:ObjectProperty>
    <!-- http://www.semanticweb.org/ontologies/2011/1/Ontology1298894565306.owl#concernedWith -->
    <owl:ObjectProperty rdf:about="#concernedWith">
        <rdf:type rdf:resource="&owl;FunctionalProperty"/>
    </owl:ObjectProperty>
    <!-- http://www.semanticweb.org/ontologies/2011/1/Ontology1298894565306.owl#conjectionBetween -->
    <owl:ObjectProperty rdf:about="#conjectionBetween">
        <rdf:type rdf:resource="&owl;FunctionalProperty"/>
    </owl:ObjectProperty>
```

```xml
<!-- http://www.semanticweb.org/ontologies/2011/1/Ontology1298894565306.owl#contains -->
<owl:ObjectProperty rdf:about="#contains">
    <rdf:type rdf:resource="&owl;FunctionalProperty"/>
</owl:ObjectProperty>

<!-- http://www.semanticweb.org/ontologies/2011/1/Ontology1298894565306.owl#continuingTo -->
<owl:ObjectProperty rdf:about="#continuingTo">
    <rdf:type rdf:resource="&owl;FunctionalProperty"/>
</owl:ObjectProperty>

<!-- http://www.semanticweb.org/ontologies/2011/1/Ontology1298894565306.owl#conversationAmong -->
<owl:ObjectProperty rdf:about="#conversationAmong">
    <rdf:type rdf:resource="&owl;FunctionalProperty"/>
</owl:ObjectProperty>

<!-- http://www.semanticweb.org/ontologies/2011/1/Ontology1298894565306.owl#doing -->
<owl:ObjectProperty rdf:about="#doing"/>

<!-- http://www.semanticweb.org/ontologies/2011/1/Ontology1298894565306.owl#employeeIn -->
<owl:ObjectProperty rdf:about="#employeeIn">
    <rdf:type rdf:resource="&owl;InverseFunctionalProperty"/>
</owl:ObjectProperty>

<!-- http://www.semanticweb.org/ontologies/2011/1/Ontology1298894565306.owl#exploreImpactOf -->
<owl:ObjectProperty rdf:about="#exploreImpactOf">
    <rdf:type rdf:resource="&owl;FunctionalProperty"/>
</owl:ObjectProperty>
```

```xml
            <owl:someValuesFrom rdf:resource="#ComputerApplication"/>
      </owl:Restriction>
    </owl:equivalentClass>
    <rdfs:subClassOf rdf:resource="#EducationOfComputerScience"/>
    <rdfs:comment
        >The level of knowledge and ability of using computer applications rather computer programming.</rdfs:comment>
  </owl:Class>
  <!-- http://www.semanticweb.org/ontologies/2011/1/Ontology1298894565306.owl#ComputerOperator -->
  <owl:Class rdf:about="#ComputerOperator">
    <rdfs:subClassOf rdf:resource="#Operator"/>
    <rdfs:comment
        >Someone who works to manage computer system in computer room.</rdfs:comment>
  </owl:Class>
```

Appendix M: Lessons learned

Lessons learnt.

As the research is training and search, during this journey I gained lots of new skills and fortify others. First point was thinking about what is the topic of our research will be to identify the problem and motivations. That required starting literature review to determine the area of investigation . Actually my tendency is about working on semantic web: many question was rising until I read about Smith Barry's article which titled "Ontology: An Introduction "this article gave my an inspiration of how ontology can be also, it capture my interest about the ontologies and its role in developing semantic web.

As ontology required software engineers it need as well experts to evaluate it. From this point I was thought about the best way to fined experts on the subject that has been chosen. Which shined the idea of designing a special website compose a number of a valuable professionals in Information Science rather use existing on like linked in face book or so on. The reason that made me thinking of designing website emerged from:

i. Employ a virtual community of practice as knowledge management tool to capture the knowledge that embedded in experts' mind.
ii. The combination of the community itself contains of a group of specialists in the same area around the world. This combination will add a sort of variety in terms of they are came from different background, culture and languages. Thus it will lead to enrich the ontology.

I learnt how to design website. The designing began from the scratch as the research has not experience to design websites before which required to learn more and more about HTML, XML, HXML, PHP , Jave scripts and MySQL database. by searching through books, articles and websites.

- Working In the community takes few months to invite people to participate start by :
    i. Create database contains (1270) name from Information science and computer science from different university around the world including Huddersfield university.
    ii. Sending an invitation letter to invite them to participate in the experimental study.
- Cultivation ontocop by Send emails and developing the website in the same time. Prepare topics to be discussed in the ontocop. Arrange online chatting with experts .Working on database+ Prepare member's profiles. Getting started to encourage participants to register at the Forum.

iii. - During this stage I have attend Consortium (UKAIS) Academy of Information system annual conference in Oxford on 10. March 2010 and prepare second conference paper.
iv. Attending more workshops as Academic writing, preparing for Viva

- For Creating Ontology of Information Science (OIS)
    b. It is required to attend Introduction to ontology in OWL at Manchester University 19 – 20 May 2009 to learn more about ontology and to improve myself to fish this project. Also, I searched at different area of ontology tools, languages, methodologies and evaluation methods.

Attending GATE Training Course and Developer Sprint May 2010 from10-14.May 2010 Sheffield University.

    c. Building the taxonomy, this required to survey the classification system to develop the theoretical base in the project.